Economics and Psychology

CESifo Seminar Series

Edited by Hans-Werner Sinn

See http://mitpress.mit.edu for a complete list of titles in this series.

Economics and Psychology

A Promising New Cross-Disciplinary Field

edited by
Bruno S. Frey and Alois
Stutzer

CESifo Seminar Series

The MIT Press
Cambridge, Massachusetts
London, England

ML

MIT Press books may be purchased at special quantity discounts for business or sales
promotional use. For information, please e-mail special_sales@mitpress.mit.edu or write
to Special Sales Department, The MIT Press, 55 Hayward Street, Cambridge, MA 02142.

This book was set in Palatino on 3B2 by Asco Typesetters, Hong Kong, and was printed
and bound in the United States of America.

Library of Congress Cataloging-in-Publication Data

Economics and psychology : a promising new cross-disciplinary field / edited by Bruno
S. Frey and Alois Stutzer.
    p.   cm. — (CESifo seminar series)
Includes bibliographical references and index.
ISBN 978-0-262-06263-3 (hardcover : alk. paper) 1. Economics—Psychological aspects.
I. Frey, Bruno S. II. Stutzer, Alois.
HB74.P8E333   2007
330.01'9—dc22   2007000956

10 9 8 7 6 5 4 3 2 1

Contents

Series Foreword

This book is part of the CESifo Seminar Series. The series aims to cover topical policy issues in economics from a largely European perspective. The books in this series are the products of the papers and intensive debates that took place during the seminars hosted by CESifo, an international research network of renowned economists organized jointly by the Center for Economic Studies at Ludwig-Maximilians-Universität, Munich, and the Ifo Institute for Economic Research. All publications in this series have been carefully selected and refereed by members of the CESifo research network.

List of Contributors

Matthias Benz is Research Fellow at the Center for Research in Economics, Management and the Arts, Zurich, and member of the editorial staff at the Neue Zürcher Zeitung.

Meghana Bhatt is a graduate student at the California Institute of Technology.

Iris Bohnet is Associate Professor of Public Policy at the Kennedy School of Government, Harvard University.

Colin F. Camerer is Axline Professor of Business Economics at the California Institute of Technology.

Bruno S. Frey is Professor of Economics at the University of Zurich.

Simon Gächter is Professor of the Psychology of Economic Decision Making at the University of Nottingham.

Ralph Hertwig is Professor of Psychology at the University of Basel.

Ming Hsu is a graduate student at the California Institute of Technology.

Richard Layard is Emeritus Professor of Economics at the London School of Economics and Director of the Well-Being Programme at the Centre for Economic Performance.

Stephan Meier is a Senior Economist at the Research Center for Behavioral Economics and Decision Making at the Federal Reserve Bank of Boston.

Felix Oberholzer-Gee is Andreas Andresen Associate Professor of Business Administration at the Harvard Business School.

Alois Stutzer is Assistant Professor in the Faculty of Business and Economics at the University of Basel.

I   Introduction

1

Economics and Psychology: Developments and Issues

Bruno S. Frey and Alois
Stutzer

The interface between economics and psychology contains imports and exports: elements from psychology are introduced into economics, and vice versa. Since the authors are economists, only the influence of psychology on economics is discussed here. The reverse influence is left to psychologists to consider, but our general impression is that so far rather few economic elements have been brought into psychology.

The developments and issues covered here are based on our personal evaluation and the selection is strongly shaped by our research interests. No effort toward "objectivity," if it were even possible, is made. Rather, we advance our own opinions in order to stimulate the discussion, knowing that other scholars would focus on different aspects and evaluate them differently.[1]

We understand the field of economics and psychology as an interaction of the two individual disciplines in several dimensions: exchange of scientific insights, improvements of empirical methods, and personal scholarly exchange. This is a broader view of the interface between the two disciplines than the introduction of behavioral decision research (a subfield of psychology) into economics, sometimes called "behavioral economics." Economics and psychology is not restricted to behavioral aspects[2] but extends beyond, for instance, to reported subjective evaluations such as those undertaken in happiness research.

We briefly cover four areas of interface between economics and psychology: anomalies, experiments, motivation, and happiness.

1.1 Anomalies

Rarely has a field in economics been so strongly dominated by one set of authors as has been the case with anomalies. "Prospect Theory" by Kahneman and Tversky, published in *Econometrica* (1979), has been one of the most cited articles in economics. The psychologist Kahneman therefore rightly received the Nobel Prize in Economics.[3]

Tversky and Kahneman's article attracted the attention of a large number of economists by providing an alternative to the classical economic approach of subjective expected utility maximization. Moreover, particular elements of prospect theory, such as "loss aversion," became widely known and were applied to a vast number of different issues. Both have become part of modern economics despite the fact that most scholars consider them incompatible with neoclassical theory (to which many of them otherwise adhere). This does not necessarily mean that prospect theory has become part of the undergraduate syllabus; indeed, many microeconomics textbooks still choose to disregard it.[4]

The dominance of Tversky and Kahneman's approach has perhaps overshadowed other work by psychologists in this vein. An example is the work of Gigerenzer (2000), who claims that many of the effects contradicting subjective expected utility (SEU) theory essentially disappear when the formulation of uncertainty in terms of probabilities is substituted by a frequency formulation. Gigerenzer also argues that many of the heuristics used by individuals, which at first sight appear inconsistent with rationality, are perfectly compatible with the broader view of bounded rationality.

The anomalies or paradoxes found in psychology (and partly also in economics as, e.g., by Allais 1953) have been introduced into economics mostly in two ways. The first approach analyzes the question of which human cognitive limits lead to which behavior anomalies. This research uses primarily laboratory experiments and has produced convincing evidence that under a wide set of conditions individuals are subject to anomalies as compared to perfect or full rationality. The second approach deals axiomatically with the question of how far formal decision theory must be adjusted in order to integrate these anomalies into economic theory. The purpose is to transform "anomalies" into "regularities."

A third possible approach has, however, been rather neglected. It analyzes the incentives produced when individuals are subject to anomalies. This incentive approach studies the question of how individuals *react* when anomalies appear.[5] On the one hand, persons subject to anomalies often become at least partly aware of them and realize that they suffer a utility loss and would benefit from avoiding them. The extent to which they are able to *guard* against utility reducing behavior depends on the available technologies or on the marginal benefits and costs of doing so. On the other hand, when individuals are prone to anomalies, other actors have an incentive to *exploit* this irrationality. Whether this interaction leads to an aggregate outcome consistent with the prediction of rational models or whether it generates large deviations from it depends on the structure of interaction (Fehr and Tyran 2005). If an individual *i* buys, sells, or produces more of a good, an individual *j* might either have an incentive to decrease her demand or supply (i.e., strategic substitutability prevails between actions) or to increase it (i.e., there is strategic complementarity between actions). With strategic substitutability, a minority of rational agents can be sufficient to produce a rational outcome, while with complementarity a small fraction of irrational agents can lead to strong deviations from market fundamentals, as observed with the stock market bubble in the late 1990s.

As a result, the equilibrium extent of observable anomalies depends on a set of institutional conditions determining the benefits and cost of guarding and exploiting. In general, anomalies are unlikely to be fully eliminated by such interaction; they are *transformed*. It seems that few laboratory experiments have taken this interaction sufficiently into account. An exception are market experiments, some of which suggest that anomalies are eliminated under perfect competition (List 2003). However, the market is only one decision-making system; individuals act under many other conditions so that in equilibrium anomalies appear in different extent and form.

1.2 Experiments

Laboratory experiments are psychologists' bread and butter. Although economists have long thought this technique could not be applied to their discipline, attitudes have changed dramatically. Today laboratory experiments are widely accepted and used. Sessions at conferences are devoted solely to this technique, and there exist specialized societies and journals on experimental economics.[6]

The familiar advantages of lab experiments lie mainly in the possibility of controlled intervention for causal inference, an aspect that is key for social science research and that paved the way to detecting anomalies and understanding the content of human preferences, thus spurring some of the most influential economic research in the last decade. As always, there are drawbacks, but they seem to be less well known than the advantages. The reason may be an economic one. In order to run experiments outside the questionable classroom setting, a costly laboratory is necessary. The founding and running of a lab requires corresponding budgets. In order to get budgets assigned, the researchers must write applications selling the importance of experiments for their research. Success in receiving funding virtually locks researchers into using the lab in their research. They therefore tend to see social issues mainly or even exclusively in terms of a potential lab experiment. To secure their position, they are reluctant to accept criticism of this method by outsiders, let alone to raise doubt themselves. There is indeed a difference between this empirical approach and standard econometrics, which uses officially published statistics. Both the data and the computers nowadays are readily available, normally without charge to the investigators. They therefore are less committed to using the corresponding technique.

Laboratory experimenters have to some extent become a self-contained group whose major preoccupation is maintaining the high internal validity of their experiments, or what Harrison and List (2004, 1029) call "the passion for abstract scripts." The quest for as context-free and abstract experimental conditions as are possible does not provide more general findings if the context matters for the subjects' behavior. Correspondingly, little emphasis has been put on external validity; in other words, on the question of what the experiment and its results mean outside the lab. Some people perceive a non-negligible portion of laboratory experiments as dictated by self-defined issues internal to the discipline, consisting in small variations around some basic game such as the ultimatum or the dictator game. This might well be true for other areas of economics, too. However, as a result, experimental economics has to some extent disassociated itself from the rest of economics and has less influence than it otherwise could.

A few economists engaged in laboratory experiments are well aware of these limitations and have faced the challenge to find the most appropriate combination of empirical approaches to research questions. Examples are the combination of surveys and experiments (e.g., Dohmen et al. 2005) or of field data and experiments (e.g., Fehr and Götte 2007). Conventional laboratory experiments have also been opened by using nonstandard subject pools (i.e., not only students), and more important by going into the field (see the survey by Harrison and List 2004). The extent of control is reduced by taking the commodity, the task, and the information set the subjects can use from the field (framed field experiments), or where the subjects do not know that they are in an experiment and do these tasks naturally (natural field experiment). Another step outside the constraints of the lab are social experiments where government agencies or other institutions undertake new programs whose consequences are studied (for surveys, see Ferber and Hirsch 1978, 1982; Hausman and Wise 1985). This development should be welcomed and should not be seen mainly in terms of a loss of experimental condition control. Indeed, it can be argued that abstract laboratory experiments fail to control for the contexts the subjects impose on themselves when solving the tasks. At the same time, this development raises the relevance of experimental research for general economic and social issues, and the results can be linked more easily to econometric research based on official statistics and surveys.

1.3 Motivation

Psychology has helped economists to overcome the narrow concept of the *homo oeconomicus*, particularly the assumption that human beings always and everywhere pursue their selfish interest. It has now been firmly established by experimental and field research that humans are well capable of higher motives such as altruism and reciprocal fairness (see, e.g., Fehr and Schmidt 2003 and Meier, chapter 3, for surveys). Pro-social behavior has been found to be important under many conditions. Not surprisingly it is crucial with respect to donations and volunteering (see, e.g., Frey and Meier 2004; Meier and Stutzer 2007). This is no small step forward, not least because it makes economics more palatable to adherents of other scholarly disciplines, who often tend to dismiss rational choice reasoning because of its too-cynical view of human nature.

Another fruitful input from psychology into economics has been the notion of *procedural utility.* It has been convincingly demonstrated that people do not only value outcomes but also the way by which they are reached. Sometimes they are prepared to accept an inferior outcome if they feel that the process has been administered in a fair way (Lind and Tyler 1988). In social interaction, intentions also matter (Falk, Fehr, and Fischbacher 2000). Procedural utility is relevant in a great number of social and economic contexts, such as democratic participation in economic policy or enterprises, or in the way taxpayers are treated (see the survey by Frey, Benz, and Stutzer 2004).

Psychologists have also influenced economists' thinking by pointing out the importance of intrinsic motivation. This opens the door to a broader view of incentives, which in economics was restricted to extrinsic factors, often to monetary compensation. Intrinsic motivation may be due to internalized norms or to the pleasures of pursuing a task as such. Field research has been able to establish that many economic activities and reactions can be better understood by accepting the existence of intrinsic motivation than by artificially concocting some extrinsic motive. An example is entrepreneurs whose main incentive to become independent is the larger work autonomy, an intrinsic value. They are prepared to choose this more risky work despite the fact that, on average, their income is lower and their work load higher (e.g., Benz 2005).

The existence of intrinsic motivation as an additional incentive is not the only thing that matters. Perhaps even more important is crowding theory's insight that extrinsic and intrinsic motivations cannot simply be summed up as was assumed in microeconomic theory. Rather, the use of extrinsic motivators can crowd out or crowd in intrinsic motivation, depending on identifiable conditions (Frey 1992; Gneezy and Rustichini 2000). For economics, crowding out is more relevant than crowding in because it may result in a reversal of the fundamental relative price effect: paying individuals can perversely induce them to work less by undermining work morale. This negative effect may be attributed to various causes. Some scholars prefer to see it as an informational response (Bénabou and Tirole 2003), while others resort more directly to the reasons given in the psychological literature (see, e.g., Frey 1997; referring to Deci, Koestner, and Ryan 1999).

Crowding theory has important implications for principal agent theory, a cornerstone of the corporate governance literature (surveys are given by Gibbons 1998; Prendergast 1999; Becht, Bolton, and Röell 2003). Principal agent theory's common argument is that monetary compensation of employees should be aligned as closely as possible to their performance. This argument has spawned, or at least stimulated, the pay-for-performance movement, which has extended beyond the corporate sector, especially to public bureaucracy (there known as "New Public Management, or NPM"). However, recent huge scandals surrounding the management of large corporations in the United States and elsewhere have forced a reconsideration. Observers have become aware of the danger that a focus on monetary compensation as an incentive instrument may undermine work morale as well as honorable behavior—with potentially far-reaching political and social consequences. Measures to maintain and foster employees' intrinsic motivation, possibly by a stronger emphasis on selection, provide an alternative to reliance on monetary compensation as an incentive instrument (see Frey and Osterloh 2002).

1.4 Happiness

As a result of the ordinal revolution of the 1930s, traditional economics was totally convinced that utility cannot and need not be measured—that view still exists today, and not only in economics textbooks. Psychology has taught us a different lesson. For a long time, psychologists discussed under what conditions happiness measures can reliably indicate individual well-being. This brought economics "back to Bentham" (Kahneman, Wakker, and Sarin 1997; more generally, Kahneman, Diener, and Schwarz 1999). Some insightful economists such as Sen (1986) have for a long time harshly criticized the serious limits of analyzing human behavior by revealed preference alone. However, this had little effect on economics teaching and research as long as utility was thought to be unmeasurable.

At present, psychologists inform economists about several different measurement methods for approximating utility. Most often used are global self-evaluation questions as included in representative surveys such as the Eurobarometer, the World Values Survey, or national household panels. Other measures are based on experience sampling, the Day Reconstruction Method, and the U-index (Kahneman and Krueger 2006). Yet another approach uses brain scanning and thus links to the new field of neuroeconomics (Davidson, Shackman, and Maxwell 2004; Camerer, Loewenstein, and Rabin 2005). These techniques do not measure the same aspects of individual well-being. Surveys on life satisfaction, for instance, are best suited to capture long-term global life evaluations while brain scanning captures short-term positive and negative affects.

Economics and psychology has become truly interdisciplinary in the empirical analysis of reported life satisfaction. Personality, sociodemographic characteristics, culture, economic circumstances (in particular income, unemployment, and inflation), and institutional factors (e.g., the type and extent of democracy and political decentralization) have been identified as determinants of life satisfaction in cross-section and time series analyses (surveys are provided in Frey and Stutzer 2002a,b). Two aspects have come to the fore:

• Adaptation and relative evaluations have been shown to be of great significance for many determinants, in particular for the influence of income and unemployment, but also marriage, on happiness (Clark 2003; Stutzer 2004; Layard 2005; Stutzer and Frey 2006). Adaptation and relative evaluations may possibly be understood in terms of the same cognitive and unconscious processes of comparisons to other states and other persons.

• Causation between circumstances and happiness often runs in both directions. For example, higher incomes provide higher subjective well-being, but more satisfied persons are also more successful in social and economic life and tend to have higher incomes (Lyubomirsky, King, and Diener 2005). Similarly, unemployed individuals are markedly less happy, but unhappy people are less likely to get a job or to remain employed. While this dual causation is well-recognized, it is difficult to analyze, in particular when there are serious data restrictions.

Research on happiness allows us to study many issues in the interface of economics and psychology. Two examples must suffice:

• The utility provided by public goods can be empirically evaluated. The existing methods of capturing the willingness to pay have serious shortcomings and need to be complemented. Methods relying on reflections in prices presume a flexible and near-perfect market, which in most countries does not typically exist for housing prices or rents, as well as for wages. Contingent valuation methods rely on questions about the willingness to pay for a specific public good and therewith are prone to bias individuals' answers. In some cases they are induced to think for the first time about the issue ("What are you willing to pay to prevent an oil spill in an Alaskan sound?"). Some researchers are aware of the danger of directing attention and unwillingly producing a Hawthorne effect, but it is difficult to avoid (see Harrison and List 2004). In contrast, as the happiness data are collected independently of any particular public good, this possible bias is circumvented. The new approach can be applied to many different public goods, as has been shown in the cases of airport noise or terrorism (Frey, Luechinger, and Stutzer 2004; van Praag and Baarsma 2005).

• Individual decisions with few exceptions involve future utilities. Economic theory has assumed as a matter of course that individuals correctly predict what amount of utility will be derived from future consumption. Indeed, standard microeconomics has solved the problem by assuming that preferences are unchanged and therefore present utility from an alternative is the same as future utility from it.

Psychologists have adduced convincing arguments that this assumption is way off the mark (Loewenstein and Schkade 1999; Wilson and Gilbert 2003). Individuals seriously mispredict the future utility of commodities. As included already in van Praag (1968), people overestimate the utility they will derive from future income. For economics the essential point is that the extent and direction of misprediction varies between commodities. While the future utility of material goods tends to be overestimated, the future utility of social interaction tends to be underestimated. Empirical research suggests that as a result people tend to devote too much time to work and too little time to family and friends. According to their own evaluation, they reach a lower level of well-being than they could if they were not subject to such systematic misprediction (Stutzer and Frey, chapter 7 in this volume).

1.5   Conclusions

This introduction has achieved its goal if the reader has become aware that together economics and psychology is a vibrant and fruitful field. We have argued that psychology has had a strong impact on economics: it has helped to substitute the assumption of complete rationality by isolating anomalies in individual behavior; it has made experiments a valid and widely accepted method of research; it has broadened the view of human nature by showing pro-social, intrinsic, and procedural aspects in people's preferences; and by showing that utility can be measured it has produced important knowledge about what people care for. The danger that economics and psychology becomes an additional playground for exhibiting one's mathematical prowess is perhaps smaller than in other areas because psychologists' influence has from the very beginning introduced a strong empirical (experimental) orientation.

We have argued that remarkable insights have already been reached but at the same time we are fully aware that in so many respects we still know so little. The field is wide open for future research.

Notes

We are grateful to Christine Benesch, Matthias Benz, Simon Lüchinger, Stephan Meier, Susanne Neckermann and Anna Winestein for helpful comments.

1. See the surveys dealing with economics and psychology, examples being Schoemaker (1982) and Rabin (1998, 2002). The authors have also provided a survey of their own; see Frey and Stutzer (2001).

2. The research in behavioral economics is described as follows: "Most of the papers modify one or two assumptions in standard theory in the direction of greater psychological realism" (Camerer and Loewenstein 2004, 3). For a survey and a discussion of the advances in behavioral economics, see Camerer, Loewenstein, and Rabin (2004) and Fudenberg (2006).

3. It may be argued that this has also been the case for Herbert Simon and his concept of "bounded rationality," but Simon was no pure psychologist, having graduated in political science.

4. The first three textbooks we checked and did not find a reference to prospect theory were Jehle and Reny (2001), Mas-Colell, Whinston, and Green (1995), and Varian (1992).

5. See Conlisk (1996, 684), and the more general earlier attempt by Frey and Eichenberger (1994).

6. See Sugden (2005).

References

Allais, Maurice. 1953. "Le Comportement de l'Homme Rationnel Devant de Risque: Critique des Postulats et Axiomes de l'École Americaine." *Econometrica* 21: 503–546.

Becht, Marco, Patrick Bolton, and Ailsa Röell. 2003. "Corporate Governance and Control." In *Handbook of the Economics of Finance*, vol. 1A, ed. George M. Constantinides, Milton Harrison, and Rene M. Stulz, 1–109. Amsterdam: Elsevier North-Holland.

Bénabou, Roland, and Jean Tirole. 2003. "Intrinsic and Extrinsic Motivation." *Review of Economic Studies* 70, no. 3: 489–520.

Benz, Matthias. 2005. "Entrepreneurship as a Non-Profit-Seeking Activity." IEW Working Paper No. 243, University of Zurich.

Camerer, Colin, and George Loewenstein. 2004. "Behavioral Economics: Past, Present, Future." In *Advances in Behavioral Economics*, ed. Colin Camerer, George Loewenstein, and Matthew Rabin, 3–51. New York: Russell Sage Foundation.

Camerer, Colin, George Loewenstein, and Drazen Prelec. 2005. "Neuroeconomics: How Neuroscience Can Inform Economics." *Journal of Economic Literature* 43, no. 1: 9–64.

Camerer, Colin, George Loewenstein, and Matthew Rabin. 2004. *Advances in Behavioral Economics.* New York: Russell Sage Foundation.

Clark, Andrew E. 2003. "Unemployment as a Social Norm: Psychological Evidence from Panel Data." *Journal of Labor Economics* 21, no. 2: 323–351.

Conlisk, John. 1996. "Why Bounded Rationality?" *Journal of Economic Literature* 34, no. 2: 669–700.

Davidson, Richard J., Alexander J. Shackman, and Jeffrey S. Maxwell. 2004. "Asymmetries in Face and Brain Related to Emotion." *Trends in Cognitive Sciences* 8, no. 9: 389–391.

Deci, Edward L., Richard Koestner, and Richard M. Ryan. 1999. "A Meta-Analytic Review of Experiments Examining the Effects of Extrinsic Rewards on Intrinsic Motivation." *Psychological Bulletin* 125, no. 6: 627–668.

Dohmen, Thomas J., Armin Falk, David Huffman, Uwe Sunde, Jürgen Schupp, and Gert G. Wagner. 2005. "Individual Risk Attitudes: New Evidence from a Large, Representative, Experimentally-Validated Survey." IZA Discussion Paper No. 1730, Bonn, Germany.

Falk, Armin, Ernst Fehr, and Urs Fischbacher. 2000. "Testing Theories of Fairness— Intentions Matter." IEW Working Paper No. 63, University of Zurich.

Fehr, Ernst, and Lorenz Götte. 2007. "Do Workers Work More When Wages Are High? Evidence from a Randomized Field Experiment." Forthcoming in *American Economic Review*.

Fehr, Ernst, and Klaus M. Schmidt. 2003. "Theories of Fairness and Reciprocity: Evidence and Economic Applications." In *Advances in Economics and Econometrics*, vol. 1, ed. Mathias Dewatripont, Lars Peter Hansen and Stephen J. Turnovsky, 208–257. Cambridge: Cambridge University Press.

Fehr, Ernst, and Jean-Robert Tyran. 2005. "Individual Irrationality and Aggregate Outcomes." *Journal of Economic Perspectives* 19, no. 4: 43–66.

Ferber, Robert, and Werner Z. Hirsch. 1978. "Some Experimentation and Economic Policy: A Survey." *Journal of Economic Literature* 16, no. 4: 1379–1414.

Ferber, Robert, and Werner Zvi Hirsch. 1982. *Social Experimentation and Economic Policy*. Cambridge: Cambridge University Press.

Frey, Bruno S. 1992. "Tertium Datur: Pricing, Regulating and Intrinsic Motivation." *Kyklos* 45, no. 2: 161–184.

Frey, Bruno S. 1997. *Not Just for the Money: An Economic Theory of Personal Motivation*. Cheltenham: Elgar.

Frey, Bruno S., Matthias Benz, and Alois Stutzer. 2004. "Introducing Procedural Utility: Not Only What, But Also How Matters." *Journal of Institutional and Theoretical Economics* 160, no. 3: 377–401.

Frey, Bruno S., and Reiner Eichenberger. 1994. "Economic Incentives Transform Psychological Anomalies." *Journal of Economic Behavior and Organization* 23, no. 2: 215–234.

Frey, Bruno S., Simon Luechinger, and Alois Stutzer. 2004. "Valuing Public Goods: The Life Satisfaction Approach." IEW Working Paper No. 184, University of Zurich.

Frey, Bruno S., and Stephan Meier. 2004. "Pro-Social Behavior in a Natural Setting." *Journal of Economic Behavior and Organization* 54, no. 1: 65–88.

Frey, Bruno S., and Margit Osterloh, eds. 2002. *Successful Management by Motivation: Balancing Intrinsic and Extrinsic Motivation*. New York: Springer.

Frey, Bruno S., and Alois Stutzer. 2001. "Economics and Psychology: From Imperialistic to Inspired Economics." *Revue de Philosophie Économique* 4: 5–22.

Frey, Bruno S., and Alois Stutzer. 2002a. *Happiness and Economics: How the Economy and Institutions Affect Well-Being*. Princeton, NJ: Princeton University Press.

Frey, Bruno S., and Alois Stutzer. 2002b. "What Can Economists Learn from Happiness Research?" *Journal of Economic Literature* 40, no. 2: 402–435.

Fudenberg, Drew. 2006. "Advancing beyond 'Advances in Behavioral Economics.'" *Journal of Economic Literature* 44, no. 3: 694–711.

Gibbons, Robert. 1998. "Incentives in Organizations." *Journal of Economic Perspectives* 12, no. 4: 115–132.

Gigerenzer, Gerd. 2000. *Adaptive Thinking: Rationality in the Real World*. Oxford: Oxford University Press.

Gneezy, Uri, and Aldo Rustichini. 2000. "Pay Enough or Don't Pay at All." *Quarterly Journal of Economics* 115, no. 3: 791–810.

Harrison, Glenn W., and John A. List. 2004. "Field Experiments." *Journal of Economic Literature* 42, no. 4: 1009–1055.

Hausman, Jerry A., and David A. Wise. 1985. *Social Experimentation*. Chicago: University of Chicago Press.

Jehle, Geoffrey A., and Philip J. Reny. 2001. *Advanced Microeconomic Theory*. Boston: Addison-Wesley.

Kahneman, Daniel, Ed Diener, and Norbert Schwarz, eds. 1999. *Well-Being: The Foundations of Hedonic Psychology*. New York: Russell Sage Foundation.

Kahneman, Daniel, and Alan B. Krueger. 2006. "Developments in the Measurement of Subjective Well-Being." *Journal of Economic Perspectives* 20, no. 1: 3–24.

Kahneman, Daniel, and Amos Tversky. 1979. "Prospect Theory: An Analysis of Decision under Risk." *Econometrica* 47, no. 2: 263–291.

Kahneman, Daniel, Peter P. Wakker, and Rakesh Sarin. 1997. "Back to Bentham? Explorations of Experienced Utility." *Quarterly Journal of Economics* 112, no. 2: 375–405.

Layard, Richard. 2005. *Happiness: Lessons from a New Science*. New York: Penguin.

Lind, Edgar Allan, and Tom R. Tyler. 1988. *The Social Psychology of Procedural Justice*. New York: Plenum Press.

List, John A. 2003. "Does Market Experience Eliminate Market Anomalies?" *Quarterly Journal of Economics* 118, no. 1: 41–71.

Loewenstein, George, and David A. Schkade. 1999. "Wouldn't It Be Nice? Predicting Future Feelings." In *Well-Being: The Foundation of Hedonic Psychology*, ed. Daniel Kahneman, Ed Diener, and Norbert Schwarz, 85–105. New York: Russell Sage Foundation.

Lyubomirsky, Sonja, Laura King, and Ed Diener. 2005. "The Benefits of Frequent Positive Affect: Does Happiness Lead to Success?" *Psychological Bulletin* 131, no. 6: 803–855.

Mas-Colell, Andreu, Michael D. Whinston, and Jerry R. Green. 1995. *Microeconomic Theory*. New York: Oxford University Press.

Meier, Stephan, and Alois Stutzer. 2007. "Is Volunteering Rewarding in Itself?" Forthcoming in *Economica*.

Prendergast, Canice. 1999. "The Provision of Incentives in Firms." *Journal of Economic Literature* 37, no. 1: 7–63.

Rabin, Matthew. 1998. "Psychology and Economics." *Journal of Economic Literature* 36, no. 1: 11–46.

Rabin, Matthew. 2002. "A Perspective on Psychology and Economics." *European Economic Review* 46, no. 4–5: 657–685.

Schoemaker, Paul J. H. 1982. "The Expected Utility Model: Its Variants, Purposes, Evidence and Limitations." *Journal of Economic Literature* 20, no. 2: 529–563.

Sen, Amartya K. 1986. "The Standard of Living." In *Tanner Lectures on Human Values*, Volume VII, ed. Sterling McMurrin, 1–51. Cambridge: Cambridge University Press.

Stutzer, Alois. 2004. "The Role of Income Aspirations in Individual Happiness." *Journal of Economic Behavior and Organization* 54, no. 1: 89–109.

Stutzer, Alois, and Bruno S. Frey. 2006. "Does Marriage Make People Happy, or Do Happy People Get Married?" *Journal of Socio-Economics* 35, no. 2: 326–347.

Sugden, Robert. 2005. "Experiment, Theory, World: A Symposium on the Role of Experiments in Economics." *Journal of Economic Methodology* 12, no. 2: 177–184.

van Praag, Bernard M. S. 1968. *Individual Welfare Functions and Consumer Behavior: A Theory of Rational Irrationality*. Amsterdam: North-Holland.

van Praag, Bernard M. S., and Barbara E. Baarsma. 2005. "Using Happiness Surveys to Value Intangibles: The Case of Airport Noise." *Economic Journal* 115, no. 500: 224–246.

Varian, Hal R. 1992. *Microeconomic Analysis*. New York: Norton.

Wilson, Timothy D., and Daniel T. Gilbert. 2003. "Affective Forecasting." In *Advances in Experimental Social Psychology*, vol. 35, ed. M. Zanna, 345–411. New York: Elsevier.

II

Pro-Social Behavior and
Trust

2   Conditional Cooperation: Behavioral Regularities from the Lab and the Field and Their Policy Implications

Simon Gächter

2.1   The Problem of Voluntary Cooperation

A well-known fact from the theory of public goods is that voluntary provision will lead to an inefficient undersupply (Samuelson 1954). The reason is the famous free rider problem: since, by definition of a public good, an agent can benefit from it even if he or she has not contributed to it, everyone has an incentive to hope that others will provide the public good. More specifically, a rational and selfish agent will equate only his or her private marginal benefits to the marginal costs of the public good, whereas efficiency requires that the sum of marginal benefits should equal the marginal costs. Thus there exists a tension between individual and collective rationality, which is prototypical for many cooperation problems. This tension lies at the heart of the matter in such diverse areas as warfare, environmental protection, management of commons, tax compliance, corruption, voting, participation in collective actions like demonstrations and strikes, donations to charities, teamwork, collusion between firms, embargoes and consumer boycotts, and so on.

While the logic of self-interest is straightforward, the data seem to be at odds with the free rider hypothesis derived under the joint assumptions of rationality and selfishness. The fact that people vote even in anonymous situations, take part in collective actions, often do not overuse common resources, care for the environment, mostly do not evade taxes on a large scale, and donate to public radio and charities suggests that the strict self-interest hypothesis is inconsistent with the degree of voluntary cooperation we observe around us.

How can we explain this? What are the implications for public policy and management? This chapter outlines some possible answers to both these questions. Our main sources of information are controlled laboratory and field experiments.[1] As I will show in this chapter, the main finding from a large body of experiments conducted in a variety of settings in the last three decades is that there is much more cooperation than predicted by standard theory (Ledyard 1995). Yet the experiments also show that voluntary cooperation is fragile in the sense that in repeatedly played public goods games cooperation declines over time.

How can we explain (the fragility of) voluntary cooperation? One important explanation is that people have "warm-glow" preferences; in other words, they have some positive utility simply from the act of contributing (e.g., Andreoni 1990). A second explanation is that many people have altruistic preferences—they want to benefit others. A third reason is errors—people make mistakes (e.g., Anderson, Goeree, and Holt 1998). In a clever design, Palfrey and Prisbrey (1997) test for warm-glow, altruism, and errors and find that altruism does not explain contributions, but some people have warm-glow preferences. Errors are important as well and explain why in repeated experiments contribution rates typically decline.

It should be noted that both motives—altruism and warm glow—are independent from other people's cooperation behavior. A set of recent experiments has cast doubt on this assumption. A large number of people are "conditionally cooperative"—they cooperate if they believe others cooperate as well. Yet a significant fraction of people is best characterized as free riders. In summary, recent evidence suggests that there is considerable heterogeneity with respect to people's cooperation preferences; in other words, there are types of players.

In section 2.3 I take up the issue of preference heterogeneity and discuss four of its predicted consequences:

(1) *Voluntary cooperation is fragile* This holds in particular without further institutional remedies, like possibilities for communication, punishment, or assortative interactions. The reason is that conditional cooperators who experience free riding will stop cooperating themselves.

(2) *Social interaction effects exist in voluntary cooperation* This means conditional cooperators will adapt their behavior to the group they are in. If other group members shirk, they shirk as well; if others cooperate, they cooperate as well. These social interaction effects mean that people's behavior is influenced by their group.

(3) *Group composition with respect to types matters for voluntary cooperation* For instance, if conditional cooperators know the other group members are cooperators as well, then they should be able to maintain high cooperation levels. The team spirit of like-minded cooperators should suffice to maintain high cooperation. Similarly, free riders who know that others are free rider types as well are predicted to defect.

(4) *Belief management matters for voluntary cooperation* Conditional cooperators cooperate by definition, if they believe others cooperate as well. Hence, any factor influencing beliefs will affect cooperation behavior.

I present evidence from new experiments designed to test these predictions. The evidence from these experiments unequivocally supports the importance of conditional cooperation and preference heterogeneity in understanding cooperation behavior. I see the experiments as behavioral models that may help us understand important field phenomena. In section 2.4 I therefore interpret field evidence on tax evasion, bribery, welfare fraud, attitudes toward the welfare state, charitable giving, and work morale in the light of the four behavioral models.

These findings on the importance of conditional cooperation and preference heterogeneity have consequences for theory and policy. If people are largely motivated by warm-glow preferences, and if the decay in contributions is due to reduced errors, then the modeling approach might be different than if people were free riders or conditional cooperators whose interaction explained the decay in contributions. In the former case, a modeling approach where errors figure prominently might be the preferable one (see, e.g., Anderson, Goeree, and Holt 1998). In the latter case, a theory of social preferences might be chosen (see, e.g., Camerer 2003; Fehr and Schmidt 2003; and Sobel 2005 for surveys of models, and Tyran and Sausgruber 2006 for a policy application). The findings also have consequences for public policy and management. I discuss them in section 2.5. Section 2.6 concludes.

2.2 Conditional Cooperation in the Lab and the Field

I start by presenting some stylized facts from laboratory experiments (section 2.2.1). This will only be a sketch and the interested reader may wish to consult Ledyard (1995) and Gächter and Herrmann (2005) for more complete accounts of important results from economic experiments. Dawes (1980) discusses evidence from social psychological experiments. I will discuss recent field experiments that are consistent with the lab findings in section 2.2.2. Section 2.2.3 presents evidence that behavior in the lab is consistent with naturally occurring field behavior.

2.2.1 Evidence from the Laboratory

The linear public goods game (or voluntary contribution mechanism) has proved extremely useful for testing the free rider hypothesis in the lab. In a typical linear public goods experiment, n people form a group. All group members are endowed with z tokens. Each subject i has to decide independently how many tokens (between 0 and z) to contribute to a common project (the public good). The contributions of the whole group are summed up. The experimenter then multiplies the sum of contributions by $\alpha > 1$ and distributes the resulting amount equally among the four group members. Thus each subject i's payoff is

$$\pi_i = z - g_i + \frac{\alpha}{n} \sum_{j=1}^{n} g_j, \quad j = 1, \ldots, n, \ \alpha > 1, \ \alpha/n < 1. \tag{1}$$

The first term $(z - g_i)$ indicates the payoff from the tokens not contributed to the public good (the "private payoff"). The second term is the payoff from the public good. Each token contributed to the public good becomes worth $\alpha > 1$ tokens. The resulting amount is distributed equally among the n group members—irrespective of how much an individual has contributed. Thus an individual benefits from the contributions of other group members, even if he or she has contributed nothing to the public good. A rational and selfish individual therefore has an incentive to keep all tokens for him- or herself, since his or her return per token from the public good is only $\alpha/n < 1$, whereas it is 1 if he or she keeps the token. By contrast, since $\alpha > 1$, the group as a whole is best off if everybody contributes all z tokens.

Figure 2.1 depicts a typical finding of a public goods experiment where the exact same game is repeated ten times. Subjects, who play in groups of four, know about the repetition. In each period each subject receives 20 tokens and decides how many of them to keep or contribute to the public good. After each round subjects are informed about what the other three group members have contributed. Figure 2.1 shows the resulting cooperation patterns in a "stranger" condition,

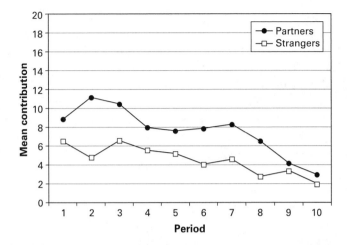

Figure 2.1
Contributions to a public good in constant groups (partners) and randomly changing groups (strangers) over ten repetitions. *Source*: Fehr and Gächter (2000).

where group members change randomly from round to round, and a "partner" condition, in which groups stay constant for all rounds.

Figure 2.1 illustrates two stylized facts from dozens of public goods experiments. First, people contribute substantially more than theoretically predicted. In most experiments, partners contribute more than strangers (see Keser and van Winden 2000 and Andreoni and Croson 2008 for an overview). The significance of this and related findings is that people are immediately able to distinguish whether they are in a situation requiring strategic cooperation (the partner condition) or not (the stranger condition) and to adapt their behavior accordingly.

The second stylized fact is that cooperation is very fragile and tends to collapse with repeated interactions. Why is this so? One explanation is that people have altruistic or warm-glow preferences, but also have to learn how to play this game. Since errors can only go in one direction, any erroneous decision looks like a contribution. Palfrey and Prisbrey (1997) test these explanations and find that the data are inconsistent with altruism. They find some evidence for warm-glow preferences but also conclude that people learn and commit fewer errors over time, which is why contributions decline.

Notice that warm glow, altruism, and errors are motivations that are independent of others' contributions. Psychologists have long argued that people's cooperation behavior depends on what others do (e.g.,

Kelley and Stahelski 1970). Using the methodology of experimental economics, Keser and van Winden (2000) were among the first economists to argue for the prevalence of conditional cooperation. Croson (2002) went one decisive step further by eliciting beliefs about other group members' contributions. She found a very high and statistically significant correlation of beliefs and contributions: subjects who expected others to contribute a lot were more likely to contribute high amounts than were subjects who expected others to free ride. This observation clearly suggests that people's contribution behavior is *not* independent of what they expect others to do. Thus, Croson's findings are consistent with conditional cooperation.

Croson (2002) did not look at individual behavior. Her observation is that, on average, people behave conditionally cooperatively in that their contributions and beliefs are positively correlated. Fischbacher and Gächter (2006) also elicited beliefs and replicated Croson's finding of a positive correlation between beliefs and contributions. At the individual level they find subjects who show a positive correlation between beliefs and contributions, whereas other subjects contribute zero even if they believe that others contribute positive amounts.

There are at least three problems with using the correlation between beliefs and contributions as an indicator of conditional cooperation. First, beliefs evolve endogenously in the experiment and are thus beyond the control of the experimenter. Second, a free rider who believes others contribute zero and actually contributes nothing him- or herself is observationally equivalent to a pessimistic conditional cooperator who only contributes a little because he or she believes others will free ride. Third, people may project their behavioral tendencies unto others; in other words beliefs may reflect a "false consensus effect" (see, e.g., Kelley and Stahelski 1970; Orbell and Dawes 1993).

Fischbacher, Gächter, and Fehr (2001) and Fischbacher and Gächter (2006) circumvent these problems by using a revealed preference method in their public goods games to infer people's contribution preferences as a function of other group members' contributions. Therefore, the subjects in their experiment do not choose one contribution but a contribution as a *function* of other group members' average contribution. The public goods game is played in groups of four subjects and the payoff function is again the same as in (2.1). The game is played just once to avoid confounds with strategic considerations. Every subject has to indicate a contribution conditional on others' average contribution; in other words, for each of the twenty-one possible values of the average of others' contribution, subjects have to enter the number of tokens they want to contribute.

Fischbacher, Gächter, and Fehr (2001) and Fischbacher and Gächter (2006) classify their subjects according to their contribution function (for details see their papers). A subject is called a free rider if and only if he or she contributes zero in all twenty-one cases. A subject is called a conditional cooperator if the contribution schedule is a positive function of the others' average contribution. A somewhat peculiar type is the triangle contributor, whose contribution increases when others' contributions are low and decreases for higher levels of others' contributions. Figure 2.2 illustrates the average contribution function of the different types in the experiments of Fischbacher and Gächter.

More than half of all subjects are conditional cooperators. Twenty-three percent are free riders. The rest are either triangle contributors or nonclassifiable others. Fischbacher, Gächter, and Fehr (2001) got a very similar distribution of types and even of average contribution patterns.

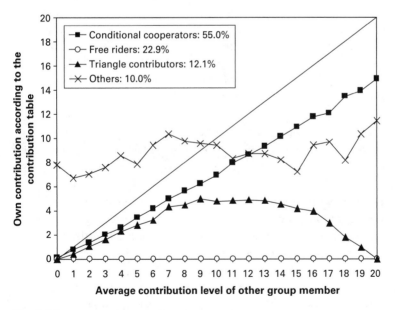

Figure 2.2
Average contribution function of types: Free riders, Conditional cooperators, Triangle contributors, and Others. Observations on the diagonal would correspond to a perfect conditional cooperator. *Source*: Fischbacher and Gächter (2006).

Ockenfels (1999), Bardsley and Moffatt (forthcoming), Burlando and Guala (2005), Muller et al. (2005), Ones and Putterman (forthcoming), and Page, Putterman, and Unel (2005) also find evidence for hetero-geneous cooperation preferences in related experimental designs. These studies differ in so many details that a straightforward com-parison of the distribution of the different types is not possible. Yet in almost all studies most subjects are classified as free riders or condi-tional cooperators, with the latter constituting the majority.

In summary, the evidence from the laboratory unambiguously shows that there is much more cooperation than is predicted by standard theory. Moreover, we find strong evidence that many people's attitude toward voluntary cooperation is conditional on other people's coopera-tion. This suggests that warm glow is not a dominant motivation. Fur-thermore, many people contribute more the more others contribute. This fact speaks against pure altruism explanations, which predict that people reduce their own contributions when informed that others al-ready contribute to the public good.

A second important finding is that people's contribution preferences are heterogeneous. While a large number of people seem to be condi-tional cooperators, a significant fraction of subjects is best character-ized as free riders. Some others show more complicated patterns. In section 2.3 I will discuss experiments that test directly for implications of preference heterogeneity. Before I do so, I will discuss evidence from the field.

2.2.2   Evidence from Field Experiments

Field experiments offer a great opportunity to test the behavioral rele-vance of laboratory findings in naturally occurring contexts (see also Harrison and List 2004). In this section I discuss a few field experi-ments that present results consistent with the lab evidence.

A first interesting study is by Frey and Meier (2004). Their subjects are University of Zurich students. Each semester each student is asked upon registering whether, in addition to the tuition fee, he or she would like to donate to two funds—one that helps needy students with cheap loans, and one supporting foreign students. A donation to the loans fund costs 7 Swiss francs (roughly €4.70), while one to the foreign student fund is 5 Swiss francs. Students can either donate these fixed amounts or not donate; intermediate donations are not possible. The data set comprises 37,624 students. For the field experiment, 2,500 nonfreshmen students were randomly selected; 2,000 of them received information about what others did. One thousand students received the information that a high percentage of others (64 percent) made a donation in the past; the remaining 1,000 students got the information that a relatively low number (46 percent) made a donation in the past.[2] Using 500 students, Frey and Meier elicited expectations about the fraction of students who make a donation.

The results are consistent with theories of conditional cooperation. First, students who expect a larger number of others to donate are more likely to donate. The correlation between expressed expectations and actual donation is 0.34 ($p < 0.001$). Second, a logit analysis shows that those students who received the information that 64 percent of others had donated in the past are more likely to donate than those who received the information that only 46 percent donated.

Heldt (2005) uses a similar idea as Frey and Meier (2004) to test for conditional cooperation. In his natural field experiment, subjects are tourists who use a cross-country skiing slope. They are then asked to make a donation for the slope's preparation. Heldt also manipulates the information people get. He finds that those who are informed that 70 percent of other tourists donated to the preparation of the slope contributed significantly more than those who did not get that information. Thus this behavior is consistent with conditional cooperation.

The study by Martin and Randal (2005) is similar in spirit. In their natural field experiment, conducted in a museum in New Zealand, visitors could donate to the museum by putting money into a transparent box. The experimenters manipulated whether there was money in the box or not. Consistent with conditional cooperation, they found that people donate significantly more when there is money in the box than when it is empty.

Shang and Croson (2005) conducted a field experiment on donations to a public radio station, which is a naturally occurring public good. The study was similar in spirit to Frey and Meier (2004). In a fundraising drive, people who called in to make a donation (to renew their membership) were confronted with what others had donated in the past. Specifically, in the experimental condition (but not in the control condition) the experimenter read the following sentence: "We had another member, they contributed $75 [$180 or $300]," and right after that "How much would you like to pledge today?" Then the callers could make their pledge (any amount they wished). In total, 538 members called to make a donation. The benchmark for donation decision is the previous year's fund drive, in which the average amount donated was $135 and the median amount, $75. The amounts used as the treatments correspond to the 50th percentile ($75), the 85th percentile ($180), and the 90th percentile ($300) in the previous fund drive. The results again support conditional cooperation. Callers who were confronted with a previous pledge of $300 donated significantly more than people in the control condition who were not confronted with that information; callers who received the $75 or $180 information, respectively, also contributed more than the control group, but this effect is not significant.[3]

In summary, the results from field experiments support the importance of conditional cooperation in the field. In the next section I briefly discuss a study that tests to what extent the same person behaves conditionally cooperatively inside and outside of the lab. This is an interesting question, because lab experiments are sometimes criticized for their lack of external validity.

2.2.3   Connections between the Lab and the Field

To gather information about the connection between lab and field behavior, the subjects in Benz and Meier (2005) took part in a lab experiment where they made a donation decision. The same subjects were observed in a naturally occurring environment—the donation decisions to two student support funds as described above and analyzed by Frey and Meier (2004). In one experiment ($n = 99$), called "social funds," the donation was to exactly the same funds as in the naturally occurring situation; in a second experiment ($n = 83$), called "charities," the donation was to another charity unrelated to the university.

The results show that lab and naturally occurring behavior are correlated. In the social funds experiment, the correlation between the average donation in the experiment and the average donation in the past four semesters is 0.28 ($p < 0.01$). In the charities experiment the correlation is very similar (0.27; $p < 0.01$). A more refined statistical analysis that controls for sociodemographic variables in a multivariate regression supports the main findings. Thus, although the lab is an artificial environment, one can observe behavior also triggered in a naturally occurring environment.

A second interesting study on the connection between lab and field behavior was done by Carpenter and Seki (2005), who combined the advantages of both environments in a very innovative way. The subjects of their study were Japanese fishermen who took part in a lab experiment, but who were also observed in their daily fishing activities.

Specifically, Carpenter and Seki collected data from fishing hauls, which they related to measures of the fishermen's social preferences. Carpenter and Seki use a finitely repeated public goods experiment with and without opportunities for social disapproval to statistically derive five measures of social preferences for each fisherman: his level of unconditional cooperation; his conditional cooperation; the propensity to disapprove; the fisherman's response to received social disapproval; and finally, the level of the unconditional response to disapproval. The results show that fishing productivity is significantly related to the experimentally derived measures of social preferences.

In my view, the results by Benz and Meier (2005) and Carpenter and Seki (2005) strongly underscore the complementarity between the lab and the field. In both the lab and the field we observe real behavior. In the lab we observe behavior in an artificial environment, whereas in a naturally occurring situation behavior takes place in a context-rich environment. Depending on the research question, context-richness and artificiality are either drawbacks or advantages. The lab's advantage is that we can observe motivations and behavioral patterns with a degree of clarity most often not feasible outside the lab. The fact that we have observed conditional cooperation in tightly controlled lab experiments supports the interpretation of the field results as stemming from conditional cooperation. The observation of conditional cooperation in the field tells us that the psychology of conditional cooperation carries over from the lab to the field.

In the following section I will use the power of the lab to test the implications of conditional cooperation and preference heterogeneity. I see these experiments as four behavioral models that might help us interpret naturally occurring field situations in policy-relevant domains like tax morale or welfare state policies, but also in managerial domains such as workplace behavior. The four models will also help me guide my discussion of consequences for public policy and management.

2.3   Four Consequences of Conditional Cooperation and Preference Heterogeneity

I will present four experiments in this section that test four implications of conditional cooperation and preference heterogeneity in general. The testable consequences are that (1) in groups where group members are randomly selected *voluntary cooperation is fragile*; (2) *there are group interaction effects*, meaning that people adapt their cooperation behavior to the relevant group they belong to; (3) *group composition matters*—in groups composed of like-minded types (groups composed of either cooperators or free riders) we should see starkly different cooperation patterns; and (4) *belief management matters*—in other words, factors that shift the belief about how much others contribute will influence contribution behavior. I discuss these four hypotheses and their experimental support in turn.

2.3.1 Voluntary Cooperation Is Fragile

I provide evidence in this section that heterogeneous motivations in randomly composed groups will lead to fragile cooperation. The reason is that free riders presumably do not contribute to the public good, while the conditional cooperators' contributions might be nonminimal, depending on their belief about other group members' contributions. Subjects learn the other team members' contributions during the repeated interaction. The free riders have no reason to react to that information. The conditional cooperators, on the other hand, will update their beliefs. Given that the average conditional cooperator does not fully match the others' contribution, the reaction will most likely be a decrease in contributions. There is no reason to expect that the remaining types (triangle contributors and others) will behave in a way that offsets the negative trend.

To test this argument rigorously, Fischbacher and Gächter (2006) combined the elicitation of contribution functions described above with a standard ten-period public goods game. The experiment was conducted in the stranger mode, meaning in every period the groups of four were formed randomly out of all twenty-four subjects present in a session. As predicted, contributions actually fell over time in all six sessions (from 40 percent initially to 10 percent on average by the last period).

Is this decline actually due to the interaction of heterogeneously motivated types? Stringent support for this conjecture comes from using the elicited contribution functions for predicting contributions. Recall that the strategies asked subjects to indicate how much they were prepared to contribute to the public good for all feasible average contribution levels of the other group members. In the standard ten-period public goods game Fischbacher and Gächter (2006) also elicited in each period each subject's *belief* about the other group members' contributions. Therefore, we can—given a stated belief about other

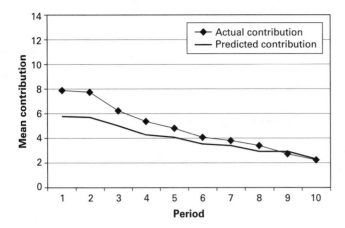

Figure 2.3
Average actual contributions and predicted contributions derived from beliefs and schedules. *Source*: Fischbacher and Gächter (2006).

group members' average contribution—*predict* what a subject should contribute to the public good if he or she would be perfectly consistent with his or her elicited contribution function. Figure 2.3 depicts the actual average contributions in the ten rounds of the public goods game and the predicted contributions as a result of stated beliefs and contribution schedules.

Although average predicted contributions are too low compared with actual contributions, we find that predicted contributions, which are derived from the contribution functions and the elicited beliefs, decline and converge to the actual pattern. This result therefore supports the argument that preference heterogeneity leads to unstable cooperation.

2.3.2 There Are Social Interaction Effects in Cooperation

If people are motivated by conditional cooperation, this may give rise to a social interaction effect, which occurs if an individual changes his or her behavior as a function of his or her respective group members' behavior. Identifying social or group interaction effects (often also called "neighborhood" or "peer effects") is notoriously difficult (Manski 2000). The ideal data set would observe the same individual at the same time in different groups, which are identical—apart from having different group members. Obviously this is impossible in the field. By contrast, in the lab it is possible to come very close to this counterfactual state. In an experiment, one is able to observe decisions of the

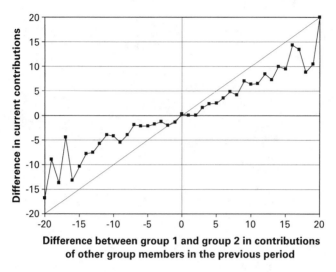

Figure 2.4
Social interaction effects: difference in own contribution as a function of the group members' contributions in the two groups. *Source*: Falk, Fischbacher, and Gächter (2005).

same subject at the same time in two economically identical environments. Social interactions—the fact that a person is systematically affected by the behavior of his or her group members—are the only reason to behave differently in these two environments. Falk, Fischbacher, and Gächter (2005) test this idea in a design where every subject is simultaneously a member of two groups, group 1 and group 2, which provide two independent public goods. The two groups consist of three group members each and are identical except that for each subject the other two group members in both groups are different people. Group composition stays constant for the twenty periods of the game. Falk, Fischbacher, and Gächter speak of a social interaction effect if the following holds: the larger the *difference* in contributions of group members in group 1 and group 2 in the previous period, the larger is the *difference* in current contributions of a group member to the two groups. Figure 2.4 provides the evidence from the 126 subjects who participated in this experiment.

The results provide unambiguous support for the social interaction hypothesis. In a given period a majority of subjects contributes more to the group that has contributed more in the previous period. This result holds for all fourteen independent units of observations, a result that is very unlikely to be due to chance ($p < 0.00007$).

2.3.3 Group Composition Matters

We have seen that a mixture of conditional cooperators and free riders is unfavorable for reaching cooperation in the public goods game. According to our third conjecture, conditional cooperators would presumably prefer to play the game with like-minded cooperators. Cooperation should be easy if the team players know they are among like-minded group members. Similarly, if the "true game" subjects are playing is a game where cooperation is one of the equilibria (free riding being another one), then knowing that others are like-minded cooperators should make it easy for subjects to coordinate on cooperation and to prevent free riding. Likewise, if free rider types know they are among other free riders, free riding should be paramount.

Gächter and Thöni (2005) conducted an experiment where subjects (105 in their version) play in groups of like-minded people. Like-mindedness refers to the type of subject according to classification as a free rider or a cooperator. The experiment starts with a three-person one-shot public goods game. When all subjects have chosen their contribution the subjects are ranked according to that contribution. Then the subjects are reassigned to new groups of three subjects. The reassignment works as follows: the three subjects with the highest contribution in the one-shot public goods game constitute the first group. The subjects with the fourth- to sixth-highest contribution are in the second group, and so on. Finally, the three least cooperative subjects find themselves in the last group. The subjects are informed about the reassignment procedure only after they finish the first game. Then the subjects learn the contributions their new group members chose in the one-shot public goods game. In the new group subjects play a ten-period public goods game. It is also important to note that the subjects do not know what the reassignment mechanism will be when choosing their contribution in the one-shot public goods game. Therefore, a high contribution in this first game credibly reveals a cooperative attitude.

The left panel of figure 2.5 shows the results of the main treatment. The maximal contribution in this game is 20. For expositional ease the groups are divided into three classes (top, middle, and low) according to their average contribution in the one-shot public goods game. The three graphs show the average contribution during the ten periods, separated by class. The unconnected dots in period zero depict the average contribution in the one-shot public goods game, which determines the group composition. The classes remain clearly separated over all periods. The groups in the top class consist to a large degree

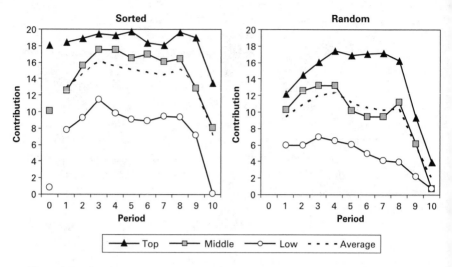

Figure 2.5
Left panel: average contributions over the ten periods for the top, middle, and low class
in the sorted treatment. The unconnected dots in period zero are the average contributions in the ranking treatment. Right panel: average contribution of the most, intermediate, and least cooperative groups over the ten periods. *Source*: Gächter and Thöni (2005).

of subjects who contributed their entire endowment in the one-shot
public goods game. These groups manage to maintain almost full cooperation until the penultimate period. The contributions of the middle
class (consisting of subjects with intermediate contributions in the one-
shot public goods game) show a similar pattern on a somewhat lower
level. Surprisingly, the subjects in the low class, who almost all chose a
contribution of zero in the one-shot public goods game, also manage to
reach a certain level of cooperation in the repeated game. There are
two explanations for this observation. First, if uncooperative subjects
know that they are among fellow uncooperatives then it is clear there
are no cooperative subjects to free ride on. This presumably motivates
even uncooperative subjects to contribute in order to encourage the
other free riders to contribute as well. A second related reason is that,
in contrast to a one-shot game, a ten-period repeated game induces
even free riders to strategically feign cooperation. Yet by the final period feigning cooperation does not pay off anymore, and consequently
the contributions of these free rider subjects drop to zero.

The right panel of figure 2.5 shows the results from a control experiment. Groups are formed randomly in this experiment, meaning there
is no reassignment according to cooperativeness. In order to make the

two treatments comparable, the data is still separated into the three classes of the top, middle, and lowest third with respect to their mean contribution levels. The separation now merely reflects the fact that there is variance in the contributions. Subjects in these control experiments are able to maintain a high level of contributions in all terciles until period 8; only in the penultimate and final periods do contributions drop to rather low levels. This "endgame effect" is typical for repeated public goods experiments in which groups are fixed for a finite number of periods (see, e.g., Keser and van Winden 2000).

Cooperation in the top class of the sorted treatment is much higher than the average contribution in the random treatment (dotted line in the right panel). However, the real value of the sorting mechanism becomes clear if we compare the top class with the most cooperative third of the groups in the random treatment. The average contribution of the top class of like-minded groups is significantly higher than the average contribution of the most cooperative third of the groups in the random treatment.

In summary, to be among like-minded people strongly affects cooperation behavior of all types. Related experiments suggest a similar conclusion. In Gunnthorsdottir, Houser, and McCabe (2007), subjects were regrouped as a function of their contributions but subjects were not aware of this. In Ones and Putterman (forthcoming) and Page, Putterman, and Unel (2005) subjects learned about others' contributions and were then regrouped according to the subjects' preferences. In all experiments regrouping made a significant difference relative to random groupings. Thus, for reasons of preference heterogeneity the "ecology of collective action," as Ones and Putterman aptly put it, matters a lot for the efficiency of voluntary cooperation.[4]

2.3.4   Belief Management Matters

Since the belief about others' contributions is important for conditional cooperators, our fourth conjecture says that any factor that alters these beliefs will influence cooperation. In the experiments of Fischbacher and Gächter (2006), for instance, beliefs evolved endogenously and mimicked the decline in cooperation. To test how beliefs can be influenced, Gächter and Renner (2005) developed a leader-follower design in a group of four players who stayed together for ten rounds (the number of rounds was known to the subjects). Specifically, one group member was designated as the leader. All group members had the same payoff function (see formula 2.1). The sole difference between the

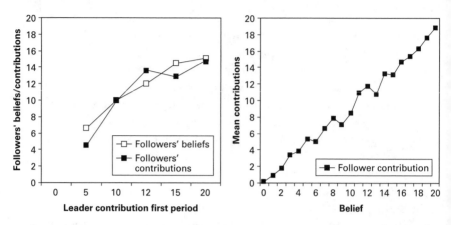

Figure 2.6
Left panel: leader's contribution in the first period and followers' beliefs and actual contributions in the first period. Right panel: relationship between beliefs and followers' actual contributions over all rounds. *Source*: Gächter and Renner (2005).

leader and the followers was that the leader made the first contribution decision. The followers observed the leader's contribution before they decided simultaneously about their own contributions. Gächter and Renner also elicited the followers' beliefs about the other followers' contributions. This allowed them to determine how the leader's contribution influences the beliefs about other followers' contributions.

The line with the open squares in the left panel of figure 2.6 shows that the leader's contribution in the first period positively influences the followers' beliefs about other followers' contributions. The first period is particularly interesting because the followers have not yet made any observation about the other followers' actual contributions. The more the leader contributes in the first period, the higher are the followers' beliefs about what other followers will contribute. This is the main and most direct evidence that a leader manages the followers' beliefs. In their actual contributions followers match their beliefs quite closely (see the line with the filled squares).

Using the data from all periods, the right panel of figure 2.6 shows that followers' beliefs and actual contributions are highly positively correlated. An econometric analysis reveals that these beliefs result from two sources: in a given period $t > 1$, beliefs are highly significantly positively correlated with the leader's contribution in this period. Yet beliefs are also highly significantly positively correlated with what the other followers contributed in the *previous* period $(t-1)$.

Moreover, quantitatively, the followers' contributions in $t - 1$ are more important than the leader's contribution for the followers' beliefs about other followers' contributions in period t. Thus there is an important path dependency in contributions. If the leader contributed little in the first period, followers are likely to contribute a small amount as well. This observation will—in addition to the leader's contribution—shape beliefs about other followers' contributions. In turn beliefs are—as the right panel of figure 2.6 shows—positively correlated with actual contributions. In other words, a bad start will make it very hard for the leader to lead his group by good example to high contribution levels. By contrast, a bold leader who sets a good example right from the beginning will positively influence followers' beliefs and contributions.

In summary, in this section I presented four experiments testing four implications of conditional cooperation and preference heterogeneity in general. As discussed earlier, I see these experiments as behavioral models that reveal something of the behavioral logic of conditional cooperation and preference heterogeneity. In the final two sections, I will therefore use these behavioral models to look at field phenomena and to discuss implications for public policy and management.[5]

2.4   Understanding Field Phenomena

2.4.1   Charitable Giving
During the war in former Yugoslavia three Austrian charity organizations set up the fund-raising campaign "Nachbar in Not" to finance food, clothes, and medical aid for the war victims. People donated more than 950 million Austrian schillings (approximately 70 million Euro) during the three years of the campaign to "Nachbar in Not" alone—donations to other charity organizations are not included. "Licht ins Dunkel" by the Austrian Broadcasting Corporation (ORF) is another example of a very successful and very large charitable fund-raising campaign that has for many years run around Christmas.

In both campaigns it was standard practice to list the names, hometowns, and donated amount of *all* donors who supported the campaigns, either on television or in newspapers. Donations by well-known politicians and celebrities were particularly prominently featured. The results from the field experiments discussed in section 2.2 and the lab results on how leader contributions can shape followers' contributions suggest that fund-raising organizers did not only rely on people's feelings of altruism, compassion, and warm glow, but also on conditional cooperation. Seed money effects are a related phenomenon that at least in part exploits the psychology of conditional cooperation (List and Lucking-Reiley 2002). Likewise, fundraisers often make a symbolic gift to the donor. Reciprocity as a form of conditional cooperation predicts that nicer gifts will lead to higher donations. Falk (2004) tests this prediction in a field experiment and finds it unambiguously supported.

Conditional cooperation is of course not the only reason why people donate to charities (see Andreoni 2006 and Vesterlund 2006 for extensive reviews). People certainly also contribute for signaling reasons (Glazer and Konrad 1996), social approval (e.g., Andreoni and Petrie 2004; Soetevent 2005), or because observing others provides information about the charity (Romano and Yildirim 2001; Vesterlund 2003). Our results suggest that genuine conditional cooperation may be an important determinant of people's philanthropy, in addition to all other motivations.

2.4.2   Tax Morale, Benefit Fraud, and Corruption

Norms of reciprocity and conditional cooperation might also influence tax morale. Tax morale is an interesting case because taxes are typically used to finance public goods from which one benefits even if one has not paid taxes. Indeed, there is evidence both from the field and the lab that people pay more taxes than the standard economic model of tax evasion predicts (e.g., Andreoni, Erard, and Feinstein 1998; Webley et al. 1991; Torgler 2002). Our results suggest that, controlling for detection probabilities, conditional cooperators will be more likely to evade taxes (or falsely claim welfare benefits) if they have the impression that many others do the same. Too many cheaters can spoil tax morale. The evidence is consistent with this prediction. People are less likely to cheat on their taxes or to commit benefit fraud if others behave honestly (e.g., Cialdini 1989; Slemrod 1992; Andreoni, Erard, and Feinstein 1998; Rothstein 2000). Frey and Torgler (2004) provide the most direct evidence on the relevance of conditional cooperation for tax morale. They use data from the European Values Survey and conduct a multivariate analysis across 30 countries (with at least 1000 individuals per country). Frey and Torgler find a positive correlation between people's tax morale (measured by a question about whether cheating on tax is justified if you have the chance) and people's perception of how many others cheat on taxes.[6] While Frey and Torgler cannot prove causation in their data, the results from the strategy method experiments by Fischbacher, Gächter, and Fehr (2001) and Fischbacher and Gächter (2006) suggest that causality goes from beliefs about others' cheating to their own cheating rather than vice versa.

The prevalence of corruption also seems to be influenced by motivations similar to those of conditional cooperation (see Abbink, Irlenbusch, and Renner 2002 for an experiment and further references to the literature). There are also important social interaction effects in these phenomena (Bertrand, Luttmer, and Mullainathan 2000; van der Klaauw and van Ours 2003), which is predicted by conditional cooperation and our model on these social interaction effects (section 2.3.2).

A particularly interesting observation is that the perception of the fairness of the tax system matters (Seidl and Traub 2001). Likewise, treatment by authorities apparently is an important determinant for people's tax morale (Pommerehne and Weck-Hannemann 1996; Frey 1997; Goette and Kucher 1998; Scholz and Lubell 1998; Feld and Frey 2002; Torgler 2003; Cummings et al. 2005; Alm and Torgler 2006). For instance, Cummings et al. (2005) present results from laboratory experiments they conducted in Botswana and South Africa. The experiments demonstrate that differences in the fairness of tax administration, perceived fiscal exchange, and attitudes toward the government can explain observed differences in compliance. Cummings et al. show that the experimental results are robust by replicating them for the same countries using survey responses measuring tax compliance.

How can our models explain such findings? First, there may be a direct effect from the concerned individual, who may reciprocate unfair treatment by authorities and/or the tax system with lower tax morale, simply because the taxpayer resents the unfair treatment (Smith 1992). Second, much like in the leadership experiments discussed in section 2.3.4, which showed that the leader strongly shapes the beliefs followers hold about other followers' behavior, tax authorities may have an indirect effect via beliefs about other taxpayers' behavior. The reason is that if many people share similar feelings and experiences, then this will lower the belief that others have a high tax morale, further undermining tax morale. Similarly, the government's trust in the honesty of its citizens may lead to a direct effect of "trust breeds trust" (Feld and Frey 2002), presumably because people like to be considered trustworthy. Again, if such feelings are widespread, they may shape beliefs about other citizens' tax morale and hence reinforce taxpayer morale.

A further interesting observation is that tax evasion at the Swiss cantonal level is higher in cantons where citizens have more direct democratic rights (e.g., Torgler 2005). According to our models, direct democratic procedures may positively influence tax morale. This is because direct democracy may affect beliefs about other people's tax morale when a tax law is passed in a referendum. A referendum signals people's opinion about a topic, and the dissemination of opinions via the result of a referendum may shape people's beliefs about others' behavior. Feld and Tyran (2002) tested this intuition in an experiment and found support for it.

2.4.3 Solidarity and Support for the Welfare State
Observers of welfare state policies (e.g., Wax 2000; Fong 2001; Fong, Bowles, and Gintis 2005; Lindbeck, Nyberg, and Weibull 1999) point out that many people hold reciprocity norms akin to the conditional cooperation observed in our experiments. Fong, Bowles, and Gintis (2002) even argue that "people support the welfare state because it conforms to deeply held norms of reciprocity and conditional obligations to others." There is evidence that people resent certain welfare policies if they think the recipient is a free rider who could earn his or her own living (Wax 2000; Fong, Bowles, and Gintis 2005). In their paper on tax payer resentment (i.e., the resentment against financing welfare payments), Besley and Coate (1992, 175) quote a notable British columnist, Lynda-Lee Porter, who neatly expresses the psychology of such resentment: "Our bronzed, healthy, young hedonistic army of self-unemployed are holidaying by the sea at our expense this year and, yes I do resent it. I resent working to support the idle loafers who have a laugh at our expensively generous system which allows them to get away with legalised plunder."

2.4.4 Work Morale
Business practitioners agree that "work morale" (i.e., loyalty, initiative, creativity, helping others, zest for the job, etc.) is crucial for productivity (Bewley 1999, 2005). Our models predict that work morale is strongly shaped by the behavior of management and coworkers. First, there may be social interaction effects in that people adapt their work morale to those of their peers. Empirical evidence supports this prediction (Ichino and Maggi 2000; Falk and Ichino 2006).

Additionally, our leadership model, discussed in section 2.3.4, and further experiments on leadership (e.g., Potters, Sefton, and Vesterlund

2004; Güth et al. 2004) suggest that managers may strongly influence morale and voluntary cooperation. To our knowledge there is no systematic evidence available, but some telling anecdotal evidence supports the point. For instance, Lawrence Weinstein, the head of Unisys, said in the wake of the Enron scandal, "Once you as a CEO go over the line, then people think it's okay to go over the line themselves."[7] This quote clearly expresses the conviction that leading by example matters for the ethical behavior of employees. Moreover, our results from section 2.3.4 suggest that a CEO's behavior may have long-lasting consequences on company morale and culture because of path-dependency effects.

Finally, our finding from section 2.3.3 that group composition matters may explain why companies sometimes fire workers, despite knowing that firing looks like a policy of management by threats. Yet Bewley (1999) notes that companies fire shirkers and incompetents to reestablish the work morale of the rest. Our models can explain this. Recall that the experimental findings reported above suggest that in heterogeneous groups contributions decline to low levels because the conditional cooperators stop cooperating once they experience free riding. If conditional cooperators know that they are among like-minded cooperators, cooperation can be established at very high levels. In a company context, this may mean that even a few shirkers can undermine work morale. Motivated workers may prefer that free riders are fired because they do not like being taken advantage of by their colleagues and because it reestablishes beliefs about others' team spirit.

2.5   Consequences for Public Policy and Management

In this section I briefly discuss policy implications that follow from the experimental findings and the four behavioral models discussed earlier. I first look at implications for public policy (section 2.5.1) and then at consequences for management (section 2.5.2).

2.5.1   Public Policy

Public policy is relevant mainly in the domains covered in sections 2.4.2 and 2.4.3. A first observation is that behavior by leaders—politicians and top officials—may matter strongly for citizens' morale. Leaders are belief managers, among other things. Leading by example strongly shapes beliefs about what others are doing, as the experiments in section 2.3.4 show. Therefore, there is a "multiplier effect," because a bad example (dishonesty in tax matters, corruption, or unethical behavior in other domains) may not only have direct effects on the concerned individual, but may also have indirect belief effects on how others will react. Moreover, there may be strong path-dependency effects, which may adversely affect morale in the long run. Leaders should thus be role models for whom there are higher moral standards than for normal citizens. Leaders in particular should be forced to resign quickly if there is confirmed evidence of dishonesty and inappropriate behavior.

Belief management happens not only through leaders, but also through things like the perceived fairness of the tax system, fair treatment by authorities, and direct democratic participation rights. The experimental results discussed above suggest that these factors are very important and should be strengthened. Tax reforms should improve the fairness of the tax system (based on careful evidence on how fairly the tax system is perceived) not only because fairness is desirable in its own right, but also because of its indirect effect on beliefs about other citizens' tax morale. A similar conclusion holds for the reform of tax authorities. How tax authorities publicly deal with tax evasion may strongly shape people's beliefs about the prevalence of tax evasion and thereby, as shown by Frey and Torgler (2004), influence tax morale (see also Kahan 2005). For instance, tax authorities should not only put tax evaders in the limelight, but they should also communicate that the large majority of citizens pay their dues.[8] Direct democratic participation rights may also have a strong effect on tax morale (see, e.g., Feld and Frey 2002; Feld and Tyran 2002; Torgler 2005; Torgler and Schaltegger 2005). People value participation for reasons of procedural fairness (Benz 2005). Also, the referenda results communicate people's norms and values for many issues and thereby shape people's beliefs about others' norms and values. For constitutional reasons, granting direct democratic rights is admittedly not an easy task in representative democracies.

The experimental results from sections 2.3.1 and 2.3.3 suggest that free riders trigger reduced cooperation. Cooperation unravels when free riders are not punished because the conditional cooperators reduce their cooperation as well. Experiments have shown that this result can be overturned if targeted punishment of free riders is possible (e.g., Fehr and Gächter 2000) or if the free riders are excluded from the group (Gächter and Thöni 2005, section 3.3; Cinyabuguma, Page, and Putterman 2005). If there is punishment, free riders have an incentive to cooperate and cooperators do not feel cheated. Cooperators therefore are happy to cooperate. This suggests that policy should aim to punish free riding (i.e., tax evasion, benefit fraud, and corruption). The experiments described above suggest that the goal should be to punish the free riders and at the same time to maintain the cooperators' optimistic beliefs by reassuring them that they will not be duped by the free riders. Thus they will continue to uphold their morale together with other like-minded cooperators.

Yet, apart from the legal implementation (which might be relatively simple), this is no easy task at all given the behavioral regularities discussed above. Punishment may entail monitoring and a general distrust of citizens. This is problematic for two reasons. First, there is evidence that monitoring may crowd out intrinsic motivation and reciprocal behavior (Frey 1993, 1997; Bohnet, Frey, and Huck 2001; Fehr and Gächter 2002). Second, monitoring may express distrust (Falk and Kosfeld 2006), which, in addition to the crowding-out effect, may have detrimental effects on beliefs about the tax morale of other taxpayers. Thus, in order to avoid the negative side effect of distrusting most citizens, policies should aim to punish big offenders severely and treat mild offenders (provided they are not serial offenders) mildly (by not using the full force of penal law, for instance). This has two advantages. First, strong sanctions have a deterrence effect, and they also reassure the honest citizens that large-scale antisocial behavior will be punished, which reduces the so-called sucker effect. Second, by trusting citizens and by fostering the fairness of the tax system and the tax authorities, the possible crowding out of intrinsic motivation and voluntary cooperation may be avoided.

The problem is complicated by the possibility that the game people actually play is one with multiple equilibria (see also Kahan 2005). Endemic cheating is an equilibrium, since conditional cooperators will also cheat if everyone else cheats. With multiple equilibria different policies may be required depending on the equilibrium currently in effect. A society with a good equilibrium of high trust, good tax morale, and low corruption must secure this equilibrium through policies that selectively punish the cheaters and maintain the conditional cooperators' good faith. If a society is trapped in a bad equilibrium, straightforward penalties and monitoring may be required to improve. Much more research is yet needed to understand what an optimal policy looks like in the presence of preference heterogeneity and multiple equilibria.

2.5.2 Management

The conclusions for management are very similar to those for public policy. First, managers, especially top managers, should be aware that they are role models who set an example and may strongly shape corporate cultures through path dependency in behaviors. Like politicians, they should therefore be held to high ethical standards.

Next, the problem of punishing shirkers in an organization is similar to the problem of how to treat antisocial behavior in the public policy domain. Management by threats will not create loyalty and may undermine intrinsic motivation and voluntary cooperation. Therefore, firing shirkers according to procedurally fair standards (Bewley 1999; Benz 2005) may help maintain high work morale among a team-spirited workforce.

Last, since group composition effects matter strongly for cooperative behavior, hiring team-spirited people is crucial if teamwork is important on the job. Composing teams of like-minded team players can help maintain high cooperation levels without any threat or negative side effects of monitoring and distrust.

2.6 Concluding Remarks

I have discussed experimental evidence from the lab and the field that shows many people are conditional cooperators, whereas others are best characterized as free riders. I believe that this sort of preference heterogeneity helps us better understand important phenomena in the field, like tax morale and attitudes toward the welfare state. Since, if many people are conditional cooperators, beliefs about others' behavior are highly relevant for voluntary cooperation, policy should not only take into account the incentive effects on an individual's behavior, but also how policy affects the beliefs and behavior of the majority of citizens, who are conditional cooperators. The evidence discussed in this chapter can only be considered a starting point. Much more research is needed for a proper understanding of the policy consequences of conditional cooperation and preference heterogeneity.

Notes

This chapter is part of the MacArthur Foundation Network on Economic Environments and the Evolution of Individual Preferences and Social Norms. Helpful comments by the seminar participants at the CESifo Summer Institute on Economics and Psychology in Venice, 2005, and by the editors and two anonymous referees are highly appreciated.

1. The laboratory allows for a degree of control not often feasible in a naturally occurring field situation. In all the experiments I will discuss below, participants earned considerable amounts of money that depended on their decisions. Thus, the laboratory allows observation of real economic behavior under controlled circumstances and also permits causal inferences often not feasible from naturally occurring data. See Kagel and Roth (1995) and Camerer (2003) for excellent overviews of experiments in economics and game theory and Guala (2005) for a discussion of the methodology of experimental economics.

2. No deception was involved because real frequencies (resulting from different time periods) were used.

3. A referee of this paper suggested that a potential problem might be callers' concern about their self-image and how they look in the eyes of the receiver of the call.

4. See Ones and Putterman (forthcoming) and Gächter and Thöni (2005) for a further discussion of the related literature.

5. See Falk (2003), Fehr and Fischbacher (2002), and Kahan (2005) for related discussions and further examples.

6. Cheaters may also entertain a self-serving belief about how many others cheat on their taxes, to justify their own misbehavior. Thus, causality may not run from beliefs about the prevalence of cheating in the population, but cheating may induce self-serving beliefs. I am grateful to a referee for suggesting this possibility.

7. Quoted from *The Economist*, July 27, 2002, p. 58.

8. An anonymous referee suggested, citing the following anecdotal evidence, that communication might be very important. India's 1997 tax amnesty has been seen as a financial success (it raised $2.5 billion from over 350,000 individuals). The tax amnesty was accompanied by intensive media activity. Celebrities such as sport and film stars promoted participation in the amnesty program, which contributed greatly to its success.

References

Abbink, K., B. Irlenbusch, and E. Renner. 2002. "An Experimental Bribery Game." *Journal of Law, Economics and Organization* 18, no. 2: 428–454.

Alm, J., and B. Torgler. 2006. "Culture Differences and Tax Morale in the United States and in Europe." *Journal of Economic Psychology* 27, no. 2: 224–246.

Anderson, S. P., J. K. Goeree, and C. Holt. 1998. "A Theoretical Analysis of Altruism and Decision Error in Public Goods Games." *Journal of Public Economics* 70: 297–323.

Andreoni, J. 1990. "Impure Altruism and Donations to Public Goods: A Theory of Warm-Glow Giving." *Economic Journal* 100: 464–477.

Andreoni, J. 2006. "Philanthropy." In *Handbook on the Economics of Giving, Reciprocity and Altruism*, ed. L.-A. Gerard-Varet, S.-C. Kolm, and J. M. Ythier, 1201–1269. Amsterdam: Elsevier.

Andreoni, J., and R. Croson. 2008. "Partners versus Strangers: Random Rematching in Public Goods Experiments." Forthcoming in *Handbook of Experimental Economic Results*, ed. C. Plott and V. Smith. Amsterdam: Elsevier.

Andreoni, J., B. Erard, and J. Feinstein. 1998. "Tax Compliance." *Journal of Economic Literature* 36: 818–860.

Andreoni, J., and R. Petrie. 2004. "Public Goods Experiments without Confidentiality: A Glimpse into Fund-Raising." *Journal of Public Economics* 88: 1605–1623.

Bardsley, N., and P. Moffatt. Forthcoming. "The Experimetrics of Public Goods: Inferring Motivations from Contributions." *Theory and Decision*.

Benz, M. 2005. "The Relevance of Procedural Utility for Economics." Mimeo., University of Zurich.

Benz, M., and S. Meier. 2005. "Do People Behave in Experiments as in Real Life? Evidence from Donations." Mimeo., University of Zurich.

Bertrand, M., E. Luttmer, and S. Mullainathan. 2000. "Network Effects and Welfare Cultures." *Quarterly Journal of Economics* 115, no. 3: 1019–1055.

Besley, T., and S. Coate. 1992. "Understanding Taxpayer Resentment." *Journal of Public Economics* 48: 165–183.

Bewley, T. 1999. *Why Don't Wages Fall in a Recession?* Cambridge, MA: Harvard University Press.

Bewley, T. 2005. "Fairness, Reciprocity and Wage Rigidity." In *Moral Sentiments and Material Interests: The Foundations of Cooperation in Economic Life*, ed. H. Gintis, S. Bowles, R. Boyd, and E. Fehr, 303–338. Cambridge, MA: MIT Press.

Bohnet, I., B. S. Frey, and S. Huck. 2001. "More Order with Less Law: On Contract Enforcement, Trust, and Crowding." *American Political Science Review* 95: 131–144.

Burlando, R., and F. Guala. 2005. "Heterogeneous Agents in Public Goods Experiments." *Experimental Economics* 8, no. 1: 35–54.

Camerer, C. 2003. *Behavioral Game Theory*. Princeton: Princeton University Press.

Carpenter, J. P., and E. Seki. 2005. "Do Social Preferences Increase Productivity? Field Experimental Evidence from Fishermen in Toyama Bay." IZA Discussion Paper No. 1697.

Cialdini, R. 1989. "Social Motivations to Comply: Norms, Values and Principles." In *Tax Payer Compliance*, ed. J. A. Roth, J. T. Scholz, and A. Dryden Witte, 200–227. Philadelphia: University of Pennsylvania Press.

Cinyabuguma, M., T. Page, and L. Putterman. 2005. "Cooperation under the Threat of Expulsion in a Public Goods Experiment." *Journal of Public Economics* 89: 1421–1435.

Croson, R. 2002. *Theories of Altruism and Reciprocity: Evidence from Linear Public Goods Games*. Mimeo., University of Pennsylvania.

Cummings, R., J. Matinez-Vazquez, M. McKee, and B. Torgler. 2005. "Effects of Tax Morale on Tax Compliance: Experimental and Survey Evidence." Working Paper No. 05-16, International Studies Program, Andrew Young School of Policy Studies, Georgia State University.

Dawes, R. 1980. "Social Dilemmas." *Annual Review of Psychology* 31: 169–193.

Falk, A. 2003. "*Homo Oeconomicus* versus *Homo Reciprocans*: Ansätze für ein neues Wirtschaftspolitisches Leitbild?" *Perspektiven der Wirtschaftspolitik* 4, no. 1: 141–172.

Falk, A. 2004. "Charitable Giving as a Gift Exchange: Evidence from a Field Experiment." Discussion Paper IZA-DP No. 1148, Bonn.

Falk, A., U. Fischbacher, and S. Gächter. 2005. "'Living in Two Neighborhoods'—Social Interaction in the Lab." Working Paper No. 150, Institute for Empirical Research in Economics, University of Zurich.

Falk, A., and A. Ichino. 2006. "Clean Evidence on Peer Pressure." *Journal of Labor Economics* 24, no. 1: 39–57.

Falk, A., and M. Kosfeld. 2006. "The Hidden Costs of Control." *American Economic Review* 96, no. 5: 1611–1630.

Fehr, E., and U. Fischbacher. 2002. "Why Social Preferences Matter—The Impact of Non-Selfish Motives on Competition, Cooperation and Incentives." *Economic Journal* 112: C1–C33.

Fehr, E., and S. Gächter. 2000. "Cooperation and Punishment in Public Goods Experiments." *American Economic Review* 90, no. 4: 980–994.

Fehr, E., and S. Gächter. 2002. "Do Incentive Contracts Undermine Voluntary Cooperation?" Working Paper No. 34, Institute for Empirical Research in Economics, University of Zurich.

Fehr, E., and K. Schmidt. 2003. "Theories of Fairness and Reciprocity: Evidence and Economic Applications." In *Advances in Economics and Econometrics. Theory and Applications.* Vol. I, ed. Matthias Dewatripont, Lars Hansen, and Stephen Turnovsky, 208–257. Cambridge: Cambridge University Press.

Feld, L., and B. S. Frey. 2002. "Trust Breeds Trust: How Taxpayers are Treated." *Economics of Governance* 3: 87–99.

Feld, L., and J.-R. Tyran. 2002. "Tax Evasion and Voting: An Experimental Analysis." *Kyklos* 55, no. 2: 197–222.

Fischbacher, U., S. Gächter, and E. Fehr. 2001. "Are People Conditionally Cooperative? Evidence from a Public Goods Experiment." *Economics Letters* 71: 397–404.

Fischbacher, U., and S. Gächter. 2006. "Heterogeneous Social Preferences and the Dynamics of Free Riding. CeDEx Discussion Paper Series No. 2006-01, University of Nottingham.

Fong, C. 2001. "Social Preferences, Self-Interest, and the Demand for Redistribution." *Journal of Public Economics* 82: 225–246.

Fong, C., S. Bowles, and H. Gintis. 2005. "Reciprocity and the Welfare State." In *Moral Sentiments and Material Interests: The Foundations of Cooperation in Economic Life*, ed. H. Gintis, S. Bowles, R. Boyd, and E. Fehr, 277–302. Cambridge, MA: MIT Press.

Frey, B. S. 1993. "Shirking or Work Morale? The Impact of Regulating." *European Economic Review* 37: 1523–1532.

Frey, B. S. 1997. "A Constitution for Knaves Crowds out Civic Virtues." *Economic Journal* 107: 1043–1053.

Frey, B. S., and S. Meier. 2004. "Social Comparisons and Pro-Social Behavior. Testing 'Conditional Cooperation' in a Field Experiment." *American Economic Review* 94, no. 5: 1717–1722.

Frey, B. S., and B. Torgler. 2004. "Taxation and Conditional Cooperation." CREMA Working Paper 2004-20, Center for Research in Economics, Management and the Arts, Basel, Switzerland.

Gächter, S., and B. Herrmann. 2005. "Human Cooperation from an Economic Perspective." In *Cooperation in Primates and Humans: Mechanisms and Evolution*, ed. P. M. Kappeler and C. P. van Schaik, 279–303. Heidelberg: Springer.

Gächter, S., and E. Renner. 2005. "Leading by Example in the Presence of Free Rider Incentives." Mimeo., University of Nottingham.

Gächter, S., and C. Thöni. 2005. "Social Learning and Voluntary Cooperation among Like-Minded People." *Journal of the European Economic Association* 3: 303–314.

Glazer, A., and K. A. Konrad. 1996. "A Signaling Explanation for Private Charity." *American Economic Review* 86, no. 4: 1019–1028.

Goette, L., and M. Kucher. 1998. "Trust Me: An Empirical Analysis of Taxpayer Honesty." *Finanzarchiv* 55: 429–444.

Guala, F. 2005. *The Methodology of Experimental Economics*. Cambridge: Cambridge University Press.

Gunnthorsdottir, A., D. Houser, and K. McCabe. (2007). "Dispositions, History and Contributions in Public Goods Experiments." *Journal of Economic Behavior and Organization* 62: 304–315.

Güth, W., V. Levati, M. Sutter, and E. van der Heijden. 2004. "Leadership and Cooperation in Public Goods Experiments." Mimeo., Max Planck Institute, Jena.

Harrison, G., and J. List. 2004. "Field Experiments." *Journal of Economic Literature* 42: 1009–1055.

Heldt, T. 2005. "Conditional Cooperation in the Field: Cross-Country Skiers' Behavior in Sweden." Mimeo., Dlarna University and Uppsala University, Sweden.

Ichino, A., and G. Maggi. 2000. "Work Environment and Individual Background: Explaining Regional Shirking Differential in a Large Italian Firm." *Quarterly Journal of Economics* 115, no. 3: 1057–1090.

Kagel, J., and A. E. Roth, eds. 1995. *Handbook of Experimental Economics*. Princeton, NJ: Princeton University Press.

Kahan, D. 2005. "The Logic of Reciprocity: Trust, Collective Action, and Law." In *Moral Sentiments and Material Interests: The Foundations of Cooperation in Economic Life*, ed. H. Gintis, S. Bowles, R. Boyd, and E. Fehr, 339–378. Cambridge, MA: MIT Press.

Kelley, H., and A. Stahelski. 1970. Social Interaction Basis of Cooperators' and Competitors' Beliefs about Others." *Journal of Personality and Social Psychology* 16: 190–197.

Keser, C., and F. van Winden. 2000. "Conditional Cooperation and Voluntary Contributions to Public Goods." *Scandinavian Journal of Economics* 102, no. 1: 23–39.

Ledyard, J. 1995. "Public Goods: A survey of Experimental Research." In *Handbook of Experimental Economics*, ed. J. Kagel and A. E. Roth, 111–194. Princeton, NJ: Princeton University Press.

Lindbeck, A., S. Nyberg, and J. Weibull. 1999. "Social Norms and Economic Incentives in the Welfare State." *Quarterly Journal of Economics* 114, no. 1: 1–35.

List, J., and D. Lucking-Reiley. 2002. "The Effects of Seed Money and Refunds on Charitable Giving: Experimental Evidence from a University Capital Campaign." *Journal of Political Economy* 110, no. 1: 215–233.

Manski, C. 2000. "Economic Analysis of Social Interactions." *Journal of Economic Perspectives* 14, no. 3: 115–136.

Martin, R., and J. Randal. 2005. "Voluntary Contributions to a Public Good: A Natural Field Experiment." Mimeo., Victoria University, Wellington, New Zealand.

Muller, L., M. Sefton, R. Steinberg, and L. Vesterlund. 2005. "Strategic Behavior and Learning in Repeated Voluntary-Contribution Experiments." CeDEx Working Paper No. 2005-13, University of Nottingham.

Ockenfels, A. 1999. "Fairness, Reziprozität und Eigennutz—Ökonomische Theorie und Experimentelle Evidenz." *Die Einheit der Gesellschaftswissenschaften* 108: 111–194.

Orbell, J. M., and R. M. Dawes. 1993. "Social Welfare, Cooperators' Advantage, and the Option of Not Playing the Game." *American Sociological Review* 58, no. 6: 787–800.

Ones, U., and L. Putterman. Forthcoming. "The Ecology of Collective Action: A Public Goods and Sanctions Experiment with Controlled Group Formation." *Journal of Economic Behavior and Organization.*

Page, T., L. Putterman, and B. Unel. 2005. "Voluntary Association in Public Goods Experiments: Reciprocity, Mimicry and Efficiency." *Economic Journal* 116: 1032–1052.

Palfrey, T. R., and J. E. Prisbrey. 1997. "Anomalous Behavior in Public Goods Experiments: How Much and Why?" *American Economic Review* 87: 829–846.

Pommerehne, W., and H. Weck-Hannemann. 1996. "Tax Rates, Tax Administration and Income Tax Evasion in Switzerland." *Public Choice* 88: 161–170.

Potters, J., M. Sefton, and L. Vesterlund. 2004. "Leading-by-Example in Voluntary Contribution Games: An Experimental Study." CeDEx Working Paper No. 2004-01, University of Nottingham.

Romano, R., and H. Yildirim. 2001. "Why Charities Announce Donations: A Positive Perspective." *Journal of Public Economics* 81, no. 3: 423–447.

Rothstein, B. 2000. "Trust, Social Dilemmas and Collective Memories." *Journal of Theoretical Politics* 12, no. 4: 447–501.

Samuelson, P. 1954. "The Pure Theory of Public Expenditures." *Review of Economics and Statistics* 36, no. 4: 387–389.

Scholz, J. T., and M. Lubell. 1998. "Trust and Taxpayers: Testing the Heuristic Approach to Collective Action." *American Journal of Political Science* 45: 160–178.

Seidl, C., and S. Traub. 2001. "Taxpayers' Attitudes, Behaviour, and Perception of Fairness." *Pacific Economic Review* 6, no. 2: 255–267.

Shang, J., and R. Croson. 2005. "Field Experiments in Charitable Contribution: The Impact of Social Influence on the Voluntary Provision of Public Goods." Mimeo., Wharton University.

Slemrod, J., ed. 1992. *Why People Pay Taxes: Tax Compliance and Enforcement.* Ann Arbor: University of Michigan Press.

Sobel, J. 2005. "Interdependent References and Reciprocity." *Journal of Economic Literature* 43: 392–436.

Soetevent, A. 2005. "Anonymity in Giving in a Natural Context—A Field Experiment in 30 Churches. *Journal of Public Economics* 89: 2301–2323.

Smith, K. W. 1992. "Reciprocity and Fairness: Positive Incentives for Tax Compliance." In *Why People Pay Taxes: Tax Compliance and Enforcement*, ed. J. Slemrod, 223–250. Ann Arbor: University of Michigan Press.

Torgler, B. 2002. "Speaking to Theorists and Searching for Facts: Tax Morale and Tax Compliance in Experiments." *Journal of Economic Surveys* 16, no. 5: 657–683.

Torgler, B. 2003. "Tax Morale, Rule-Governed Behavior and Trust." *Constitutional Political Economy* 14: 119–140.

Torgler, B. 2005. "Tax Morale and Direct Democracy." *European Journal of Political Economy* 21: 525–531.

Torgler, B., and C. Schaltegger. 2005. "Tax Amnesties and Political Participation." *Public Finance Review* 33, no. 3: 403–431.

Tyran, J.-R., and R. Sausgruber. 2006. "A Little Fairness May Induce a Lot of Redistribution in Democracy." *European Economic Review* 50, no. 2: 469–485.

van der Klaauw, B., and J. van Ours. 2003. "From Welfare to Work: Does the Neighborhood Matter?" *Journal of Public Economics* 87: 957–985.

Vesterlund, L. 2003. "The Informational Value of Sequential Fundraising." *Journal of Public Economics* 87: 627–657.

Vesterlund, L. 2006. "Why Do People Give?" In *The Nonprofit Sector*, 2nd ed., ed. R. Steinberg and W. W. Powell, 568–588. New Haven, CT: Yale University Press.

Wax, A. 2000. "Rethinking Welfare Rights: Reciprocity Norms, Reactive Attitudes, and the Political Economy of Welfare Reforms." *Law and Contemporary Problems* 63: 257–298.

Webley, P., H. Robben, H. Elffers, and D. Hessing. 1991. *Tax Evasion: An Experimental Approach*. Cambridge: Cambridge University Press.

3

A Survey of Economic Theories and Field Evidence on Pro-Social Behavior

Stephan Meier

3.1 Introduction

Standard economic theory predicts that public goods are often under-provided because individuals will free ride on the contributions of others since they cannot be excluded from using the public good. An enormous number of decision situations can be characterized as public good problems. For example, people free ride on the efforts of others to protect the environment; no consumer puts effort into fighting for reduced tariff rates because everyone profits from the resulting lower prices; people let others organize community events; no one donates blood because, if needed, he or she will receive blood anyway; people do not enforce social norms (e.g., not to litter in a public park) because they think that others should do it; and so on. All these individual calculations result in suboptimal outcomes: too little environmental protection, no reduction in tariff rates, no community events, too few blood donors, and nobody who enforces social norms. In general, people will not contribute a sufficient amount of money or time to provide the socially optimal amount of public goods.

In reality, people free ride less often than is predicted by standard economic theory. People behave in a number of situations not according to narrow self-interest, but rather pro-socially: for instance, most people actually pay their taxes, a fact that cannot be explained by relying on strict self-interest axioms (e.g., Andreoni, Erard, and Feinstein 1998). Due to the low probability of having the decisive vote, the expected utility of voting is close to zero and standard economic theory predicts that few people will show up at the ballot boxes; yet individuals do vote (e.g., Mueller 2003). In the political process, voters express their preferences for income redistribution in a way that goes beyond financial self-interest (e.g., Shabman and Stephenson 1994).

Under certain circumstances people are able to prevent the overuse of a common-pool resource (Ostrom 1990). And a large part of open source software production is difficult to explain by relying on strict self-interested behavior (see Osterloh, Rota, and Kuster 2003).

According to standard economic theory, people should take advantage of any opportunity to exploit society or another individual—but they do not. In various situations in the political sphere, in firms, or in the family, people are "rent leavers," meaning that they "do not invest in something that is unproductive for others but that would increase their own income" (Bohnet and Frey 1997, 711). Individuals therefore contribute substantial amounts of money and time to public goods.[1] The self-interest hypothesis has also been rejected in a large number of laboratory experiments (see Ledyard 1995; Camerer 2003). A recent study of experimental ultimatum games in 15 small-scale societies around the world reveals that "the canonical model of the self-interested material pay-off maximizing actor is systematically violated" (Henrich et al. 2001, 77).

As a result of these findings, economists have turned to psychologists, who have studied pro-social behavior for quite a long time. Consequentially, a large number of economic theories have evolved to explain people's pro-social behavior and the variation in their respective behavior. This paper surveys economic theories of pro-social behavior. In each subsection, one specific theory is investigated and predictions for behavior are derived. The hypotheses are then confronted with existing empirical evidence. The empirical findings presented are mainly based on field and survey evidence rather than on laboratory experiments, but laboratory studies are also referred to where appropriate. Fehr and Schmidt (2003), Camerer (2003), and Konow (2003) offer other good surveys of theories of fairness and reciprocity with a focus on experiments as sources of evidence.

Contributions to public goods may be explained by relying on extended versions of the self-interest model. People may contribute to a public good if it is a precondition of receiving a private good (Olson 1965). Automobile lobby groups like the AAA, for example, provide breakdown services, insurance, and reductions in hotel prices to their members. Donors to arts organizations may gain access to special events, gala dinners, or choice seats in the opera house they support; they may even have exhibition halls named after them. In addition to the fringe benefits, volunteers may receive job experience and a social network. Or donations may be driven by a desire to signal wealth in order to increase one's prestige (Glazer and Konrad 1996; Harbaugh 1998). Despite the fact that prestige is not a material good, the important aspect of the "prestige motive" is that people instrumentally behave pro-socially to get an external reward. But theories based on extended self-interest cannot explain the full range of pro-social behavior. Even in anonymous situations and in last rounds of interaction where no material fringe benefit can be expected, people often behave pro-socially. Although some economists are reluctant to accept that the self-interest hypothesis has its limits, the bulk of empirical evidence on pro-social behavior requires that theories explaining human behavior go beyond self-interest.

The survey proceeds as follows: section 3.2 presents the three most important sets of theories on nonselfish or "other-regarding" behavior: outcome-based pro-social preference models, theories based on the norm of reciprocity, and approaches focusing on the relevance of self-identity. Section 3.3 focuses on the importance of the institutional environment in explaining variations in pro-social behavior. Section 3.4 presents evidence for the effect of relative prices on pro-social behavior. Section 3.5 discusses the heterogeneity of individuals with respect to pro-social behavior and the importance of such differences for an economic analysis of pro-social behavior. In section 3.6, the relationship between utility and pro-social behavior is discussed. Section 3.7 draws conclusions for policy and formulates remaining open questions.

3.2   Theories beyond Self-Interest

Adam Smith, who praised the selfishness of individuals in *The Wealth of Nations*, did not believe that only selfish motives matter for human beings. In his first book, *The Theory of Moral Sentiments*, Smith wrote: "How selfish soever man may be supposed, there are evidently some principles in his nature, which interest him in the fortune of others, and render their happiness necessary to him, though he derives nothing from it, except the pleasure of seeing it" (1759, 3). In recent years, various models have been developed in order to map out *how* man is interested in the fortune of others and whether these motives can systematically explain pro-social behavior. Three groups of prominent models can be broadly distinguished: (1) outcome-based *pro-social preference* theories assume that an individual's utility depends directly on the utility of other people; (2) theories of *reciprocity* are based on the notion that individuals behave in a friendly manner when they are treated benevolently, and, conversely, they act meanly when treated badly; and (3) a third group of approaches stresses the importance of *self-identity* for pro-social behavior.

3.2.1 Outcome-Based Pro-Social Preferences

Theories of pro-social preferences are based on the notion that people care about the well-being of others. In the three most prominent formulations of pro-social preferences, the utility of others can either (1) influence one's utility directly (pure altruism theories), (2) influence one's utility partly because helping others produces a "warm glow" (impure altruism theories), or (3) have an effect on one's utility that depends on the difference between one's own and another's well-being (theories of inequality aversion).

3.2.1.1 Pure altruism Altruism theories assume that others' consumption or utility positively affects an individual's own utility (e.g., Becker 1974). People thus behave pro-socially or contribute to a public good because they enjoy the well-being of others. Altruistic preferences are used to explain a wide range of pro-social behavior: donations (Smith, Kehoe, and Cremer 1995), volunteering (Unger 1991), behavior in the workplace (Rotemberg 1994), and contributions in laboratory experiments like dictator games (Eckel and Grossman 1996; Andreoni and Miller 2002).

Altruism theories assume that individuals enjoy seeing the well-being of others increase independently of the source of the improvement. This leads to the hypothesis that people will contribute positive amounts to public goods but their contributions are inversely related to the contributions of others. If other private individuals contribute to the public good, or the state contributes, then people will reduce their contribution to the same extent (e.g., Roberts 1984).

Altruism theories' prediction that contributions by others will completely crowd out an individual's own contribution has been criticized on the basis of both theoretical considerations and empirical facts. From a theoretical point of view, for example, it can be argued that in large groups, no altruist would contribute to a public good since he or she could free ride on the contributions of others (Sugden 1982; Andreoni 1988; Croson 1998). But in reality, people donate to large charities like the Red Cross or Amnesty International. In empirical research, it is difficult to support the one-to-one crowding-out of private contributions by public grants. Government spending has been found to crowd out private contributions, but the crowding-out is far from complete (dollar-for-dollar); it lies in the range of zero to one-half (see Andreoni 2006 for an excellent survey).[2]

3.2.1.2 Impure altruism Because pure altruism theories do not make empirically accurate predictions with respect to crowding-out effects, Andreoni (1990) extends the altruism model with a "warm glow" motive for giving. People care not only about the recipient's utility but receive some private goods benefit from their pro-social behavior per se. In comparison with the private goods benefit (e.g., prestige), the warm glow is purely internal, derived from the donor's own knowledge of his pro-social behavior. Psychologically, various underlying motivations may cause the ultimately egoistic warm glow, such as self-reward, negative state relief, or guilt reduction (for a survey, see Bierhoff 2002). In the case of volunteering, self-determination and increased self-esteem may be intrinsically rewarding motives. In models of impure altruism, crowding-out is never perfect because donors still receive a benefit from the donation per se. The prediction of the impure altruism model better fits the observation that givers do not see public grants as perfect substitutes for private contributions.[3] Nevertheless, the model of warm-glow giving still predicts that people will partly reduce their own contributions when other agents or the government increases their share to the public good.

Theories of both pure and impure altruism also assume stable interdependent preferences. According to these theories, people will therefore exhibit stable behavior. However, this prediction is at odds with at least two empirical observations. First, pro-social behavior erodes with repetition in most experimental studies (e.g., Dawes and Thaler 1988). Altruism theories are not able to explain the decay of pro-social behavior. Second, people do not always behave pro-socially to increase the well-being of others. Sometimes they consciously reduce others' utility by punishing their behavior, which is inconsistent with altruistic preferences (Fehr and Gächter 2000a). To cope with these behavioral irregularities, models of inequality aversion focus on the relative well-being rather than absolute utility levels.

3.2.1.3 Inequality aversion Models of inequality aversion assume that one's relative standing in the income distribution is important. According to the model of Fehr and Schmidt (1999), people do not like inequality.[4] Inequality is particularly disturbing when a subject's pay-off is smaller than that of other subjects. Such models attempt to explain why, on the one hand, people behave altruistically toward others worse off than they are, while on the other hand they punish those who are better off than they are.[5] A number of studies in experimental economics have investigated this phenomenon and found that people's behavior in various situations can indeed be explained by inequality aversion (Fehr and Schmidt 1999). However, people are also driven by other motives than inequality reduction. Charness and Rabin (2002), for example, let subjects in a number of simple games choose between an equal payoff (e.g., 400 and 400) and an unequal but often more efficient payoff (750 for the recipient and 400 for the dictator). The authors find "a strong degree of respect for social efficiency, tempered by concern for those well off" (849); in other words, the more unequal but socially efficient outcome is often chosen. Whether people are more concerned with social welfare than with inequality has to be investigated further, possibly using a broader set of games than simple dictator games. Other studies argue that inequality aversion is inadequate to explain a whole range of pro-social behavior (Engelmann and Strobel 2004).

The next set of models extends these outcome-based models by capturing the importance of intentions.

3.2.2 Reciprocity and Conditional Cooperation

The aforementioned theories of pro-social preferences assume that people value only the distributional consequences of their own and others' behavior. In theories of reciprocity, people are also concerned about the intentions leading other people to their choices. We talk of reciprocity when individuals act in a more pro-social manner in response to the friendly behavior of others, and in a hostile way in response to unfriendly behavior (Rabin 1993; Falk and Fischbacher 2006; Dufwenberg and Kirchsteiger 2004). The reciprocity model has recently gained much attention. It has been claimed that "[p]ractically all life in society includes and implies reciprocities, and reciprocity has been seen as the basic glue that makes people constitute groups or societies" (Kolm 2000, 115). A substantial number of studies in experimental economics (e.g., Fehr and Gächter 2000b) supplement the evidence, provided by other social sciences, indicating that reciprocity is an important factor in pro-social behavior. In public good games, the option for reciprocally punishing free riders sustains high contribution rates even with repetition (Fehr and Gächter 2000a). This is not trivial, as contributions in public good games normally converge to full free riding over time. Individuals do indeed undertake the costly punishment of free riders. The more a subject's contribution is below the average of group contributions, the more heavily he or she is punished.

There is also evidence for reciprocity and its influence on pro-social behavior outside the laboratory. Fong (2001) interprets survey data about support for redistribution as evidence of reciprocity's importance. People who believe that the needy are those who have been beset by unfortunate external circumstances are more in favor of redistribution. In contrast, people who believe that the poor are not doing their share to escape poverty are more likely to be against redistribution (see also Bowles, Fong, and Gintis 2006). This reflects the view that if the poor don't give, or try to give, their share to society, they should not receive aid. However, it is also possible that people who are generally selfish will legitimize their behavior by assuming that welfare recipients are able but unwilling to help themselves. In a second study, Fong (2003) addresses this caveat by randomly matching welfare recipients reporting different work morals to potential donors. The results show that people who indicate in a pre-experiment survey that helping the poor is important are especially sensitive to the laziness of welfare recipients. On the one hand, they give large amounts to people who have a high work ethic, while on the other hand they reduce their share substantially when confronted with a lazy person. People who do not indicate in the pre-experiment survey that helping the poor is important are significantly less sensitive to a recipient's laziness.

The principle of reciprocity seems to be important in various fields, from merchandising to political "logrolling" (a number of examples can be found in Cialdini 1993), tax compliance (Smith 1992), tipping in restaurants (Seligman et al. 1985; Conlin, Lynn, and O'Donoghue 2003), and effort in the workplace (e.g., Akerlof 1982; Frey 1993; Fehr, Gächter, and Kirchsteiger 1997). To test the effects of reciprocal norms in charitable giving, Falk (2004) conducted a large-scale field experiment where potential donors were given either no gift, a small gift, or a large gift in the solicitation letter. The relative frequency of donations increases by 75 percent among those receiving a large gift as compared to the no gift treatment. If a person receives a gift from a potential aid recipient, the norm of reciprocity seems to require a donation. For interactions between donors and recipients, the principle of reciprocity thus seems to play a substantial role. For the norm of reciprocity, it may be a question not only of the relationship between the donor and a single recipient, but also whether reciprocity affects social interactions *between* donors.

One implication of reciprocity theories is that people react positively to the behavior of others. When a group of people has to decide whether to contribute to a public good, individuals will judge the behavior of others as kind or not, and adjust their behavior accordingly. If individuals observe that others behave pro-socially, they will do so as well. No one likes being the only one who contributes to a good cause, and no one likes being the victim of others' free riding. The most distinctive prediction from such a theory is that individual i's probability of contributing to a public good *increases* when the percentage of individuals j ($j = 1, \ldots, n; j \neq i$) who contribute increases within a given group. The prediction stands in contrast to the prediction made by altruism theories, where a negative relationship is expected between an individual's own behavior and the contributions of others in his group.

The idea of conditionality in theories of reciprocity is crucial. Individuals are defined as conditional cooperators when the positive correlation discussed above applies (a survey by Gächter on conditional cooperation is chapter 2 of this book). Evidence in favor of conditional cooperation can show that expectations about the behavior of others positively correlate with one's own behavior. For example, there is a large literature showing that people's (self-reported) tax compliance correlates with their estimate of other people's noncompliance (e.g., Frey and Torgler 2004). However, this kind of evidence does not reveal the direction of causality. It may be the case that expectations do not trigger behavior, but rather that behavior influences expectations. Such a "false consensus" effect (Dawes, McTavish, and Shaklee 1977; Ross, Greene, and House 1977; Marks and Miller 1987) can occur because one projects one's own behavior onto others, or because behavior needs to be justified.

In a laboratory experiment, which allows one to vary the group's average behavior at random, Fischbacher, Gächter, and Fehr (2001) solved the causality problem by using the strategy method. Subjects in their laboratory public good game have to decide how much to give to a public account based on the contributions of others. The study concludes that roughly 50 percent of subjects increase their contribution if the others do so as well. In contrast to most studies about conditional cooperation, which are based on laboratory experiments, Andreoni and Scholz (1998) provide a non-laboratory study, finding that one's own donation depends on the donations of one's reference group. The results show that if the contributions of those in one's social reference group increase by an average of 10 percent, the expected rise in one's own contribution is about 2 to 3 percent. However, because the reference group in this study is constructed on socioeconomic characteristics, it does not provide a direct test of how people react to the behavior of others.

Frey and Meier (2004) found supporting evidence of conditional cooperation in a field experiment. Students at the University of Zurich are asked each semester whether they want to contribute to two social funds. In the field experiment, students are randomly informed either that many other students contribute (64 percent of the student population) to the two funds or that few other students contribute (46 percent). As this information is either based on the average over the last ten years (the lower contribution rate) or on the behavior in the previous semester (the high contribution rate), no deception was involved. The analysis shows that people increase their pro-social behavior if faced with many other students who do the same.[6]

In an interesting field experiment on tax compliance, Wenzel (2001) first asked taxpayers about their own tax compliance and about others' norms and behavior with regard to paying taxes. Then in the field experiment, he informed a subgroup of these taxpayers about their misperception of others' behavior. Taxpayers actually wrongly think that most others act less honestly than they themselves do. When people are informed in the experiment that others are more honest than they expected them to be, they subsequently significantly reduced their claims for tax reductions (in their actual behavior) compared to the control group. This result can be interpreted as evidence that people behave conditionally based on what others do.[7] Heldt (2005) presents evidence in support of conditional cooperation in the field. In an innovative study, he found that cross-country skiers are more likely to contribute to the maintenance of the slopes if confronted with the knowledge that many other skiers do. Shang and Croson (2005) show in a field experiment that people increase their financial contribution in a National Public Radio campaign when informed about a high contribution from the previous donor.[8] A positive correlation has also been found in a situation where money is collected in a community using a list of others in the neighborhood who had already donated.

The longer the list, the higher the willingness to contribute (Reingen 1982).

These studies do not necessarily show that the perceived good intentions of other people caused individuals' pro-social behavior. Reciprocity models, however, explicitly assume this. Recent laboratory studies have therefore analyzed the effect of intentions per se. The evidence supports the notion that intentions matter. For example, Blount (1995) reports that subjects in an ultimatum game accept lower offers when the offer is generated by a random mechanism than when it is chosen deliberately by another party. Various other studies support the finding that the process and particularly the intentions behind another party's actions are crucial for reciprocity (see Charness and Levine 2003 and the references therein). How those intentions are perceived often depends on the particular situation. Bohnet and Meier (2005) show that framing effects in a trust game changes the perception of the other parties' intentions. As a result reciprocal behavior changes dramatically. In summary, there are a number of studies supporting the influence of reciprocity, and therefore intentions, on pro-social behavior in the lab and in the field.

3.2.3 Self-Identity

Recently, economists recognized the importance of self-identity for human behavior (Akerlof and Kranton 2000). People do not only care about their reputation with others, but also want to have a good self-image. They therefore undertake certain activities—pro-social activities—in order to self-signal their good traits.

Bodner and Prelec (2003) and Bénabou and Tirole (2004) present two recent models in which self-identity is a crucial element in explaining pro-social behavior. The important difference to outcome-based models is that people do not necessarily care about the outcome of a pro-social behavior per se, but their behavior affects their self-identity. Whether pro-social behavior actually produces a good self-image thus depends on at least two factors: first, what is considered to be "good," and second, in what circumstances a pro-social action is a valuable signal of one's good traits.

The social norm defines what constitutes a good action. Managing self-identity therefore often means conforming to the social norm in one's reference group (e.g., Bernheim 1994). The results discussed previously, which found that people contribute to a public good based on other people's behavior, are therefore consistent with a theory based on self-identity. In order to fully understand why people behave pro-socially in one but not the other situation, models of pro-social behavior need to incorporate people's expectations of what is perceived to be appropriate.

The context in which a decision is made crucially influences whether a pro-social activity is a needed and/or valuable signal in preserving one's self-identity. As will be discussed later in more detail, a financial incentive to behave pro-socially might, for example, make the signal less valuable. The pro-social action might not be attributed solely to good traits, but might be influenced by extrinsic motivation. As a result, the level of pro-social behavior might be lower than without a financial incentive (Bénabou and Tirole 2004). The context might also allow people to behave selfishly without attributing it to a greedy trait. In such situations, people might be much more willing to behave selfishly. Murnighan, Oesch, and Pillutla (2001) find in a simple dictator game that the reduction of the potential options—to split from 0 to 10 in increments of 1, to two options, a selfish $(10,0)$ and the equal split $(5,5)$—decreases the fair split significantly. Reducing the options allows subjects to construe the (unfairer) outcome as largely outside their control and thus preserve their self-identity (see also Dana, Weber, and Xi Kuang 2004; Dana, Cain, and Dawes 2005). As will be discussed in more detail in the following chapter, the institutional environment might therefore have a huge impact on people's pro-social behavior. The context could allow people to attribute the same decision either to a greedy or to an altruistic trait, and as a consequence affect their decision in the first place.

3.3 Institutional Environment

For pro-social behavior, the institutional environment in which people decide to contribute to public goods is crucial (e.g., Ostrom 2000; Sobel 2002, 146–149). The institutional environment, which constitutes the context in which people decide, can matter even though the decisions remain the same in terms of material payoffs. Such context-dependent pro-social behavior has been labeled "institutional framing" by Isaac, Mathieu, and Zajac (1991).

The institutional environment's influence on pro-social behavior can be twofold. On the one hand, the context calibrates the salience of motives like altruism and reciprocity. In a situation where a mechanism exists to punish free riders, the norm of reciprocity will be more important than in the absence of this institutional feature. On the other hand, the institutional environment can trigger motives which go beyond altruism and reciprocity, as evidence presented by Bohnet and Frey (1999) and Frey and Bohnet (1995) suggests. In a dictator game they allow for one-way identification, meaning that the dictator sees the recipient but not vice versa. This institutional change increases the willingness to cooperate dramatically. Such a shift in behavior cannot be explained by reciprocity, because according to these theories identification should not change the behavior in the decision situation. Giving in dictator games may therefore not be caused solely by reciprocity (e.g., Hoffman, McCabe, and Smith 1996) or even altruism (e.g., Johannesson and Persson 2000).

The effect of contextual factors on pro-social behavior is supported in various experiments in which framing the same decision differently has a critical influence on decisions (e.g., Andreoni 1992; Cookson 2000). Because framing effects are significant, most experimentalists try to avoid using verbal cues in their decision settings. However, verbal framing is not the only contextual factor influencing human pro-social behavior. Real-life social contexts contain a variety of cues that shape individuals' beliefs about the appropriate set of rules. This is closely related to findings in ultimatum game experiments conducted in 15 small-scale societies: "[...] the preferences over economic choices [...] are shaped by the economic and social interactions of everyday life" (Henrich et al. 2001, 77). The institutional environment can have at least two distinctive effects, which I will now discuss.

The institutional environment changes the salience of a social norm Institutional settings as well as framing effects change the focus of what is considered fair behavior in a certain situation. The context helps to evaluate which set of values to use. Whether people share 10 dollars that they have received as a gift or, by contrast, that they have had to earn, influences the "generosity" of the donor considerably. In dictator games between students, an equal split of the total seems to be the norm. When the same amount of money has to be shared with a charity, the amount given is on average much larger (Eckel and Grossman 1996). According to Bohnet and Frey (1999), the contextual setting can influence the social distance and thereby vary the empathy between the actors. Charities have long recognized the importance of reducing social distance between donor and recipient. It is well known that people are more willing to help an identifiable victim (Schelling 1984;

Small and Loewenstein 2003), like a specific child in the Third World, than to support a project that tries to improve the overall situation of children in poor countries. More generally, contextual factors not only change the social distance between individuals, but also influence the salience of a social norm in contributing to a public good. It can be hypothesized that "the greater the extent to which a decision is taken in a social context, the more relevant manners become" (Bohnet and Frey 1999, 44).

The institutional environment varies the degree of (potential) social sanctions The context in which people decide to contribute to a public good affects the extent of social sanctions when the social norm is violated. Even in anonymous situations, people may follow the internalized social norm because they otherwise suffer from guilt, shame, or fear. According to Trivers (1971), internalized norms are a reaction to social sanctions in case of the violation of a norm. Even the suspicion that someone dislikes one's behavior can trigger compliance (Loewenstein 2000). But social sanction, for example, in the form of social approval or disapproval, is most important if each person's identity is revealed. In situations where anonymity is lifted, pro-social behavior is expected to be the most pronounced (Rege and Telle 2004). Soetevent (2005) examines the role of anonymity in a field experiment in Dutch churches. Either closed collection bags or open collection baskets were randomly used for the collection of offerings. The open baskets, where the neighbors on each side can identify the donor's contribution, increase contribution in the service's second offering by 10 percent. Interestingly, people started to give larger coins when open baskets were used.

To illustrate the importance of the institutional environment, three different phenomena will be discussed that substantially influence pro-social behavior: property rights, in-group effects, and communication.

Property rights The perception of what constitutes a fair allocation is shaped greatly by the way property rights are assigned (see Frey and Bohnet 1995). Imagine the following situation in two different environments: you submit an academic paper for a prize, as does your colleague. In one setting, the independent jury chooses your paper to receive a $1,000 prize. In the other setting, the independent jury could not choose between your paper and your colleague's paper, but a lottery was used to determine that you will receive the cash prize. Would you share the prize money with your colleague? You probably would only in the situation where you received the money by luck. The way of assigning the property right changes the principles of what is perceived as fair. Cherry, Frykblom, and Shogren (2002) investigated whether in a laboratory dictator game the allocation differed when earned wealth was divided compared to unearned wealth given by the experimenter. In the treatment where people received $40 as a gift, only 15 percent offered nothing to the recipients. In sharp contrast, when people had to earn the $40, which was to be divided by answering some questions, 70 percent of the subjects offered nothing to the other person. It seems that less generosity can be expected when people attribute the received property rights to a variable they can influence (e.g., effort). In contrast, when the assignment of a property is based on factors that cannot be influenced (e.g., luck), an equal sharing is perceived to be fairer (Hoffman and Spitzer 1985; Konow 2000). One should expect that the stronger the property rights that are assigned, the less likely individuals will be to share their wealth.

In-group effects   The institutional environment may shape the formation and salience of groups. For example, whether individuals are faced with a decision to behave pro-socially in their own firm or in a supermarket is critical to their decision (see, e.g., Carpenter, Burks, and Verhoogen 2003). There is some evidence suggesting that people tend to cooperate more with their in-group (e.g., other members of the same fraternity) than with individuals not part of their in-group (like members of other fraternities) (see, e.g., Kollock 1998). Even a minimal definition of groups (e.g., those who prefer Kandinsky over Klee) has been found sufficient to create a group identification that has a significant influence on the division of money in an experimental setting (Tajfel 1981). In-group effects can also been found outside the laboratory. The more equal and less fragmented a community is in terms of ethnicity and race, the greater is its willingness to participate in social organizations and activities (Alesina and La Ferrara 2000), and the greater is its acceptance of income redistribution (Luttmer 2001). One reason for the higher contribution rates in in-groups may be that, in a defined group, individuals have a biased perception about members of their own group and those of the out-group. In the case of redistribution, people may attribute a group member's poverty to external circumstances (such as bad luck), whereas a poor outcome for a non-group member tends to be attributed to poor personal characteristics. Goette, Huffman, and Meier (2006) use random assignment to real social groups to isolate the effect of group membership. They found more cooperation and altruistic punishment within random assigned groups, but no hostility effects toward out-group members. The tendency to help in-group members may also be due to other reasons, like reciprocity, social pressure, or sociobiological motives.

Communication   A number of studies have empirically shown that communication is important for cooperation in social dilemmas (for a meta-analysis, see Sally 1995), despite the fact that no enforceable agreements can be made and communication is therefore viewed as "cheap talk" (Farrel and Rabin 1996). Communication fulfills two important functions. First, people get to know the other people involved; after just a few minutes of talking, the subjects' expectation of others' cooperative behavior increases significantly in accuracy (Frank, Gilovich, and Regan 1993b). If people believe that the other group members will act pro-socially, their willingness to contribute increases (consistent with inequality aversion and conditional cooperation). Communication, however, has to be face-to-face to affect the judgment of others; when communication is only allowed via a computer, the effects on cooperation are smaller (Ostrom 2000). Second, communication provides an opportunity for subjects to ask other individuals what they will do. Most subjects in experiments where communication is allowed try to make agreements about mutual behavior (Frey and Bohnet 1995). Even though such agreements can never be enforced, people seldom violate them. People seem to feel obliged to stick to their promises because the inconsistency of breaking a promise has high psychic costs.[9] "The Importance of Being Asked" can be demonstrated for the decision to volunteer (Freeman 1997), to donate money (Long 1976), to participate in political demonstrations (Opp 2001), and even for the rescue of Jews in World War II (Varese and Yaish 2000). The importance of being asked is due not only to selection (people who look like potential volunteers are asked). The request carries some social pressure with it, and therefore people are more likely to be persuaded by a personal request than by written requests. The closer the relationship to the requester, the higher the probability of contributions (Freeman 1997).

In this section, we demonstrated that the institutional environment affects pro-social behavior in various respects. There is, however, still insufficient understanding of how and when institutional factors influence pro-social behavior more or less strongly.

3.4 Monetary Incentives and Pro-Social Behavior

From an economic point of view, people's pro-social behavior should depend on the relative cost: the more expensive pro-social behavior is, the less it should be undertaken. This is a feature of all the models discussed in the previous sections. Relative prices and incentives can be understood as important factors in the institutional environment discussed earlier. In this section, the effects of monetary incentives on pro-social behavior are investigated in more detail.

When people react systematically to changes in the cost of pro-social behavior, this creates the opportunity to subsidize pro-social behavior in order to increase it. In the case of charitable giving, donors can either get a rebate on their donations or their donation can be matched. While the first mechanism is often implemented by the possibility of deducting charitable giving from taxable income, the second mechanism is often implemented by firms that match their employees' donations. Such monetary incentives to increase pro-social behavior can of course be implemented in all areas where pro-social behavior is involved: volunteering, littering, organizational citizenship behavior, and so on.

In what follows, two contradictory effects of monetary incentives on pro-social behavior are presented: (1) according to the ordinary *relative price effect*, pro-social behavior will increase when monetary incentives are provided; (2) in certain circumstances, monetary incentives may, however, decrease intrinsic motivation to undertake the pro-social behavior due to a *motivational crowding-out effect* (Frey 1997b). The net effect of monetary incentives on pro-social behavior may be positive or negative in such circumstances, depending on the magnitude of the two effects. Under specific conditions, the relative price effect can thus be reversed.

3.4.1 Relative Prices of Pro-Social Behavior

The importance of the relative price effect for pro-social behavior can be illustrated by the opposition of very wealthy U.S. citizens to a recent tax reform proposal. A group of rich citizens centered around Bill Gates, the founder of Microsoft, has been arguing against the introduction of a new tax law that would basically lower the tax burden for wealthy people (Gates and Collins 2002).

A substantive literature attempts to analyze whether the presumption that people react to the price of giving is founded on a solid empirical basis (for a survey, see Andreoni 2004). Two results of this branch of research are worth mentioning.

First, estimated price elasticities support the hypothesis that the price of giving is important for pro-social behavior. The estimated elasticities vary from −0.4 to −3.0, but most fall in a range from −1.0 to −1.3 (Andreoni 2004). Recent studies based on panel data find somewhat lower price elasticities in the range from −0.51 to −1.26 (e.g., Auten, Sieg, and Clotfelter 2002). This means, for example, that the elimination of tax deductibility for charitable contributions would increase the price of a unit of giving for a taxpayer, formerly faced with a marginal tax rate of 30 percent, from 0.7 to 1.0. Calculating the effect equivalently, charitable contributions would decrease between 15 and 36 percent.[10] Matching people's donations, which is another way of changing the relative price of giving, also increases the willingness to behave pro-socially (Meier 2005a). Matching is even shown to be a more powerful subsidy mechanism than a rebate (Eckel and Grossman 2003, 2005). Laboratory studies show that another form of pro-social behavior, norm enforcement, also reacts to the changes in prices as if punishment was a normal good (Carpenter 2002; Putterman and Anderson 2006).

Second, substitutes and complements have to be taken into account when analyzing the relative price effect on pro-social behavior. Charitable contributions, for example, can be made in money (charitable giving) or in time (volunteering). If monetary giving and volunteer labor are complements, the above-mentioned tax deduction would also increase volunteering. If, however, people move away from volunteering when prices for cash contributions decrease, the benefits of such a decrease would be overestimated by ignoring the effect on volunteering. Contrary to standard economic theory, contributions of time and money are mostly found to be gross complements (Brown and Lankford 1992; Freeman 1997).[11] The effect of a price reduction on pro-social behavior is therefore understated by focusing solely on monetary giving.

3.4.2   Motivational Crowding Effect

The relative price effect, however, does not always hold. In certain situations, a motivational crowding-out effect can work against the relative price effect (Frey 1997b). This is of considerable importance for pro-social behavior. Incentives may undermine or even crowd out an intrinsic motivation to behave pro-socially (Bénabou and Tirole 2004).

The motivational crowding effect was known in psychology long before economists started to think seriously about the "hidden costs of reward" (Lepper and Greene 1978) or the "corruption effect" (Deci 1975). In an early insight, Titmuss's book *The Gift Relationship* (Titmuss 1970) argues that monetary incentives for blood donors will undermine their motivation and reduce the amount of blood donated overall. While Titmuss did not present any empirical evidence, a considerable amount of evidence has since been collected on the motivational crowding-out effect (for an extensive survey, see Frey and Jegen 2001). In psychology, the large number of experimental studies has led to several meta-analyses that in general support the finding that (external) incentives have detrimental effects on intrinsic motivation (e.g., Deci, Koestner, and Ryan 1999).[12] In economics, the few studies that explicitly test the crowding-out effect cover a wide range of activities involving pro-social behavior. This section limits discussion to the three cases of volunteering, civic duties, and trust relationships.

The introduction of monetary incentives has been found to reduce the work motivation of volunteers (Frey and Goette 1999; Gneezy and Rustichini 2000a). Frey and Goette show in an econometric study that, while the size of the offered financial reward raises the number of hours volunteered, the mere fact that financial compensation is provided significantly reduces the amount of volunteering. Volunteers receiving the median amount of monetary incentive work less than either people who receive a large reward or those who receive no reward at all, a result that supports the crowding-out effect and has, of course, important implications for policies regarding volunteer work. The evidence points especially to two important aspects of the crowding effect.

First, the introduction of (external) incentives dramatically shifts the perception of the decision situation. In a situation with extrinsic incentives, people seem to behave in an "exchange mode," where they make strategic considerations and start to calculate ("I'm not working for only $5 per hour, am I?") (Gneezy 2003). In contrast, in a situation without external incentives, people seem rather to behave in a "moral mode" where pro-social behavior is rewarded internally, such as with a warm glow (Heyman and Ariely 2004).

Small amounts of extrinsic incentives in particular are expected to have large negative effects on observed pro-social behavior, because with large extrinsic incentives the relative price effect will dominate. This is supported in a field experiment by Gneezy and Rustichini

(2000a), who offered extrinsic incentives to children who voluntarily collected monetary donations. Small extrinsic incentives are found to reduce the motivation of volunteers significantly, while the effort increases when large incentives are offered. This effect can be observed with negative incentives (fines) as well as with positive incentives (rewards) (Gneezy 2003).

Other important crowding effects have been discovered for activities requiring intrinsic motivation in the form of civic duty. Frey and Oberholzer-Gee (1997) investigate motivational crowding out in the context of siting locally undesirable projects (so-called Not In My Backyard, or NIMBY, problems). Economic theory proposes a simple solution for such projects, which are often socially desirable but impose considerable costs on the immediate neighbors: a community that hosts the NIMBY project should be compensated by all the other communities, so that its net benefit becomes positive. Frey and Oberholzer-Gee analyzed the reaction of Swiss residents to such compensation for the acceptance of a nuclear waste depository. While more than 50 percent of the respondents agreed to host the depository without compensation, the offering of monetary incentives reduced the acceptance rate to 24 percent. The authors' favored explanation for this reduction is that the sense of civic virtue that accompanies accepting the noxious facility is crowded out by the offer of monetary compensation. A civic duty to behave pro-socially can be crowded out not only by explicit monetary incentives, but also by laws and rules. An important application of this notion is tax morale, where the crowding effect can have huge costs. Tax morale, or the motivation explaining the low rate of tax evasion in many countries, depends to a great extent on trust between the government and the citizens. A constitution that tries to discipline citizens can be perceived as distrusting and can therefore decrease civic virtue (see Frey 1997a for empirical evidence).

More generally, the introduction of monetary incentives can have considerable negative effects on trust-based pro-social behavior. In a laboratory experiment with CEOs, Fehr and List (2004) found that detrimental effects follow from external incentives. If the first player uses an external incentive in a trust game, the second player returns less money. However, the highest efficiency is reached if it is possible to implement an external incentive, but the subjects explicitly trust each other and do not use the incentive mechanism. Therefore, while in general trust is crowded out by external incentives, the existence but nonuse of incentives allows for increased pro-social behavior. Bohnet,

Frey, and Huck (2001) conducted a study where subjects must decide if they want to enter a contract without knowing whether the partner will perform. The authors report a crowding-out effect: in a situation of weak contract enforcement, performance is higher than in a situation of medium contract enforcement. Only if contract enforcement is increased well past the medium mark are contracts performed again. These findings support the notion that medium or low incentives can crowd out trust and intrinsic motivation. Falk and Kosfeld (2004) present an interesting experimental study on the dysfunctional effect of incentives. In their study, a principal's decision to control decreases agents' motivation and effort.

Extrinsic incentives do not always lead to a motivational crowding-out effect. The present state of research allows one to indicate conditions under which extrinsic incentives have more positive or more negative effects. A discussion of these identifiable conditions makes it clear that crowding effects are of particular importance for pro-social behavior.[13]

Intrinsic motivation can only be crowded out by extrinsic incentives if people have an intrinsic motivation to begin with. If, for example, people only undertake a task due to extrinsic motivation, an increase in extrinsic incentives will certainly increase effort, as predicted by standard price theory. However, to contribute time or money to a public good often involves some sort of intrinsic motivation. The introduction of external incentives to increase pro-social behavior must therefore be considered very carefully.

Motivational crowding out is expected if the external intervention is perceived as controlling (Enzle and Anderson 1993). Psychologically, extrinsic incentives can have negative effects when they reduce the perceived self-determination of individuals (Rotter 1966 and Deci 1975), or when they interfere with a relationship based on mutual trust (Rousseau 1995). However, if extrinsic incentives are applied carefully—for example, in a way acknowledging individuals' intrinsic motivation—they may not be perceived as hostile and controlling, and can even support and increase pro-social behavior (a crowding-in effect).

A motivational crowding-out effect only results in a net negative effect on behavior if it dominates the standard relative price effect. As mentioned before, this is most likely to be the case for small (positive or negative) incentives. Motivational crowding, however, is not thereby rendered irrelevant in the context of pro-social behavior. First, there are many situations where small incentives are quite important.

In the case of pro-social behavior, the introduction of small incentives is widely discussed, as in the context of volunteering. Second, the reliance on extrinsic incentives may lead to a selection of certain selfishly oriented people. Whereas for some tasks it is desirable to attract extrinsically motivated people (see, e.g., Lazear 2000), in other areas like the nonprofit or charitable sector this is not very welcome. Third, if pro-social preferences are affected permanently, pro-social behavior will not reach the original level again, even if the extrinsic incentive is removed. Meier (2005a) presents suggestive evidence from a field experiment, which shows that offering matching in a donation context increases donations in that period in which the matching was offered. However, people's willingness to contribute decreases below the original level if the matching is removed. Gneezy and Rustichini (2000b) present evidence from a field experiment indicating that the original level of pro-social behavior will not be reached even after the dysfunctional incentive is removed. Fourth, extrinsic incentives for a certain task may not only reduce the intrinsic motivation for the particular task, but also spill over to other areas (Frey and Benz 2000). This may then destroy intrinsic motivation in areas not actually subject to the external intervention. The detrimental effect of extrinsic incentives may be even worse in the dimension not directly affected.

3.5 Heterogeneity in Individuals

In standard economic theory, preferences are usually (but not always) assumed to be homogeneous. This assumption generates powerful predictions with regard to pro-social behavior. However, taking the variation in pro-social attitudes into account leads to interesting additional implications. To begin with, there are significant differences between individuals: Andreoni and Miller (2002) show in a study based on dictator games that about 47 percent of individuals can be characterized as selfish (however, only 23 percent are perfectly selfish), while the other 53 percent have to be characterized as "other regarding." Fischbacher, Gächter, and Fehr (2001) find in a public good game that 30 percent of the individuals behave like free riders and 50 percent can be characterized as conditional cooperators. I discuss the three implications of this heterogeneity below.

The *interaction of different types* of people is crucial to understanding why cooperation is stable and public goods are provided. Consider, for example, the situation in which an egoistic individual is interacting with a reciprocal individual. The presence of a reciprocal individual may change the egoist's material incentive and therefore cause the egoist to behave pro-socially. The presence of only a few reciprocal types may have a big impact on the aggregate outcome of markets and organizations (see the survey in Fehr and Fischbacher 2002). Whether a pro-social individual will cause an egoist to behave pro-socially or, conversely, a few egoists cause pro-social individuals to start free riding, is a question that depends crucially on the institutional setting.[14] To analyze the institutions that lead to one of the two situations, one has to understand how heterogeneous individuals interact.

The *institutional environment may influence individuals differently*. In analyzing the effect of a change in the institutions, it is important to take heterogeneous individuals into account. Meier (2005a) presents additional evidence from a controlled field experiment showing that only certain types of people react to a change in relative prices. In addition, people may react quite differently to the introduction of monetary incentives with respect to their motivation to behave pro-socially. Pro-socially inclined persons may reduce their intrinsically motivated pro-social behavior when external incentives are introduced, whereas a more selfishly oriented individual may increase his or her pro-social behavior to capture the extra reward.

The *evolution of heterogeneous pro-social preferences* can help one to understand how pro-social preferences can be fostered. Very little is known about this question in economics. One prominent position, however, is that education can influence pro-social behavior and probably even preferences. Economics and business students in particular are assumed to be better citizens and better future managers if they are taught some ethics instead of self-interest maximization. Economics students are portrayed as being more egotistical than noneconomists, partly because the training changes their behavior (e.g., Frank, Gilovich, and Regan 1993a and 1996). However, Frey and Meier (2003) analyze a large panel dataset and find that those who choose economics as their major already tend toward egoism when they enter. In that case, it is possible that "economists are born, not made" (Carter and Irons 1991).

3.6   How Does Pro-Social Behavior Affect Happiness?

In the history of ideas, pro-social behavior has always been linked with human welfare. In the Judeo-Christian tradition, helping others is the only way to reach the ultimate goal of happiness. However there is still no empirical evidence proving that a person who acts pro-socially is happier than a *homo oeconomicus,* who is solely concerned with his or her narrow self-interest. To answer the question of what constitutes a good life or a happy life, one has to understand how pro-social behavior influences utility (happiness). Reported subjective well-being is typically used as a proxy for utility. Frey and Stutzer (for surveys, see Frey and Stutzer 2002a and 2002b) present excellent surveys on why and how economists can learn from happiness research.

The various theories on pro-social behavior lead to different predictions concerning utility gained from such behavior. In the following, these predictions are presented alongside the scarce empirical evidence gleaned from economics and the evidence documented in psychology and sociology.

3.6.1 Inequality and Happiness

According to these theories, people's well-being increases if they observe that other people's lives are improving or that inequality, whether between two individuals or social inequality in general, is decreasing. Importantly, the increase in utility occurs independently of one's own decision, whereas according to impure altruism one's own decision is a substantial source of the warm glow coming from pro-social behavior. A few studies have investigated the overall effect of inequality, as well as the effect of other people's material well-being on individual happiness levels. Alesina, Di Tella, and MacCulloch (2005) find that people are less likely to report being happy when inequality is high. This "inequality aversion," however, is more pronounced in Europe than in the United States. Interestingly, the effect of inequality on the well-being of the poor versus the wealthy differs on the two continents. Whereas in the United States only the wealthy seem to suffer from the effect of inequality, in Europe only the poor's well-being is decreased by higher inequality. The authors interpret this result, which is inconsistent with pure inequality aversion, as an effect of differences in social mobility between European countries and the United States. Because social mobility in the United States is perceived to be higher, wealthy U.S. citizens interpret high inequality as a potential risk of falling down the scale in case of an unfortunate life event. According to the authors, poor U.S. citizens believe that they can improve their income situation substantially. In contrast, poor Europeans feel stuck in poverty. People may therefore not only care about inequality outcomes (whether the income distribution is more or less unequal), but also about the process leading to a certain result (whether it is in the individual's power to influence an outcome).[15] However, Schwarze and Härpfer (2004) find evidence consistent with inequality aversion in Germany for all income classes. In their panel survey, people's life satisfaction is inversely related to inequality on the regional level.

Charness and Grosskopf (2001) find no correlation between happiness scores and preferences for equality in dictator games. Subjects who choose more equal payoffs do not report higher well-being after the decision, nor do subjects who report higher happiness scores before the decision choose more equal payoffs. Thus the experiment does not support the hypothesis that happiness is correlated with inequality. However, overall happiness measures are explicitly designed to be relatively insensitive to minor life events. They are therefore not expected to be influenced by the results in a laboratory experiment involving low stakes. Much more research is needed to understand how others' utility levels influence one's own happiness.

3.6.2   Pro-Social Behavior and Happiness

Theories of impure altruism predict that pro-social behavior increases utility. In this branch of research, the focus is on the effect of pro-social behavior per se on subjective well-being. Various studies by psychologists and sociologists, mostly focusing on volunteering, find positive correlations between pro-social behavior and well-being (for a survey, see Wilson and Musick 1999). Volunteers report higher well-being scores than non-volunteers; they are less depressed and their mortality rate is lower than average. These effects are found to be especially true for elderly volunteers (Wheeler, Gorey, and Greenblatt 1998).

People may get a warm glow from volunteering because helping others increases either their perceived self-esteem or their self-efficacy. Volunteering may also generate a state of "flow" (Csikszentmihalyi 1990), which depends on the extent of commitment, the use of skill, and the kind of achievement involved in the task (Argyle 1999, 364–365). Alternatively, the positive effect of pro-social behavior in the form of volunteering may be due to the effect of social integration. People who feel integrated and enjoy many personal relationships are taken to be happier than people who feel lonely. According to this explanation, volunteering increases people's well-being not because they help others, but because they feel integrated. Most studies on the effects of pro-social behavior on happiness (mostly on volunteering) cannot discriminate between utility arising from the act of helping and utility arising from side effects such as social involvement. In addition, most empirical work uses cross-sectional data where participants self-assess the impact of volunteer programs. Apart from problems arising from response biases in volunteers self-assessing their own program's benefits, the direction of causality is very difficult to assess in such studies. In fact, pro-social behavior may not make people happier so much as happier people are more willing to behave pro-socially. There is some evidence that happiness affects one's willingness to help others. In a number of experiments, the mood of subjects was first manipulated, for example, by letting them "find" a coin or by letting them win in a game. Afterward the subjects had the opportunity to help in a task or to donate money to a charity. It is found that those with induced good moods were more likely to help others (Harris and Smith 1975; Isen, Horn, and Rosenhan 1997).[16]

Konow and Earley (2002) use simple dictator games to disentangle the various effects influencing the relationship between happiness and pro-social behavior. The authors ask the subjects various questions about their subjective well-being either before or after a decision about dividing an amount of money between another person and the subjects themselves. The results indicate an indirect relationship between pro-social behavior and happiness: generosity contributes to self-actualization, which in turn increases long-run happiness.

Meier and Stutzer (2004) find robust evidence that volunteers are more satisfied with their lives than nonvolunteers, based on a large-scale panel dataset for Germany. Causality is addressed by taking advantage of a natural experiment: the collapse of East Germany and its volunteer infrastructure. People who accidentally lost their opportunities for volunteering are compared to people who experienced no change in their volunteer status. Exogenously losing the opportunity to volunteer decreases people's well-being. This result establishes that part of the correlation between happiness and volunteering is because volunteering causes higher well-being.

3.7 Concluding Remarks

The evidence is overwhelming that human behavior is not solely motivated by narrow self-interest. People accept costs when engaging in pro-social activities, like voluntarily contributing money or time to public goods or enforcing social norms. Pro-social behavior is widespread and quantitatively important for economic and societal outcomes. When designing institutions, pro-social behavior has to be taken into account. If not, the institutions may not reach their intended goals.

In recent years, a number of theories have evolved that attempt to formalize pro-social behavior. The most important approaches presented in this survey can be classified into three groups: (1) those that emphasize the distributional outcome, as do theories of outcome-based pro-social preferences; (2) those that highlight the importance of the process that leads to a certain outcome (e.g., the intentions of the people involved), an aspect stressed by theories of reciprocity and conditional cooperation; and (3) those that focus on the importance of people's self-identity for pro-social behavior.

An important insight developed in this survey is the effect of the institutional environment on pro-social behavior. On the one hand, the institutional environment affects the salience of particular social norms, as well as the intrinsic motivation to behave pro-socially. On the other hand, it influences the social interaction between (egoistic and/or altruistic) individuals, as in how the violation of a social norm can be punished.

We believe that less emphasis should be given to the quest for the ultimate pro-social motivation but more to conditions which trigger one or the other of these effects. The evidence on theories of pro-social behavior is inconclusive because (1) not only do people differ substantially in their pro-social preferences, but (2) even the same people might show different patterns of pro-social behavior depending on the situation. While in some situations people are motivated by altruism or inequality aversion, in other situations people care more for the socially efficient outcome. To get a better understanding of the importance of these conditions will help to bring the various theories and their supporting evidence in line with each other.

Notes

I am grateful for helpful comments from Matthias Benz, Bruno S. Frey, Simon Gächter, Lorenz Götte, Simon Lüchinger, Alois Stutzer, and two referees. The views expressed herein are solely those of the author and not those of the Federal Reserve System or the Federal Reserve Bank of Boston.

1. Estimations for the United States show that in 1995, more than 68 percent of households contributed to charitable organizations. In 1998, these private households donated more than \$134 billion (Andreoni 2002). In the same year, more than 50 percent of all adult Americans did voluntary work, amounting to 5 million full-time equivalents

(Anheier and Salamon 1999, 58). Although the extent of charitable contributions and the engagement in volunteer work is smaller in Europe, it is still substantial: in Europe, on average 32.1 percent of the population volunteer. Taking the hours volunteered into account, this amounts to 4.5 million full-time equivalent volunteers for the ten European countries taken into consideration (Anheier and Salamon 1999, 58).

2. As fundraising and revenues from ancillary goods constitute a "necessary evil" for many managers of nonprofit organizations (see, e.g., Segal and Weisbrod 1998) government grants may not only crowd out private contributions due to donors' altruistic preferences, but they may also lower the incentive of charities to undertake fundraising activities. Andreoni and Payne (2003) have empirically established that, for arts organizations and social service organizations, part of the crowding-out indeed comes from the reduction of charities' fundraising efforts when they receive government grants. If fundraising efforts are not included in the estimations, even a low crowding-out effect is likely to be overestimated.

3. Another extension of the pure altruism model assumes that donors value making a difference (Duncan 2004).

4. For a similar model, see Bolton and Ockenfels (2000).

5. For models which introduce other motives like envy and spitefulness, see Mui (1995) and Fehr and Schmidt (2003).

6. For the effect of framing on the proportion of noncontributors vs. the proportion of contributors, see Meier (2006).

7. See also the field experiment by Blumenthal, Christian, and Slemrod (2001). However, they find no statistically significant effect to informing taxpayers that few others cheat.

8. Another field experiment that can be interpreted as evidence for conditional cooperation is presented by List and Lucking-Reiley (2002). The authors analyze the impact of seed money on charitable donations, which shows a positive correlation between the giving of others and the giving of the individual donor.

9. A large Swiss charity, for example, raises donations by announcing the donated amount on public radio. The reasons for this technique may be twofold: first, people are more willing to donate when others do so as well (conditional cooperation) and, second, it may be easier to express the intention to donate than to actually do it. Surprisingly (for an economist), most people actually donate the promised amount although no enforcement mechanism exists. Cialdini (1993, 57–113) presents many examples of how firms use people's tendency to be consistent with former commitments to sell their products or to raise donations.

10. Interestingly, men and women have different price elasticities: "(...) when it is relatively expensive to give, women are more generous than men; however as the price of giving decreases, men begin to give more than women" (Andreoni and Vesterlund 2001, 294). Bohnet (in chapter 4 of this book) finds substantial differences in the trust behavior of men and women. However, in a field experiment men were not more sensitive to a matching mechanism than were women (Meier 2005b).

11. An exception from this general result is the study by Duncan (1999).

12. For a meta-study declaring the crowding effect to be "a myth," see Eisenberger and Cameron (1996). For an evaluation of the two contradictory meta-studies, see Lepper, Henderlong, and Gingras (1999).

13. However, little is known about whether a motivational crowding out is due to a change in preferences (Frey 1997b) or to the perceived nature of the task (Bénabou and Tirole 2002), nor about how exactly intrinsic motivation is rebuilt after an extrinsic incentive is removed.

14. Because an altruist mimics the behavior of an egoist every time he or she meets one, expectations about others differ between the two types. An egoist believes that everybody is an egoist because he or she only meets people who behave egoistically, while an altruist knows that there are egoists and altruists (Kelley and Stahelski 1970). For a test of this "triangle hypothesis," see van Lange (1992).

15. The importance of processes for utility is often neglected in economics. For a survey on procedural utility, see Benz (chapter 8 in this book).

16. The negative-state-relief theory in psychology (see Cialdini, Kenrick, and Baumann 1982) proposes exactly the opposite: people in a bad mood behave more pro-socially because they think that doing good lifts the bad mood.

References

Akerlof, George A. 1982. "Labor Contracts as Partial Gift Exchange." *Quarterly Journal of Economics* 97, no. 4: 543–569.

Akerlof, George A., and Rachel E. Kranton. 2000. "Economics and Identity." *Quarterly Journal of Economics* 115, no. 3: 715–753.

Alesina, Alberto, and Eliana La Ferrara. 2000. "Participation in Heterogeneous Communities." *Quarterly Journal of Economics* 115, no. 3: 847–904.

Alesina, Alberto, Rafael Di Tella, and Robert MacCulloch. 2005. "Inequality and Happiness: Are Europeans and Americans Different?" *Journal of Public Economics* 88, nos. 9–10: 2009–2042.

Andreoni, James. 1988. "Privately Provided Public Goods in a Large Economy: The Limits of Altruism." *Journal of Public Economics* 35, no. 1: 57–73.

Andreoni, James. 1990. "Impure Altruism and Donations to Public Goods: A Theory of Warm-Glow Giving." *Economic Journal* 100, no. 401: 464–477.

Andreoni, James. 1992. "Warm-Glow Versus Cold-Prickle: The Effects of Positive and Negative Framing in Cooperation in Experiments." *Quarterly Journal of Economics* 60, no. 1: 1–21.

Andreoni, James. 2002. "The Economics of Philanthropy." In *International Encyclopedia of Social and Behavioral Sciences*, ed. N. J. Smelser and P. B. Baltes, 11369–11376. London: Elsevier.

Andreoni, James. 2006. "Philanthropy." In *Handbooks of Giving, Reciprocity and Altruism*, ed. L.-A. Gérard-Varet, S.-C. Kolm, and J. Mercier Ythier, 1201–1269. Amsterdam: Elsevier/North Holland.

Andreoni, James, Brian Erard, and Jonathan Feinstein. 1998. "Tax Compliance." *Journal of Economic Literature* 36, no. 2: 818–860.

Andreoni, James, and John H. Miller. 2002. "Giving According to Garp: An Experimental Test of the Consistency of Preferences for Altruism." *Econometrica* 70, no. 2: 737–753.

Andreoni, James, and Abigail Payne. 2003. "Do Government Grants to Private Charities Crowd out Giving or Fund-Raising?" *American Economic Review* 93, no. 3: 792–812.

Andreoni, James, and John Karl Scholz. 1998. "An Econometric Analysis of Charitable Giving with Interdependent Preferences." *Economic Inquiry* 36, no. 3: 410–428.

Andreoni, James, and Lise Vesterlund. 2001. "Which Is the Fair Sex? Gender Differences in Altruism." *Quarterly Journal of Economics* 116, no. 1: 293–312.

Anheier, Helmut K., and Lester M. Salamon. 1999. "Volunteering in Cross-National Perspective: Initial Comparisons." *Law and Contemporary Problems* 62, no. 4: 43–65.

Argyle, Michael. 1999. "Causes and Correlates of Happiness." In *Well-Being: The Foundations of Hedonic Psychology*, ed. D. Kahneman, E. Diener, and N. Schwarz, 353–373. New York: Russell Sage Foundation.

Auten, Gerald, Holger Sieg, and Charles T. Clotfelter. 2002. "Charitable Giving, Income and Taxes: An Analysis of Panel Data." *American Economic Review* 92, no. 1: 371–382.

Becker, Gary S. 1974. "A Theory of Social Interactions." *Journal of Political Economy* 82, no. 6: 1063–1093.

Bénabou, Roland, and Jean Tirole. 2002. "Intrinsic and Extrinsic Motivation." *Review of Economic Studies* 70: 489–520.

Bénabou, Roland, and Jean Tirole. 2004. "Incentives and Prosocial Behavior." Mimeo., Princeton University.

Bernheim, Douglas B. 1994. "A Theory of Conformity." *Journal of Political Economy* 102, no. 5: 842–877.

Bierhoff, Hans-Werner. 2002. *Prosocial Behaviour*. New York: Psychology Press.

Blount, Sally. 1995. "When Social Outcomes Aren't Fair: The Effect of Causal Attributions on Preferences." *Organizational Behavior and Human Decision* 63: 131–144.

Blumenthal, Marsha, Charles Christian, and Joel Slemrod. 2001. "Do Normative Appeals Affect Tax Compliance? Evidence from a Controlled Experiment in Minnesota. *National Tax Journal* 54, no. 1: 125–138.

Bodner, Ronit, and Drazen Prelec. 2003. "Self-Signaling and Diagnostic Utility in Everyday Decision Making." In *The Psychology of Economic Decisions. Vol. 1: Rationality and Well-Being*, ed. I. Brocas and J. Carrillo, 105–126. Oxford: Oxford University Press.

Bohnet, Iris, and Bruno S. Frey. 1997. "Rent Leaving." *Journal of Institutional and Theoretical Economics* 153: 711–721.

Bohnet, Iris, and Bruno S. Frey. 1999. "The Sound of Silence in Prisoner's Dilemma and Dictator Games." *Journal of Economic Behavior and Organization* 38, no. 1: 43–57.

Bohnet, Iris, Bruno S. Frey, and Steffen Huck. 2001. "More Order with Less Law: On Contract Enforcement, Trust and Crowding." *American Political Science Review* 95, no. 1: 131–144.

Bohnet, Iris, and Stephan Meier. 2005. "Deciding to Distrust." Mimeo., Kennedy School of Government, Harvard University.

Bolton, Gary, and Axel Ockenfels. 2000. "Erc—a Theory of Equity, Reciprocity and Competition." *American Economic Review* 90, no. 1: 166–193.

Bowles, Samuel, Christina Fong, and Herbert Gintis. 2006. "Reciprocity and Welfare State." In *Handbook on the Economics of Giving, Reciprocity and Altruism*, eds. J. Mercier Ythier and S.-C. Kolm, 1439–1464. Amsterdam: Elsevier.

Brown, Eleanor, and Hamilton Lankford. 1992. "Gifts of Money and Gifts of Time: Estimating the Effect of Tax Prices and Available Time." *Journal of Public Economics* 47, no. 3: 321–341.

Camerer, Colin. 2003. *Behavioral Game Theory*. Princeton: Princeton University Press.

Carpenter, Jeffrey. 2002. "The Demand for Punishment." Working Paper No. 0243, Middlebury College.

Carpenter, Jeffrey, Stephen Burks, and Eric Verhoogen. 2003. "Comparing Students to Workers: The Effect of Stakes, Social Framing, and Demographics on Bargaining Outcomes." Mimeo., Middlebury College.

Carter, John R., and Michael D. Irons. 1991. "Are Economists Different, and If So, Why?" *Journal of Economic Perspectives* 5, no. 2: 171–177.

Charness, Gary, and Brit Grosskopf. 2001. "Relative Payoffs and Happiness: An Experimental Study." *Journal of Economic Behavior and Organization* 45, no. 3: 301–328.

Charness, Gary, and David I. Levine. 2003. "The Road to Hell: An Experimental Study of Intentions." Mimeo., University of California at Santa Barbara.

Charness, Gary, and Matthew Rabin. 2002. "Social Preferences: Some Simple Tests and a New Model." *Quarterly Journal of Economics* 117, no. 3: 817–869.

Cherry, Todd L., Peter Frykblom, and Jason F. Shogren. 2002. "Hardnose the Dictator." *American Economic Review* 92, no. 4: 1218–1221.

Cialdini, Robert B. 1993. *Influence: The Psychology of Persuasion*. New York: William Morrow.

Cialdini, Robert B., D. T. Kenrick, and D. J. Baumann. 1982. "Effects of Mood on Prosocial Behavior in Children and Adults." In *The Development of Prosocial Behavior*, ed. N. Eisenberg, 339–359. New York: Academic Press.

Conlin, Michael, Michael Lynn, and Ted O'Donoghue. 2003. "The Norm of Restaurant Tipping." *Journal of Economic Behavior and Organization* 52, no. 3: 297–321.

Cookson, Richard. 2000. "Framing Effects in Public Goods Experiments." *Experimental Economics* 3, no. 1: 55–79.

Croson, Rachel. 1998. "Theories of Commitment, Altruism and Reciprocity: Evidence from Linear Public Good Games." Mimeo., Wharton School, University of Pennsylvania.

Csikszentmihalyi, Mihaly. 1990. *Flow: The Psychology of Optimal Experience*. New York: Harper Perennial.

Dana, Jason, Daylian M. Cain, and Robyn M. Dawes. 2006. "What You Don't Know Won't Hurt Me: Costly (but Quiet) Exit in Dictator Games." *Organizational Behavior and Human Decision Processes* 100, no. 2: 193–201.

Dana, Jason, Roberto A. Weber, and Jason Xi Kuang. 2004. "Exploiting Moral Wriggle Room: Behavior Inconsistent with a Preference for Fair Outcomes." Mimeo., Carnegie Mellon University.

Dawes, Robyn M., Jeanne McTavish, and Harriet Shaklee. 1977. "Behavior, Communication, and Assumptions about Other People's Behavior in a Commons Dilemma Situation." *Journal of Personality and Social Psychology* 35, no. 1: 1–11.

Dawes, Robyn M., and Richard Thaler. 1988. "Anomalies: Cooperation." *Journal of Economic Perspectives* 2, no. 3: 187–197.

Deci, Edward L. 1975. *Intrinsic Motivation*. New York: Plenum Press.

Deci, Edward L., Richard Koestner, and Richard M. Ryan. 1999. "A Meta-Analytic Review of Experiments Examining the Effects of Extrinsic Rewards on Intrinsic Motivation." *Psychological Bulletin* 125, no. 6: 627–668.

Dufwenberg, Martin, and Georg Kirchsteiger. 2004. "A Theory of Sequential Reciprocity." *Games and Economic Behavior* 47: 268–298.

Duncan, Brian. 1999. "Modeling Charitable Contributions of Time and Money." *Journal of Public Economics* 72, no. 2: 213–242.

Duncan, Brian. 2004. "A Theory of Impact Philanthropy." *Journal of Public Economics* 88, nos. 9–10: 2159–2180.

Eckel, Catherine C., and Philip J. Grossman. 1996. "Altruism and Anonymous Dictator Games." *Games and Economic Behavior* 16, no. 2: 181–191.

Eckel, Catherine C., and Philip J. Grossman. 2003. "Rebate Versus Matching: Does How We Subsidize Charitable Giving Matter?" *Journal of Public Economics* 87, nos. 3–4: 681–701.

Eckel, Catherine C., and Philip J. Grossman. 2005. "Subsidizing Charitable Contributions: A Field Test Comparing Matching and Rebate Subsidies." Mimeo., Virginia Polytechnic Institute and Station University.

Eisenberger, Robert, and Judy Cameron. 1996. "Detrimental Effects of Reward: Reality or Myth?" *American Psychologist* 51: 1153–1166.

Engelmann, Dirk, and Martin Strobel. 2004. "Inequality Aversion, Efficiency and Maximim Preferences in Simple Distribution Experiments." *American Economic Review* 94, no. 4: 857–869.

Enzle, Michael E., and Sharon C. Anderson. 1993. "Surveillant Intentions and Intrinsic Motivation." *Journal of Personality and Social Psychology* 64, no. 2: 257–266.

Falk, Armin. 2004. "Charitable Giving as a Gift Exchange: Evidence from a Field Experiment." Mimeo., Institute for Empirical Research in Economics, University of Zurich.

Falk, Armin, and Urs Fischbacher. 2006. "A Theory of Reciprocity." *Games and Economic Behavior* 54, no. 2: 293–315.

Falk, Armin, and Michael Kosfeld. 2004. "Distrust—The Hidden Cost of Control." IZA Discussion Paper No. 1203, Institute for the Study of Labor.

Farrel, Joseph, and Matthew Rabin. 1996. "Cheap Talk." *Journal of Economic Perspectives* 10, no. 3: 103–118.

Fehr, Ernst, and Urs Fischbacher. 2002. "Why Social Preferences Matter—The Impact of Non-Selfish Motives on Competition, Cooperation and Incentives." *Economic Journal* 112, no. 478: 1–33.

Fehr, Ernst, and Simon Gächter. 2000a. "Cooperation and Punishment in Public Goods Experiments." *American Economic Review* 90, no. 4: 980–994.

Fehr, Ernst, and Simon Gächter. 2000b. "Fairness and Retaliation: The Economics of Reciprocity." *Journal of Economic Perspectives* 14, no. 3: 159–181.

Fehr, Ernst, Simon Gächter, and Georg Kirchsteiger. 1997. "Reciprocity as a Contract Enforcement Device." *Econometrica* 65, no. 4: 833–860.

Fehr, Ernst, and John A. List. 2004. "The Hidden Costs and Returns of Incentives—Trust and Trustworthiness among CEOs." *Journal of the European Economic Association* 2, no. 5: 743–771.

Fehr, Ernst, and Klaus Schmidt. 1999. "A Theory of Fairness, Competition, and Cooperation." *Quarterly Journal of Economics* 114, no. 3: 817–868.

Fehr, Ernst, and Klaus Schmidt. 2003. "Theories of Fairness and Reciprocity—Evidence and Economic Application." In *Advances in Economics and Econometrics—8th World Congress, Econometric Society Monographs*, ed. M. Dewatripont, L. P. Hansen, and S. J. Turnovsky, 208–257. Cambridge: Cambridge University Press.

Fischbacher, Urs, Simon Gächter, and Ernst Fehr. 2001. "Are People Conditionally Cooperative? Evidence from a Public Goods Experiment." *Economics Letters* 71, no. 3: 397–404.

Fong, Christina. 2001. "Social Preferences, Self-Interest, and the Demand for Redistribution." *Journal of Public Economics* 82, no. 2: 225–246.

Fong, Christina. 2003. "Empathic Responsivenesss: Evidence from a Randomized Experiment on Giving to Welfare Recipients." Mimeo., Carnegie Mellon University.

Frank, Robert H., Thomas D. Gilovich, and Dennis T. Regan. 1993a. "Does Studying Economics Inhibit Cooperation?" *Journal of Economic Perspectives* 7, no. 2: 159–171.

Frank, Robert H., Thomas Gilovich, and Dennis T. Regan. 1993b. "The Evolution of One-Shot Cooperation: An Experiment." *Ethology and Sociobiology* 14: 247–256.

Frank, Robert H., Thomas D. Gilovich, and Dennis T. Regan. 1996. "Do Economists Make Bad Citizens?" *Journal of Economic Perspectives* 10, no. 1: 187–192.

Freeman, Richard B. 1997. "Working for Nothing: The Supply of Volunteer Labor." *Journal of Labor Economics* 15, no. 1: 140–166.

Frey, Bruno S. 1993. "Shirking or Work Morale? The Impact of Regulating." *European Economic Review* 37, no. 8: 1523–1532.

Frey, Bruno S. 1997a. "A Constitution for Knaves Crowds Out Civic Virtues." *Economic Journal* 107, no. 443: 1043–1053.

Frey, Bruno S. 1997b. *Not Just for the Money: An Economic Theory of Personal Motivation.* Northampton, MA: Edward Elgar.

Frey, Bruno S., and Matthias Benz. 2000. "Motivation Transfer Effect." Mimeo., Institute for Empirical Research in Economics, University of Zurich.

Frey, Bruno S., and Iris Bohnet. 1995. "Institutions Affect Fairness: Experimental Investigations." *Journal of Institutional and Theoretical Economics* 151, no. 2: 286–303.

Frey, Bruno S., and Lorenz Goette. 1999. "Does Pay Motivate Volunteers?" Mimeo., Institute for Empirical Research in Economics, University of Zurich.

Frey, Bruno S., and Reto Jegen. 2001. "Motivation Crowding Theory: A Survey of Empirical Evidence." *Journal of Economic Surveys* 5, no. 5: 589–611.

Frey, Bruno S., and Stephan Meier. 2003. "Are Political Economists Selfish and Indoctrinated? Evidence from a Natural Experiment." *Economic Inquiry* 41, no. 3: 448–462.

Frey, Bruno S., and Stephan Meier. 2004. "Social Comparisons and Pro-Social Behavior: Testing Conditional Cooperation in a Field Experiment." *American Economic Review* 94, no. 5: 1717–1722.

Frey, Bruno S., and Felix Oberholzer-Gee. 1997. "The Cost of Price Incentives: An Empirical Analysis of Motivation Crowding-Out." *American Economic Review* 87, no. 4: 746–755.

Frey, Bruno S., and Alois Stutzer. 2002a. "What Can Economists Learn from Happiness Research?" *Journal of Economic Literature* 40, no. 2: 402–435.

Frey, Bruno S., and Alois Stutzer. 2002b. *Happiness and Economics: How the Economy and Institutions Affect Well-Being.* Princeton and Oxford: Princeton University Press.

Frey, Bruno S., and Benno Torgler. 2004. "Taxation and Conditional Cooperation." Mimeo., Yale Center for International and Area Studies, New Haven, CT.

Gates, William H., and Chuck Collins. 2002. "Tax the Wealthy: Why America Needs the Estate Tax." *The American Prospect* 13, no. 11: 20–21.

Glazer, Amihai, and Kai A. Konrad. 1996. "A Signaling Explanation of Charity." *American Economic Review* 86, no. 4: 1019–1028.

Gneezy, Uri. 2003. "The W Effect of Incentives." Mimeo., University of Chicago Graduate School of Business.

Gneezy, Uri, and Aldo Rustichini. 2000a. "Pay Enough or Don't Pay at All." *Quarterly Journal of Economics* 115, no. 3: 791–810.

Gneezy, Uri, and Aldo Rustichini. 2000b. "A Fine Is a Price." *Journal of Legal Studies* 29, no. 1: 1–18.

Goette, Lorenz, David Huffman, and Stephan Meier. 2006. "The Impact of Group Membership on Cooperation and Norm Enforcement: Evidence Using Random Assignment to Real Social Groups." *American Economic Review* 96, no. 2: 212–216.

Harbaugh, William T. 1998. "The Prestige Motive for Making Charitable Transfers." *American Economic Review* 88, no. 2: 277–282.

Harris, Mary B., and Robert J. Smith. 1975. "Mood and Helping." *The Journal of Psychology* 91, no. 2: 215–221.

Heldt, Tobias. 2005. "Conditional Cooperation in the Field: Cross-Country Skiers' Behavior in Sweden." Mimeo., Uppsala University.

Henrich, Joseph, Robert Boyd, Sam Bowles, Colin Camerer, Herbert Gintis, Richard McElreath, and Ernst Fehr. 2001. "In Search of Homo Economicus: Experiments in 15 Small-Scale Societies." *American Economic Review* 91, no. 2: 73–79.

Heyman, James, and Dan Ariely. 2004. "Effort for Payment: A Tale of Two Markets." *Psychological Science* 15, no. 11: 787–793.

Hoffman, Elizabeth, Kevin McCabe, and Vernon Smith. 1996. "Social Distance and Other-Regarding Behavior in Dictator Games." *American Economic Review* 86, no. 3: 653–660.

Hoffman, Elizabeth, and Matthew L. Spitzer. 1985. "Entitlements, Rights and Fairness: An Experimental Examination of Subjects' Concepts of Distributive Justice." *Journal of Legal Studies* 14: 259–297.

Isaac, R. Mark, Deborah Mathieu, and Edward E. Zajac. 1991. "Institutional Framing and Perceptions of Fairness." *Constitutional Political Economy* 2, no. 3: 329–370.

Isen, Alice M., Nancy Horn, and D. L. Rosenhan. 1997. "Effects of Success and Failure on Children's Generosity." *Journal of Personality and Social Psychology* 27, no. 2: 239–247.

Johannesson, Magnus, and Björn Persson. 2000. "Non-Reciprocal Altruism in Dictator Games." *Economics Letters* 69, no. 2: 137–142.

Kelley, Harold H., and Anthony J. Stahelski. 1970. "Social Interaction Basis of Cooperators' and Competitors' Beliefs about Others." *Journal of Personality and Social Psychology* 16, no. 1: 66–91.

Kollock, Peter. 1998. "Transforming Social Dilemmas: Group Identity and Co-Operation." In *Modelling Rationality, Morality and Evolution*, ed. P. A. Danielson, 186–210. New York: Oxford University Press.

Kolm, Serge-Christophe. 2000. "The Theory of Reciprocity, Giving and Altruism." In *The Economics of Reciprocity, Giving and Altruism*, ed. L. A. Gérard-Varet, S.-C. Kolm and J. M. Ythier, 1–44. Houndmills: McMillan Press Ltd.

Konow, James. 2000. "Fair Shares: Accountability and Cognitive Dissonance in Allocation Decisions." *American Economic Review* 90, no. 4: 1072–1091.

Konow, James. 2003. "Which Is the Fairest One of All? A Positive Analysis of Justice Theories." *Journal of Economic Literature* 41, no. 4: 1188–1239.

Konow, James, and Joseph Earley. 2002. "The Hedonistic Paradox: Is Homo Economicus Happier?" Mimeo., Loyola Marymount University.

Lazear, Edward. 2000. "Performance Pay and Productivity." *American Economic Review* 90, no. 5: 1346–1361.

Ledyard, John O. 1995. "Public Goods: A Survey of Experimental Research." In *Handbook of Experimental Economics*, ed. J. Kagel and A. E. Roth, 111–194. Princeton: Princeton University Press.

Lepper, Mark R., and David Greene, eds. 1978. *The Hidden Costs of Reward: New Perspectives on Psychology of Human Motivation*. Hillsdale, NY: Erlbaum.

Lepper, Mark R., Jennifer Henderlong, and Isabelle Gingras. 1999. "Understanding the Effects of Extrinsic Rewards on Intrinsic Motivation—Uses and Abuses of Meta-Analysis—Comment on Deci, Koestner, and Ryan (1999)." *Psychological Bulletin* 125, no. 6: 669–676.

List, John A., and David Lucking-Reiley. 2002. "The Effects of Seed Money and Refunds on Charitable Giving: Experimental Evidence from a University Capital Campaign." *Journal of Political Economy* 110, no. 1: 215–233.

Loewenstein, George. 2000. "Emotions in Economic Theory and Economic Behavior." *American Economic Review* 90, no. 2: 426–432.

Long, Stephen H. 1976. "Social Pressure and Contributions to Health Charities." *Public Choice* 28, no. 2: 56–66.

Luttmer, Erzo F. P. 2001. "Group Loyalty and the Taste for Redistribution." *Journal of Political Economy* 109, no. 3: 500–528.

Marks, Gary N., and Norman Miller. 1987. "Ten Years of Research on the False-Consensus Effect: An Empirical and Theoretical Review." *Psychological Bulletin* 102, no. 1: 72–90.

Meier, Stephan. 2005a. "Do Subsidies Increase Charitable Giving in the Long Run? Matching Donations in a Field Experiment." Mimeo., Institute for Empirical Research in Economics, University of Zurich.

Meier, Stephan. 2005b. "Conditions under which Women Behave Less/More Pro-Socially Than Men." Mimeo., Kennedy School of Government, Harvard University.

Meier, Stephan. 2006. "Does Framing Matter for Conditional Cooperation? Evidence from a Natural Field Experiment." *Contributions to Economic Analysis & Policy* 5, no. 2, article 1.

Meier, Stephan, and Alois Stutzer. 2004. "Is Volunteering Rewarding in Itself? Evidence from a Natural Experiment." IEW Working Paper No. 181, University of Zurich.

Mueller, Dennis C. 2003. *Public Choice III*. Cambridge: Cambridge University Press.

Mui, Vai-Lam. 1995. "The Economics of Envy." *Journal of Economic Behavior & Organization* 26: 311–336.

Murningham, J. Keith, John M. Oesch, and Madan Pillutla. 2001. "Player Types and Self Impression Management in Dictator Games: Two Experiments." *Games and Economic Behavior* 37, no. 2: 388–414.

Olson, Mancur. 1965. *The Logic of Collective Action: Public Goods and the Theory of Groups*. Cambridge, Mass.: Harvard University Press.

Opp, Karl-Dieter. 2001. "Collective Political Action." *Analyse & Kritik* 23, no. 1: 1–20.

Osterloh, Margit, Sandra Rota, and Bernhard Kuster. 2003. "Open Source Software Production: Climbing on the Shoulders of Giants." Mimeo., Institute for Research in Business Administration, University of Zurich.

Ostrom, Elinor. 1990. *Governing the Commons: The Evolution of Institutions for Collective Action*. Cambridge: Cambridge University Press.

Ostrom, Elinor. 2000. "Collective Action and the Evolution of Social Norms." *Journal of Economic Perspectives* 14, no. 3: 137–158.

Putterman, Louis, and Christopher M. Anderson. 2006. "Do Non-Strategic Sanctions Obey the Law of Demand? The Demand for Punishment in the Voluntary Contribution Mechanism." *Games and Economic Behavior* 54, no. 1: 1–24.

Rabin, Matthew. 1993. "Incorporating Fairness into Game Theory and Economics." *American Economic Review* 83, no. 5: 1281–1302.

Rege, Mari, and Kjetil Telle. 2004. "The Impact of Social Approval and Framing on Cooperation in Public Good Situations." *Journal of Public Economics* 88, nos. 7–8: 1625–1644.

Reingen, P. H. 1982. "Test of a List Procedure for Inducing Compliance with a Request to Donate Money." *Journal of Applied Psychology* 67, no. 1: 110–118.

Roberts, Russell D. 1984. "A Positive Model of Private Charity and Public Transfers." *Journal of Political Economy* 92, no. 1: 136–148.

Ross, Lee, David Greene, and Pamela House. 1977. "The 'False Consensus Effect': An Egocentric Bias in Social Perception and Attribution Processes." *Journal of Experimental Social Psychology* 13, no. 3: 279–301.

Rotemberg, Julio. 1994. "Human Relations in the Workplace." *Journal of Political Economy* 102, no. 4: 684–717.

Rotter, Julian B. 1966. "Generalized Expectancies for Internal versus External Control of Reinforcement." *Psychological Monographs* 80, entire issue.

Rousseau, Denise M. 1995. *Psychological Contracts in Organizations: Understanding Written and Unwritten Agreements.* Thousand Oaks, CA: Sage Publications.

Sally, David. 1995. "Conversation and Cooperation in Social Dilemmas: A Meta-Analysis of Experiments from 1958 to 1992." *Rationality and Society* 7, no. 1: 58–92.

Schelling, Thomas C. 1984. "The Life You Save May Be Your Own." In *Choice and Consequence: Perspectives of an Errant Economist*, ed. T. Schelling, 113–146. Cambridge, MA, and London: Harvard University Press.

Schwarze, Johannes, and Marco Härpfer. 2004. "Are People Inequality Averse, and Do They Prefer Redistribution by the State? Evidence from German Longitudinal Data on Life Satisfaction." Discussion Paper No. 407, German Institute for Economic Research (DIW) Berlin.

Segal, Lewis M., and Burton Weisbrod. 1998. "Interdependence of Commercial and Donative Revenues." In *To Profit or Not to Profit: The Commercial Transformation of the Nonprofit Sector*, ed. B. A. Weisbrod, 105–127. Cambridge: Cambridge University Press.

Seligman, Clive, Joan E. Finegan, J. Douglas Hazlewood, and Mark Wilkinson. 1985. "Manipulating Attributions for Profit: A Field Test of the Effects of Attributions on Behavior." *Social Cognition* 3, no. 3: 313–321.

Shabman, Leonard, and Kurt Stephenson. 1994. "A Critique of the Self-Interested Voter Model: The Case of a Local Single Issue Referendum." *Journal of Economic Issues* 18, no. 4: 1173–1186.

Shang, Jen, and Rachel Croson. 2005. "Field Experiments in Charitable Contribution: The Impact of Social Influence on the Voluntary Provision of Public Goods." Mimeo., Wharton School, University of Pennsylvania.

Small, Deborah A., and George Loewenstein. 2003. "Helping the Victim or Helping *the* Victim: Altruism and Identifiability." *Journal of Risk and Uncertainty* 26, no. 1: 5–16.

Smith, Adam. 1759. *The Theory of Moral Sentiments.* Amherst, NY: Prometheus Books.

Smith, Kent W. 1992. "Reciprocity and Fairness: Positive Incentives for Tax Compliance." In *Why People Pay Taxes: Tax Compliance and Enforcment*, ed. J. Slemrod, 223–250. Ann Arbor: University of Michigan Press.

Smith, Vincent H., Michael R. Kehoe, and Mary E. Cremer. 1995. "The Private Provision of Public Goods: Altruism and Voluntary Giving." *Journal of Public Economics* 58, no. 1: 107–126.

Sobel, Joel. 2002. "Can We Trust Social Capital?" *Journal of Economic Literature* 40, no. 1: 139–154.

Soetevent, Adriaan R. 2005. "Anonymity in Giving in a Natural Context—an Economic Field Experiment in Thirty Churches." *Journal of Public Economics* 89, nos. 10–11: 2301–2323.

Sugden, Robert. 1982. "On the Economics of Philanthropy." *Economic Journal* 92: 341–350.

Tajfel, Henri. 1981. *Human Groups and Social Categories Studies in Social Psychology*. London: Cambridge University Press.

Titmuss, Richard M. 1970. *The Gift Relationship*. London: Allen and Unwin.

Trivers, Robert. 1971. "The Evolution of Reciprocal Altruism." *Quarterly Journal of Biology* 46: 32–57.

Unger, Lynette S. 1991. "Altruism as a Motivation to Volunteer." *Journal of Economic Psychology* 12, no. 1: 71–100.

van Lange, Paul A. 1992. "Confidence in Expectations: A Test of the Triangle Hypothesis." *European Journal of Personality* 6, no. 5: 371–379.

Varese, Federico, and Meir Yaish. 2000. "The Importance of Being Asked: The Rescue of Jews in Nazi Europe." *Rationality and Society* 12, no. 3: 307–334.

Wenzel, Michael. 2001. "Misperception of Social Norms About Tax Compliance: A Field Experiment." Mimeo., Australian National University.

Wheeler, Judith A., Kevin M. Gorey, and Bernard Greenblatt. 1998. "The Beneficial Effects of Volunteering for Older Volunteers and the People They Serve: A Meta-Analysis." *International Journal of Aging and Human Development* 47, no. 1: 69–79.

Wilson, John, and Marc Musick. 1999. "The Effects of Volunteering on the Volunteer." *Law and Contemporary Problems* 62, no. 4: 141–168.

4   Why Women and Men Trust Others

Iris Bohnet

4.1   Introduction

Trust pervades our lives and contributes to economic, political, and organizational success. Generalized trust in others has been associated with economic growth (Knack and Keefer 1997; Zak and Knack 2001), stable democracy (Inglehart 1999), better functioning governments (LaPorta et al. 1997), social capital (Putnam, Leonardi, and Nanetti 1993; Putnam 2000), a decrease in crime (Rosenfeld, Messner, and Baumer 2001), and cooperation within and between organizations (Kramer and Tyler 1996; Ostrom and Walker 2003).

But why do people trust each other? And why might some demographic groups be more willing to trust than others? In this chapter, we focus on what motivates men and women to trust others. We adopt a definition of trust proposed by a cross-disciplinary review as "a psychological state composing the intention to accept vulnerability based on positive expectations of the intentions or behavior of another" (Rousseau et al. 1998, 395). This definition combines the notion of trust as a belief—namely, the expectation of trustworthiness (e.g., Hardin 2002)—with the view that trust is a social motivation—namely, the willingness to accept vulnerability (e.g., Kramer 1999; Mansbridge 1999). Mansbridge (1999) talks of "altruistic trust" and Kramer (1999, 573) argues that "trust needs to be conceptualized not only as a calculative orientation toward risk, but also a social orientation toward other people and toward society as a whole."

This chapter examines to what degree men and women perceive the decision of whether or not to trust another person as basically a decision under risk, based on their expectations of trustworthiness, and to what extent social preferences come into play. I distinguish between unconditional and conditional social preferences. A person's (un) will-ingness to assume vulnerability may be based on unconditional social preferences such as altruism (e.g., Batson 1991; Andreoni and Miller 2002) and inequity aversion (e.g., Loewenstein, Bazerman, and Thomp-son 1989; Fehr and Schmidt 1999; Bolton and Ockenfels 2000), or may be due to internalized norms; in other words, the psychological bene-fits or costs an individual derives from being kind or unkind to others (e.g., Andreoni 1990).[1]

Alternatively, willingness to be vulnerable may depend on the infer-ences a person makes about why a particular outcome occurred or about one's counterpart's intentions, a conditional social preference. The relevance of "causal attributions" has been noted by psychologists for a long time. Attribution theory models assert that people have a need to infer causes and to assign responsibility for outcomes. Heider (1958) introduced the notion of causal inferences as critical cognitive processes and Buss (1978) and Kruglanski (1979) focused on the rele-vance of intentionality. In a seminal paper in economics, Rabin (1993) introduced intentions into game theory.

We use two approaches to measure the relevance of social prefer-ences for trust. In study 1, we examine what fractions of the variance in observed trust are due to social preferences, risk preferences, and expectations of trustworthiness. We do this by experimentally measur-ing unconditional social preferences, attitudes to risk, and expectations and then controlling for these three possible motivators of trust *econo-metrically*. Trust is measured by the amount sent in an anonymous, one-shot investment game (Berg, Dickhaut, and McCabe 1995), social preferences by the amount sent in a triple dictator game (Kahneman, Knetsch, and Thaler 1986), risk preferences in a standard risky choice task (e.g., Eckel and Wilson 2004a), and expectations of trustworthi-ness by a simple question in an ex post experimental questionnaire. If people perceived trust mainly as a decision under risk, trust should be related to expectations of return and, possibly, their risk preferences.[2] If trust was mainly a social orientation, it should be related to social preferences.

In study 2, we examine how robust our findings from study 1 are with a different subject pool—executives instead of students—and in a different context—namely, with preplay communication instead of under anonymity. While cheap talk should not matter theoretically, a host of experimental evidence on prisoner's dilemma and public goods games suggests that it does (e.g., Bohnet and Frey 1999 and Camerer

2003 for a survey). The role of communication in the investment game has not been studied widely.

In study 3, we use a different approach and control for risk preferences and expectations of trustworthiness by *experimental design*. I compare behavior in two different games to measure the relevance of conditional social preferences for trust. I use a binary-choice trust game (e.g., Camerer and Weigelt 1988) and a binary-choice risky dictator game with identical odds and payoffs (Bohnet and Zeckhauser 2004). The only difference between the two games is that in the former the agent of uncertainty is another person, while in the latter it is nature. We ask people how high the likelihood of receiving the "high payoff" (resulting from trustworthiness, or a lucky draw in the risky dictator game) minimally has to be for them to be willing to take risk in these games. If people's willingness to take risk in the two games does not differ, they perceive trust as a decision under risk. If we find a difference in the willingness to take risk between the trust and the risky dictator game, this suggests that trust also has a social component.

Whether trust is mainly based on expectations of trustworthiness or on social preferences has policy implications. If policy makers or managers wish to raise the level of trust in society or in their organization, they need to know the determinants of trust. If trust is mainly a function of expected trustworthiness in a specific context, they should focus on the level of trustworthiness and on beliefs about that level. In contrast, if trust in that context is basically a social orientation, they should focus on fostering social preferences.

If they choose the wrong focus, policies may not only be ineffective but may even be counterproductive. Recent evidence suggests that arrangements increasing trustworthiness, such as contractual arrangements or penalties, may undermine the social motivation to trust (Bohnet, Frey, and Huck 2001; Fehr and Gächter 2003; Pillutla, Malhorta, and Murnighan 2003). For example, Sitkin and Roth (1993, 376) observed that "legalistic remedies can erode the interpersonal foundations of a relationship they are intended to bolster because they replace reliance on an individual's goodwill with objective, formal requirements." The negative effect of extrinsic incentives on intrinsic motivation is known as "crowding out" in economics and has been documented in a wide set of cases (e.g., Frey 1997; Frey and Oberholzer-Gee 1997; Frey and Jegen 2001).

Policy makers and managers should also be interested in the heterogeneity in motivation. If there are differences in the motivation to trust between demographic groups, group-specific policy interventions are called for. A sizable number of earlier studies on trust examines demographic differences in behavior but does not analyze the underlying motivations (see Croson and Gneezy 2004 for a survey).

Our findings suggest a clear gender pattern in the motivation to trust: women perceive trust as a risky choice. They base their decision of whether or not to trust on expectations of trustworthiness. When we hold expectations constant by design, women behave in a trust game basically like they behave in a risky dictator game. Men, in contrast, respond more strongly to the social component of trust. Their trust is related to both their expectations of trustworthiness and their willingness to be vulnerable. Men are less likely to take risk in a trust game than in a risky dictator game. They care about how outcomes come to be and dislike being betrayed by another person more than losing in a lottery.

Our gender findings add to a recent stream of studies that examine the motivation to trust but do not focus on the gender heterogeneity in motivation (e.g., Dufwenberg and Gneezy 2000; Cox 2004; Ashraf, Bohnet, and Piankov 2006). Recent work by Bohnet and Zeckhauser (2004) suggests the relevance of conditional social preferences for trust. Hong and Bohnet (2007) focus on the relationship between status and trust, and Bohnet, Herrmann, and Zeckhauser (2006) find that the motivation to trust strongly differs between Islamic and Western countries. Greig and Bohnet (2005a, 2005b) found that when gender is correlated with income, as is typically the case in developing (and often also in developed) countries, need becomes a strong motivator of trust.

This chapter combines various approaches to measure the relevance of gender heterogeneity in motivation for trust, including different games, techniques, and subject pools in different parts of the world. The possibility of examining the robustness of a finding under different conditions is one of the advantages of running experiments.

The chapter is organized as follows: section 4.2 introduces the experimental designs, section 4.3 presents the results, section 4.4 compares our results with theories on gender, and section 4.5 concludes.

4.2 Experimental Design

Study 1 examines behavior and motivations in an investment game with students in three countries; Russia, South Africa, and the United States. It investigates whether trust behavior is (also) related to unconditional social preferences. Study 2 builds on the design of study 1 but focuses on a different context and subject pool, namely, executives. Study 3 employs a binary-choice trust game conducted in Kuwait and the United States, among other places. It examines whether a person's willingness to accept the vulnerability inherent in trust is related to how the vulnerability was produced, by another person or by nature. The three studies build on joint work with Nava Ashraf and Nikita Piankov (Ashraf, Bohnet, and Piankov 2006), Yael Baytelman (Bohnet and Baytelman 2007), Benedikt Herrmann and Richard Zeckhauser (Bohnet, Herrmann, and Zeckhauser 2006), and Kessely Hong (Hong and Bohnet 2007). These papers focus on different aspects than gender and in particular, discuss the cross-societal comparisons in greater detail.

4.2.1   Study 1

In our investment game, a first mover, the principal, received an endowment E, of which she[3] could send any amount $X \leq E$ to her agent. Any amount sent was tripled by the experimenter, such that the agent received $3X$. The agent could return any amount $Y \leq 3X$ to her principal. Final payoffs were $(E - X + Y)$ for the principal and $(3X - Y)$ for the agent. In addition to indicating how much they wanted to send, we also asked principals to indicate what they expected to get back. In our experiments, $E = 100CU$ (currency units).

To examine the role of social motivation, a principal also played a triple dictator game. The only difference from the investment game was that the game ended after the principal's decision. Thus, final payoffs were $(E - X)$ for the principal and $(3X)$ for the agent. To measure a principal's risk preferences, principals also participated in a risky choice task. They had to indicate for six risky choice tasks whether they preferred the gamble or the certain amount. They could choose to bet on a 50 percent chance of winning 300CU or nothing, or to accept a certain amount varying between 40CU and 140CU. The more people prefer the sure thing to the gamble, the more risk averse they are. Finally, subjects were asked how much they expected to get back in the investment game.

Thus the experiment consisted of four parts, the investment game (including the trustworthiness question), the triple dictator game, a risky choice task, and a short questionnaire on demographic characteristics. The order in which the games were played was varied. Half of the subjects played the investment game first, the other half the triple dictator game. The fact that subjects would participate in several tasks was common knowledge. In an introduction page, subjects were informed that the experiment consisted of four parts, that they would receive the instructions for each part separately, that they would remain anonymous during the experiment (i.e., identified by code numbers), that they would be paired randomly for each decision, and that they would be paid according to a special procedure.

The endowment E was 100CU in our experiments. The experiments were run in three countries: Russia, South Africa, and the United States. Adjusted for purchasing power parity, this meant $E = 100$ dollars in the United States, $E = 1,000$ rubles in Russia, and $E = 400$ rands in South Africa.[4] Subjects were paid randomly at the end of the whole experiment; they did not learn about any results during the experiment. More specifically, for the investment game and the triple dictator game one principal and one agent per game were randomly selected and matched at the end of the experiment; they were paid according to their choices in the corresponding game. For the risky choice task, one person was randomly paid according to his or her choice.[5]

The experiments were conducted with 359 college students: 118 students from universities in Moscow, Russia, 129 students from universities in Capetown, South Africa, and 112 students from universities in Boston, the United States. We ran four experimental sessions in each country, two with the risky dictator game first and two with the investment game first. The experimenters who ran experiments in Russia and in South Africa also ran one session in the United States. No experimenter effects could be found in the U.S.[6] The experiment took about one hour and thirty minutes. A show-up fee of 10CU was paid and subjects earned on average an additional 22CU. The experimental design is discussed more fully in Ashraf, Bohnet, and Piankov (2006).

4.2.2 Study 2

We used a very similar protocol to that of study 1. Subjects also participated in both an investment and a triple dictator game for 100CU and we elicited expectations of trustworthiness after they had made their decisions. The main difference in design was that principals and agents were confronted with hypothetical scenarios only, and participated in a number of different scenarios. The complete design is presented in Bohnet and Baytelman (2007). The scenario of interest here indicated that principals and agents were allowed to talk to each other for five minutes before principals had to decide how much to send to their agents and agents how much to return to their principals. Participants decided hypothetically, based on the description of the scenario, and were not matched with each other or paid according to their decision.

The experiments were run with 302 senior executives participating in executive programs at the Kennedy School of Government, Harvard University. Of these participants, 63 percent came from the United States, 25 percent from Europe, and the rest from a variety of countries in Asia and Latin America; 70 percent were white, and they ranged in age from 35 to 62 years, with the median age being 44. We ran the experiments in executive programs; thus, in contrast to our student subjects, these participants knew each other before they participated in the experiment.

4.2.3   Study 3

Study 3 significantly differs from the previous two studies. We compared behavior in two different games, a binary-choice trust game and a binary-choice risky dictator game, in Kuwait and the United States, among other countries. Bohnet, Herrmann, and Zeckhauser (2006) discuss the complete study, which focuses on comparisons between several Islamic and Western countries. Hong and Bohnet (2007) present additional results for various demographic groups in the United States.

The only difference between the trust and the risky dictator game was that in the latter, it was not the second mover who decided whether to reward trust or not, but nature. In the trust game (risky dictator game), the principal decided between a sure outcome and trust (a lottery). If she chose the sure thing, she and her agent both received (S, S). If she was willing to trust (gamble), both either ended up with a moderate payoff exceeding S (M, M), or the principal received a lower payoff than if she had not trusted (accepted the lottery) and the agent the highest possibly payoff, (L, H). Thus, for the principal, $M > S > L$ and for the agent, $H > M > S$. In the trust game, the final outcomes after trust were determined by the agent. If he rewarded trust, both earned the moderate payoffs. If he betrayed trust, he received the highest and the principal the lowest possible outcome. In the risky dictator game, nature determined final payoffs. In our experiment, $S = 10CU$, $M = 15CU$, $L = 8CU$ and $H = 22CU$. A risk-neutral principal only caring about her own payoffs would be indifferent between the sure outcome and the gamble for $p' = 0.29$.

In each decision situation, we elicited each principal's *minimum acceptable probability (MAP)* of earning M for which they would prefer the gamble to the sure payoff S. We compared a principal's MAP with the likelihood of trustworthiness in a given session, p^*. We conducted the trust experiments first and then used the average p^* for the risky dictator games. In the latter, we informed principals that prior to the experiment we determined p^*, the probability of receiving M. If principals' MAPs were higher than p^*, they earned M. However, principals played the gamble with probability p^* if their MAP was lower than or equal to p^*. The higher one's MAP, the higher p^* must be for the person to be willing to gamble instead of choosing the sure outcome. Thus the less one likes one or both outcomes of the lottery, the higher will be one's MAP. This mechanism is incentive-compatible since individuals cannot affect the probability they receive in the lottery.

If the MAPs in the trust game exceeded the MAPs in the risky dictator game, we took this as evidence for social preferences. Our expectation was that it is fundamentally different to trust another person than to rely on a random device offering the same outcomes: people are averse to being betrayed. Note that the difference between the MAPs in the trust game and the risky dictator game produces a net effect, based not only on concerns about betrayal but also about trustworthiness. While a person may dislike experiencing betrayal, she may also enjoy experiencing trustworthiness. As we expected betrayal costs to outweigh trustworthiness benefits, Bohnet and Zeckhauser (2004) referred to this as "betrayal aversion."

We ran the experiments with 282 students in the United States and 158 students in Kuwait. Subjects were identified by code numbers, were anonymous to other players, and were randomly assigned to the role of principal or agent and randomly matched. The payoffs were presented to subjects in a matrix form with neutral terminology. Payoffs were given in points, which were converted 1 point:0.25 Kuwaiti dinar and 1 point:1 U.S. dollar at the end of the experiment. Our goal was to keep incentives constant across countries. We used the hourly wage of a research assistant as a guideline. Subjects earned a 10CU show-up fee and received on average an additional 13CU for an experiment that took approximately 45–60 minutes.

4.3   Results

We present the results of each study in turn.

4.3.1   Study 1
On average, women (N = 83) sent 41CU and men (N = 96) 47CU in the investment game. Both women and men who sent a positive

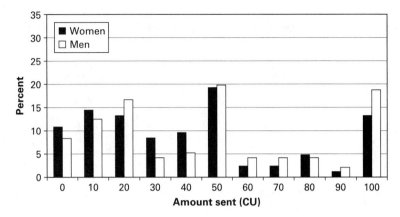

Figure 4.1
Distribution of the choices of men and women in the anonymous one-shot investment game.

amount expected the agent to return 90 percent of the amount sent to them. Thus, on average, principals did not expect to make money in this game. While we want to focus on principals' behavior here, we also shortly summarize what agents did. On average, women returned 77 percent and men returned 82 percent out of the amount sent. We did not observe any significant gender differences in agent behavior or motivation. Thus, on average, our principals were slightly too optimistic about returns.

In the triple dictator game, women sent 22CU and men 26CU on average. In our risky choice task, women chose the safe option in 4 out of 6 cases; men in 3.5 out of 6 cases. None of these differences is significant.[7] In fact, figure 4.1 illustrates that for the investment game there were basically no gender differences in the distribution of choices.

Figure 4.1 suggests considerable variation in behavior. We ran regressions to examine what might account for this variation for women and men. Table 4.1 presents the regression results. Columns 1 and 4 show that expectations of trustworthiness, measured by the fraction expected back out of the amount sent (Y/X), were strongly related to women's and men's trust. In columns 2 and 5, we added the amount given in the triple dictator game to the regression. The amounts women sent in the investment game were not related to the amounts they gave in the triple dictator game. In contrast, for men triple dictator game giving and the amounts sent in the investment game were strongly correlated. For every CU given in the triple dictator game, men gave 0.65CU in the investment game. Adding triple dictator

Table 4.1
Determinants of trust: Amount sent in the anonymous one-shot investment game (OLS)

	Women (1)	Women (2)	Women (3)	Men (4)	Men (5)	Men (6)
Expectations (Y/X)	28.16 (4.61)***	26.83 (4.61)***	36.53 (4.44)***	26.66 (5.08)***	23.00 (4.51)***	17.87 (4.88)***
Amount sent in TDG		0.26 (0.18)	0.05 (0.16)		0.65 (0.13)***	0.69 (0.14)***
Risk aversion			0.96 (2.16)			−3.17 (2.04)
Order			0.77 (5.27)			−13.73 (5.98)**
Russia			16.94 (7.95)**			11.68 (8.13)
South Africa			−5.65 (5.78)			6.20 (8.17)
Constant	21.38 (5.05)***	15.91 (5.95)***	9.47 (10.72)	26.91 (5.58)***	12.45 (5.63)**	24.53 (10.83)**
Observations	73	73	65	86	85	73
R-squared	0.35	0.37	0.60	0.25	0.43	0.49

Source: Data based on Ashraf, Bohnet, and Piankov (2006).
Note: Robust standard errors in parentheses. ***significant at 1 percent; **significant at 5 percent; *significant at 10 percent

game giving hardly helped in accounting for the variance observed for women, but almost doubled the R-squared for men.

In columns 3 and 6, we included risk preferences and a number of controls, namely, the order in which the games were played and the countries in which the experiments took place. Trust was not significantly related to risk preferences or to the country where the experiments were conducted. In fact, we found little cross-country variation in behavior and motivation. American principals sent 42CU in the trust game and 20CU in the triple dictator game, Russian principals 49CU and 25CU, and South African principals 43CU and 27CU, respectively. The inclusion of these variables affects our results only little. If anything, the gender differences in motivation increase, with expectations of trustworthiness affecting women's trust decisions more than men's, and triple dictator game giving affecting men's trust decisions more than women's.

Study 1 provides the first evidence that different motives matter for women's versus men's trust. Women perceive the trust decision as a choice under risk, based on their expectations of trustworthiness.

Expectations also matter for men, but their trust is also related to how much principals care about others in the triple dictator game.

4.3.2   Study 2

Women sent 62CU (N = 64) and men 76CU (N = 88) in the hypothetical investment game with preplay communication. Women expected to get back 1.24 times and men 1.42 times the amount sent in this version of the investment game. Thus, with communication, men sent more and expected back more than women. All principals expected to make money in this game. Female principals were slightly and male principals significantly too optimistic, with agents returning 1.1 times the amount sent on average. Women returned significantly less than men—0.93 in comparison to 1.2 times the amount sent. In the triple dictator game women sent 18CU (N = 64) and men 32CU (N = 88), again a significant difference. Thus, overall, men were more generous than women, whether they decided as principals, agents, or dictators.

Both trust and trustworthiness levels in study 2 exceed the levels observed in study 1. This may be due to cheap talk, but it may also be due to the hypothetical nature of the experiment or the differences in subject pools. Bohnet and Baytelman (2007) ran the anonymous hypothetical investment game with executives as well and found that women sent 49CU (N = 69) and men 60CU (N = 89) on average, suggesting that both men and women sent significantly more with than without communication. When we compare these results with study 1, we find that executives sent slightly more than students (for a similar result, see Fehr and List 2004).

Table 4.2 presents the results of a regression analysis. In contrast to the earlier regressions, we use amounts expected back rather than proportions expected back to measure the impact of expectations. The results are robust to either specification. We use both measures in this chapter to demonstrate this. Note, however, that when we control for amounts expected back, this variable typically accounts for most of the variance in trust. Part of this is due to a mechanical correlation as the more principals send, the more they can expect back. Even more surprisingly, we found that women's trust decisions were significantly more affected by their expectations of return but significantly less influenced by their unconditional social preferences than were men's, independent of which controls we included.

Study 2 presents a similar picture as study 1. Not only in an anonymous one-shot investment game with students, but also in a

100   Iris Bohnet

Table 4.2
Determinants of trust: Amount sent in the hypothetical investment game with preplay communication (OLS)

	Women (1)	Women (2)	Women (3)	Men (4)	Men (5)	Men (6)
Expectations (Y)	0.53 (0.04)***	0.53 (0.04)***	0.55 (0.04)***	0.38 (0.03)***	0.36 (0.03)***	0.36 (0.03)***
Amount sent in TDG		−0.04 (0.09)	0.02 (0.10)		0.17 (0.06)***	0.18 (0.06)***
Age			−1.82 (1.72)			−1.03 (2.40)
White			1.69 (5.10)			9.33 (6.05)
Europe			16.42 (11.22)			0.31 (8.46)
U.S.A.			11.99 (10.03)			−1.12 (7.25)
Constant	24.16 (3.62)***	24.95 (4.15)***	14.20 (11.53)	34.86 (3.86)***	31.12 (3.96)***	28.50 (9.70)***
Observations	64	64	64	88	88	87
R-squared	0.76	0.76	0.78	0.65	0.68	0.69

Source: Data based on Bohnet and Baytelman (2007).
Note: Robust standard errors in parentheses. *** significant at 1 percent; ** significant at 5 percent; * significant at 10 percent

hypothetical investment game with preplay communication with executives, unconditional social preferences matter for men's but not for women's trust. Women's trust is only based on their expectations of trustworthiness. This suggests that women perceive the investment game as an "investment decision," and decide based on their expectations of success while for men, additional social components come into play when confronted with the decision of how much to trust another person. In table 4.3, we present the regression results for the complete samples of studies 1 and 2. We include all controls presented in tables 4.1 and 4.2 (columns 3 and 6). The interaction variables between female and expectations (Y/X in study 1 and Y in study 2) and between female and the amounts given in the triple dictator game are all significant.

While indicative of gender differences in the motivation to trust, studies 1 and 2 have a number of shortcomings. A priori, none of these should affect men and women differently—but we still want to note them here. First, study 1 finds that attitudes to risk and trust are hardly

Table 4.3
Determinants of trust: Amount sent in studies 1 and 2 (OLS)

	Study 1 (All)	Study 2 (All)
Expectations	19.19	0.36
(Y/X in study 1; Y in study 2)	(4.49)***	(0.03)***
Amount sent in TDG	0.72	0.19
	(0.13)***	(0.06)***
Female	3.72	−7.66
	(8.49)	(6.04)
Expectations × Female	16.40	0.17
	(6.23)**	(0.05)***
Amount sent in TDG × Female	−0.57	−0.19
	(0.22)**	(0.09)*
Controls	Yes	Yes
Constant	19.47	28.43
	(8.67)**	(7.19)***
Observations	138	151
R-squared	0.51	0.73

Robust standard errors in parentheses. ***significant at 1 percent; **significant at 5 percent; *significant at 10 percent

related, a finding shared with other papers examing this relationship (e.g., Eckel and Wilson 2004a). This is in stark contrast to a large theoretical literature crossing various disciplines that expects there to be a strong relationship (e.g., Luhmann 1979; Ben-Ner and Putterman 2001; Cook and Cooper 2003). However, while they may indeed not be correlated, it may also be that we, as well as others, used a weak instrument to measure attitudes to risk (or trust, for that matter). Most notably, there is one important difference between a risky choice in a gamble and the decision of whether or not to trust—namely, the presence of a second person in the trust game. While we control for principals' social preferences in the triple dictator game, risk-taking in the presence of an agent may still differ from risk-taking if final payoffs only affect oneself. To account for this more directly, we introduced the risky dictator game in study 3.

Second, we elicited expectations of trustworthiness after principals decided how much to send their agent in the trust game. What our study has in common with other studies examining expectations is that there is no right answer for how and when to elicit expectations (e.g., Fehr et al. 2002; Eckel and Wilson 2004b). While many researchers provide incentives for accurate predictions, the evidence on whether such incentives matter is not conclusive. In both our studies, men's and women's predictions were slightly too optimistic.

Like most others, we also chose to elicit expectations after the trust choice so as to have "clean" observational data. At the same time, what people reported they expected back may just be *ex post* justifications for their behavior. If women have more of a need for consistency than men, this could have contributed to the observed gender pattern. However, we do not know of any evidence suggesting gender differences in consistency preferences.

Study 3 tries to avoid these pitfalls: it holds the riskiness of the decision task constant across games and controls for expectations by experimental design.

4.3.3 Study 3

Table 4.4 shows that both men and women in Kuwait and the United States were more likely to take risk in the risky dictator game than in the trust game. However, the difference in MAPs between the trust game and the risky dictator game is about twice as large for men than it is for women in the two countries. In Kuwait, the difference is 0.28 for men and 0.13 for women and in the United States, it is 0.19 for men and 0.07 for women. Comparing these gender differences, we find that men cared significantly more about how the outcome came to be than did women, or, put differently, men were more betrayal-averse than women (significant in Kuwait, $p < 0.1$ in the United States).

A number of additional differences are noteworthy: American men were significantly less risk-averse in the risky dictator game than were American women or Kuwaitis. In fact, as p', the probability of p that

Table 4.4
Mean MAPs in the risky dictator and the trust game, [N]

	Risky dictator game	Trust game
American women	0.44	0.51
	[38]	[55]
American men	0.32	0.51
	[48]	[50]
Kuwaiti women	0.40	0.53
	[15]	[24]
Kuwaiti men	0.46	0.74
	[25]	[15]

Sources: Data based on Bohnet, Herrmann, and Zeckhauser (2006) and Hong and Bohnet (2007).

makes a risk-neutral principal who only cares about her own payoffs indifferent between the sure outcome and the gamble, was 0.29, American men were basically risk-neutral while everyone else was significantly risk-averse in this game. Kuwaiti men demanded significantly higher MAPs than Kuwaiti women and Americans in the trust game.

We conclude that women are more likely than men to perceive the trust decision as a risky choice. While both men and women experience some betrayal aversion when confronted with another person rather than nature, men are significantly more affected by it than are women. Study 3 provides rather strong evidence for gender differences in the relevance of social preferences for trust. In contrast to studies 1 and 2, we focus on conditional social preferences here.

4.4   Discussion

By trusting, principals make their agent better off but also expose themselves to the risk of being betrayed by their agent. Such concerns about the "other," our findings suggest, mainly matter for men's trust decisions. In contrast, women perceive trust more like a gamble: they trust based on their expectations of trustworthiness. The net effect of these differences in motivation on trust is unclear. Unconditional social preferences such as altruism or warm-glow altruism should lead men to trust more than women. At the same time, men's more pronounced concerns about betrayal should induce them to trust less than women.

In addition, women and men may differ in their attitudes to risk. Generally, women have been found to be more risk averse than men—although most experiments examining attitudes to risk have been conducted in Western developed countries (see Croson and Gneezy 2004 for a survey). In study 3, we also find that American women are significantly more risk-averse than men in this context. However, this gender difference does not apply to Kuwaitis. Thus, if women were in fact more risk-averse, they would be less likely to trust than men.

Finally, women and men may have different expectations of trustworthiness. Male executives were significantly more optimistic than female executives in study 2, but we did not find any significant gender differences for the students of study 1. In other tasks, Western men have generally been found to be more optimistic or overconfident than Western women (see Croson and Gneezy 2004 for a survey). Accordingly, we might expect men to be more willing to trust.

Overall, it is unclear whether men or women should be more likely to trust, consistent with the mixed evidence we have amassed. Most studies do not suggest any gender differences in trust behavior (e.g., Croson and Buchan 1999; Ashraf, Bohnet, and Piankov 2006; Fehr et al. 2002). Buchan, Croson, and Solnick (2003) find men to be more trusting than women while Eckel and Wilson (2004b) report women to be more trusting than men when shown a photo of their counterpart, but less trusting when given only information about their counterpart's gender and preferences.

What seems obvious, based on our research, is that women's and men's trust is motivated differently. If this finding generalizes to other environments, different instruments are required to motivate women and men. For example, if social planners or managers want to increase trust, as numerous recent books such as *Restoring Trust in American Business* (Lorsch, Berlowitz, and Zelleke 2005) suggest, they would have to focus on changing the levels of trustworthiness and expectations thereof for women, but must also highlight the intrinsic benefits derived from trusting for men. The same principle applies to negotiation and conflict resolution where integrative agreements are more likely if the parties trust each other.[8] Books such as *The Cheating Culture* (Callahan 2004), which remind the reader that the recent corporate and religious violations of trust may not be exceptions but just represent the tip of the iceberg, may destroy women's trust in others while socially oriented men may still derive some intrinsic benefits from trusting.

Finally, we may wonder why we see gender differences in the motivation to trust. While our experiments show that there are substantive differences, they do not shed any light on what the reasons might be. Thus, we only offer some preliminary thoughts here. In many ways, our results suggest that women behave more rationally in the trust game than men—they mainly focus on their own and hardly care about others' payoffs, their expectations are more accurate and less optimistic than those of men, and they care less about others' intentions than do men. That men experience larger costs from betrayal than women is a possible explanation of the puzzling finding that in public goods games allowing punishment men are more likely than women to punish free riders in one-shot games or in the very last round of repeated games (e.g., Herrmann 2004, 66; Egas and Riedl 2005). Recent neuroscientific evidence suggests that men are more likely than women to derive pleasure from punishing wrong-doers (Singer et al.

2006). While women seem to use punishment to "educate" free riders, men seem to also use it to take revenge.

Is *homo oeconomicus* a she—in contrast to what many feminist theories of economics have assumed so far (e.g., Ferber and Nelson 1993)? This seems consistent with the differences in fitness-enhancing strategies employed by males and females as observed in anthropology and evolutionary biology. However, our social preference findings are not only consistent with a nature hypothesis, but also with explanations based on nurture. Theories on status and power, for example, suggest that men, or, more generally, people belonging to higher status groups, are more likely to derive a paternalistic warm glow from trusting others. Such generosity is described as a means for high status benefactors to preserve their own status (e.g., Swim and Campbell 2003). At the same time, trusting implies ceding power over one's own outcome to the agent and accepting some degree of submission to another's will. The more powerful, men, dislike being vulnerable more than do the less powerful, women (e.g., Mainiero 1986; Lips 1991).

4.5   Conclusions

Social preferences, conditional as well as unconditional, matter for men's interpersonal trust but hardly matter for women's. In this chapter, we measured the relevance of social preferences for men's and women's trust in three studies. Study 1 focused on a one-shot anonymous investment game between students in three different countries: South Africa, Russia, and the United States. It showed that independent of country of origin, our female subjects' trust is accounted for by their expectations of trustworthiness. In contrast, male students trust more, the more optimistic they are about their counterpart's trustworthiness and the more they care about others (as measured in a triple dictator game).

Study 2 is similar to the study 1 design but asked people to make hypothetical decisions in an investment game where principals and agents can talk to each other before playing the game. In addition, it used a different subject pool, namely, executives from different parts of the world. Women were again not affected by their social preferences when they decided how much to trust another person—men were. Using a different design, study 3 shed further light on how people perceive the trust decision. It found that women were more likely to perceive trust as a risky choice while men strongly differentiated between a gamble and a trust decision. When confronted with another person rather than nature, men were more betrayal-averse than women.

Thus women's behavior is more in line with the assumptions of traditional economic theory than is men's: their trust decisions are not affected by concerns about others' payoffs or intentions; they base their decisions on (relatively accurate) expectations of return and their risk preferences. Interestingly, much of the neuroscientific evidence on betrayal aversion, and more generally the dislike of unfair treatment, is based on studies of men only. For example, Kosfeld et al. (2005) found that intranasal administration of oxytocin decreased men's betrayal aversion in the investment game, and Sanfey et al. (2003) found that for men unfairness in an ultimatum game triggered activity in an area of the brain well known for its involvement in negative emotions (the anterior insula). The recent study by Singer et al. (2006) of men and women suggests that these patterns may in fact mainly apply to men.

Notes

This chapter was inspired by joint work with Nava Ashraf, Yael Baytelman, Benedikt Herrmann, Kessely Hong, Nikita Piankov, and Richard Zeckhauser and greatly benefited from discussions with Stephan Meier. Financial support from the Women and Public Policy Program at the Kennedy School of Government and the Women's Leadership Board is gratefully acknowledged.

1. For summaries of the literature on social preferences, see Fehr and Schmidt (2002) and Meier (2004).

2. Measuring risk preferences for the small amounts normally involved in experiments is tricky (see for a theoretical explanation, e.g., Rabin 2000).

3. For ease of understanding, we refer to the principal as "she" and the agent as "he."

4. We chose denominations such that the monetary incentives relative to subject income and living standards were approximately equal across countries. The experiments were conducted in 2001. The average lunch in the student cafeteria cost 5 dollars in Boston, 50 rubles in Moscow, and 20 rands in South Africa.

5. Recent evidence supports the validity of the random-choice payments method. Laury (2002) found that subjects take (high) stakes at their stated value and do not scale down to account for random payment.

6. In order to ensure equivalence of experimental procedures across countries, we followed Roth et al. (1991) on designs for cross-societal experiments and controlled for experimenter, currency, and language effects to the best of our ability.

7. Unless noted otherwise, we use the nonparametric Mann-Whitney U test to examine differences in means. We report as significant if $p < 0.05$. There are no cross-country differences in trust or giving in the dictator game (see Ashraf, Bohnet, and Piankov 2006).

8. Unfortunately, very little is known about gender differences in integrative negotiations (as opposed to distributive negotiations; see, e.g., the review by Kray and Thompson 2005).

References

Andreoni, James. 1990. "Impure Altruism and Donations to Public Goods: A Theory of Warm-Glow Giving?" *Economic Journal* 100: 464–477.

Andreoni, James, and John Miller. 2002. "Giving According to GARP: An Experimental Test of the Consistency of Preferences for Altruism." *Econometrica* 70: 737–753.

Ashraf, Nava, Iris Bohnet, and Nikita Piankov. 2006. "Decomposing Trust and Trustworthiness." *Experimental Economics* 9: 193–208.

Batson, C. D. 1991. *The Altruism Question: Toward a Social Psychological Answer.* Hillsdale, NJ: Erlbaum.

Ben-Ner, Avner, and Louis Putterman. 2001. "Trusting and Trustworthiness." *Boston University Law Review* 81: 523–551.

Berg, John, John Dickhaut, and Kevin A. McCabe. 1995. "Trust, Reciprocity, and Social History." *Games and Economic Behavior* 10: 290–307.

Bohnet, Iris, and Yael Baytelman. 2007 "Institutions and Trust: Implications for Preferences, Beliefs and Behavior." Forthcoming in *Rationality & Society.*

Bohnet, Iris, and Bruno S. Frey. 1999. "Social Distance and Other-Regarding Behavior in Dictator Games: Comment." *American Economic Review* 89: 335–340.

Bohnet, Iris, Bruno S. Frey, and Steffen Huck. 2001. "More Order With Less Law: On Contrast Enforcement, Trust and Crowding." *American Political Science Review* 89: 335–339.

Bohnet, Iris, Benedikt Herrmann, and Richard Zeckhauser. 2006. "The Requirements for Trust in Gulf and Western Countries." Working Paper, John F. Kennedy School of Government.

Bohnet, Iris, and Richard Zeckhauser. 2004. "Trust, Risk and Betrayal." *Journal of Economic Behavior and Organization* 55: 467–485.

Bolton, Gary, and Axel Ockenfels. 2000. "A Theory of Equity, Reciprocity and Competition." *American Economic Review* 90: 166–193.

Buchan, Nancy, Rachel Croson, and Sara Solnick. 2003. "Trust and Gender: An Examination of Behavior, Biases, and Beliefs in the Investment Game." Working Paper, Wharton School, University of Pennsylvania.

Buss, A. R. 1978. "Causes and Reasons in Attribution Theory: A Conceptual Critique." *Journal of Personality and Social Psychology* 36: 1311–1321.

Callahan, David. 2004. *The Cheating Culture.* New York: Hartcourt.

Camerer, Colin. 2003. *Behavioral Game Theory.* Princeton, NJ: Princeton University Press.

Camerer, Colin, and Keith Weigelt. 1988. "Experimental Tests of a Sequential Equilibrium Reputation Model." *Econometrica* 56: 1–36.

Cook, K. S., and R. M. Cooper. 2003. "Experimental Studies of Cooperation, Trust, and Social Exchange." In *Trust and Reciprocity,* ed. E. Ostrom and J. Walker, 209–244. New York: Russell Sage.

Cox, James C. 2004. "How To Identify Trust and Reciprocity." *Games and Economic Behavior* 46: 260–281.

Croson, Rachel, and Nancy Buchan. 1999. "Gender and Culture: International Experimental Evidence from Trust Games." *American Economic Review* 89: 386–392.

Croson, Rachel, and Uri Gneezy. 2004. "Gender Differences in Preferences." Working Paper, Wharton School, University of Pennsylvania.

Dufwenberg, Martin, and Uri Gneezy. 2000. "Measuring Beliefs in an Experimental Lost Wallet Game." *Games and Economic Behavior* 30: 163–182.

Eckel, Catherine C., and Rick K. Wilson. 2004a. "Is Trust a Risky Decision?" *Journal of Economic Behavior and Organization* 55: 447–466.

Eckel, Catherine C., and Rick K. Wilson. 2004b. "Conditional Trust: Sex, Race and Facial Expressions in a Trust Game." Working Paper, Virginia Polytechnic.

Egas, Martijn, and Arno Riedl. 2005. "Cooperation and Punishment in the Dutch: Evidence from a Large Internet Experiment." Presentation at the Economic Science Association meetings, Montreal, Canada.

Fehr, Ernst, Urs Fischbacher, Bernhard von Rosenbladt, Jürgen Schupp, and Gert G. Wagner. 2002. "A Nation-Wide Laboratory-Examining Trust and Trustworthiness by Integrating Behavioral Experiments into Representative Surveys." *Schmollers Jahrbuch* 122: 519–542.

Fehr, Ernst, and Simon Gächter. 2003. "Do Incentive Contracts Crowd Out Voluntary Cooperation?" Working paper No. iewwp034, Institute for Empirical Economic Research in Economics, University of Zürich.

Fehr, Ernst, and John A. List. 2004. "The Hidden Costs and Returns of Incentives—Trust and Trustworthiness among CEOs." *Journal of the European Economic Association* 2, no. 5: 743–771.

Fehr, Ernst, and Klaus Schmidt. 1999. "A Theory of Fairness, Competition and Cooperation." *Quarterly Journal of Economics* 114: 817–868.

Fehr, Ernst, and Klaus Schmidt. 2002. "Theories of Fairness and Reciprocity—Evidence and Economic Applications." In *Advances in Economics and Econometrics—8th World Congress, Econometric Society Monographs*, ed. M. Dewatripont, L. Hansen, and S. Turnovsky, 208–258. Cambridge: Cambridge University Press.

Ferber, Marianne A., and Julie A. Nelson, eds. 1993. *Beyond Economic Man: Feminist Theory and Economics*. Chicago: University of Chicago Press.

Frey, Bruno S. 1997. *Not Just for the Money: An Economic Theory of Personal Motivation*. Cheltenham: Edward Elgar.

Frey, Bruno S., and Reto Jegen. 2001. "Motivation Crowding Theory: A Survey of Empirical Evidence." *Journal of Economic Surveys* 15: 589–611.

Frey, Bruno S., and Felix Oberholzer-Gee. 1997. "The Cost of Price Incentives: An Empirical Analysis of Motivation Crowding Out." *American Economic Review* 87: 746–755.

Greig, Fiona, and Iris Bohnet. 2005a. "Is There Reciprocity in a Reciprocal-Exchange Economy? Evidence Gendered Norms from a Slum in Nairobi, Kenya." Working Paper, John F. Kennedy School of Government.

Greig, Fiona, and Iris Bohnet. 2005b. "Why Women Cooperate with Women and Not Men: Evidence from a Slum in Nairobi, Kenya." Working Paper, Kennedy School of Government.

Hardin, Russell. 2002. *Trust and Trustworthiness*. New York: Russell Sage.

Heider, F. 1958. *The Psychology of Interpersonal Relations*. New York: Wiley.

Herrmann, Benedikt. 2004. "Norms of Cooperation and Sanctioning—Comparative Experiments in Switzerland, Germany, Belarus and Russia." Doctoral Dissertation, University of Göttingen.

Hong, Kessely, and Iris Bohnet. 2007. "Status and Distrust: The Relevance of Inequality and Betrayal Aversion." Forthcoming in *Journal of Economic Psychology*.

Inglehart, Ronald. 1999. "Trust, Well-Being and Democracy." In *Democracy and Trust*, ed. Mark E. Warren, 88–120. Cambridge: Cambridge University Press.

Kahneman, Daniel, Jack Knetsch, and Richard Thaler. 1986. "Fairness as Constraint on Profit Seeking: Entitlements in the Market." *American Economic Review* 76: 728–741.

Knack, Stephen, and Philip Keefer. 1997. "Does Social Capital Have an Economic Payoff? A Cross-Country Investigation." *Quarterly Journal of Economics* 112: 1251–1288.

Kosfeld, Michael, Markus Heinrichs, Paul J. Zak, Urs Fischbacher, and Ernst Fehr. 2005. "Oxytocin Increases Trust in Humans." *Nature* 435, no. 2: 673–676.

Kramer, Roderick. 1999. "Trust and Distrust in Organizations: Emerging Perspectives, Enduring Questions." *Annual Review of Psychology* 50: 569–598.

Kramer, Roderick, and Tom R. Tyler, eds. 1996. *Trust in Organizations*. Thousand Oaks, CA: Sage.

Kray, Laura, and Leigh Thompson. 2005. "Gender Stereotypes and Negotiation Performance: A Review of Theory and Research." In *Research in Organizational Behavior Series* 26, ed. Barry Staw and Roderick Kramer, 103–182. Amsterdam: Elsevier.

Kruglanski, A. W. 1979. "Causal Explanation, Teleological Explanation: On Radical Particularism in Attribution Theory." *Journal of Personality and Social Psychology* 37: 1447–1457.

LaPorta, Raphael, Florencio Lopez-de-Silanes, Andrei Shleifer, and Robert W. Vishny. 1997. "Trust in Large Organizations." *American Economic Review* 87: 333–338.

Laury, Susan. 2002. "Pay One or Pay All: Random Selection of One Choice for Payment." Mimeo., Georgia State University.

Lips, H. M. 1991. *Women, Men, and Power*. Mountain View, CA: Mayfield Publishing.

Loewenstein, George F., Max H. Bazerman, and Leigh Thompson. 1989. "Social Utility and Decision Making in Interpersonal Contexts." *Journal of Personality and Social Psychology* 57: 426–441.

Lorsch, Jay W., Leslie Berlowitz and Andy Zelleke, eds. 2005. *Restoring Trust in American Business*. Cambridge: MIT Press.

Luhmann, Niklas. "Trust: A Mechanism for the Reduction of Social Complexity." In *Trust and Power*, ed. N. Luhmann, 1–103. New York: Wiley.

Mainiero, L. A. 1986. "Coping with Powerlessness: The Relationship of Gender and Job Dependency to Empowerment-Strategy Usage." *Administrative Science Quarterly* 31: 633–653.

Mansbridge, Jane. 1999. "Altruistic Trust." In *Democracy and Trust*, ed. Mark E. Warren, 290–309. Cambridge: Cambridge University Press.

Meier, Stephan. 2004. "A Survey on Economic Theories and Empirics on Pro-Social Behavior." Mimeo., Institute for Empirical Research in Economics, University of Zürich.

Ostrom, Elinor, and James Walker, eds. 2003. *Trust and Reciprocity*. New York: Russell Sage.

Pillutla, Madan, Deepak Malhotra, and Keith Murnighan. 2003. "Attributions of Trust and the Calculus of Reciprocity." *Journal of Experimental Social Psychology* 39, no. 5: 448–455.

Putnam, Robert D. 2000. *Bowling Alone: The Collapse and Revival of American Community*. New York: Simon & Schuster.

Putnam, Robert D., Robert Leonardi, and Raffaella Y. Nanetti. 1993. *Making Democracy Work: Civic Traditions in Modern Italy*. Princeton: Princeton University Press.

Rabin, Matthew. 1993. "Incorporating Fairness into Game Theory and Economics." *American Economic Review* 83: 1281–1302.

Rabin, Matthew. 2000. "Risk Aversion and Expected-Utility Theory: A Calibration Theorem." *Econometrica* 68: 1281–1292.

Rosenfeld, R., S. F. Messner, and E. P. Baumer. 2001. "Social Capital and Homicide." *Social Forces* 80, no. 1: 283–309.

Roth, Alvin E., Vesna Prasnikar, Masahiro Okuno-Fujiwara, and Shmuel Zamir. 1991. "Bargaining and Market Behavior in Jerusalem, Ljubliana, Pittsburgh, and Tokyo: An Experimental Study." *American Economic Review* 81: 1068–1095.

Rousseau, D., S. Sitkin, R. Burt, and C. Camerer. 1998. "Not So Different After All: A Cross-Discipline View of Trust." *Academy of Management Review* 23: 393–404.

Sanfey, A. G., J. K. Rilling, J. A. Aronson, L. E. Nystrom, and J. D. Cohen. 2003. "The Neural Basis of Economic Decision-Making in the Ultimatum Game." *Science* 300: 1755–1758.

Singer, T., B. Seymour, J. P. O'Doherty, K. E. Stephan, R. J. Dolan, and C. D. Frith. 2006. "Empathic Neural Responses Are Modulated by the Perceived Fairness of Others." *Nature* 439: 466–469.

Sitkin, S. B., and N. L. Roth. 1993. "Explaining the Limited Effectiveness of Legalistic 'Remedies' for Trust/Distrust." *Organization Science* 4, no. 3: 367–392.

Swim, J. K., and Campbell, B. 2003. "Sexism: Attitudes, Beliefs, and Behaviors." In *Blackwell Handbook of Social Psychology: Intergroup Processes*, ed. R. Brown and S. Gaertner, 218–237. Oxford: Blackwell Publishing.

Zak, Paul, and Steven Knack. 2001. "Trust and Growth." *Economic Journal* 111: 295–321.

III   Neuroeconomics

5 Neuroeconomics: Illustrated by the Study of Ambiguity Aversion

Colin F. Camerer, Meghana Bhatt, and Ming Hsu

This chapter is about the emerging field of neuroeconomics, which seeks to ground economic theory in details about how the brain works. This approach is a sharp turn in economic thought. Around the turn of the century, economists made a clear methodological choice to treat the mind as a black box and ignore its details for the purpose of economic theory (Bruni and Sugden 2007). In an 1897 letter Pareto wrote: "It is an empirical fact that the natural sciences have progressed only when they have taken secondary principles as their point of departure, instead of trying to discover the essence of things....Pure political economy has therefore a great interest in relying as little as possible on the domain of psychology" (qtd. in Busino 1964, xxiv).

Pareto's view that psychology should be ignored was reflective of a pessimism of his time about the ability to ever understand the brain.[1] As William Jevons wrote a little earlier, in 1871, "I hesitate to say that men will ever have the means of measuring directly the feelings of the human heart. It is from the quantitative effects of the feelings that we must estimate their comparative amounts."

This pessimism about understanding the brain led to the popularity of "as-if" rational choice models. Models of this sort posit individual behavior that is consistent with logical principles, but they do not put any evidentiary weight on direct tests of whether those principles are followed. For example, a consumer might act as if she attaches numerical utilities to bundles of goods and choose the bundle with the highest utility, but if you ask her to assign numbers directly her expressed utilities may not obey axioms like transitivity. The strong form of the as-if approach simply dismisses such direct evidence as irrelevant because predictions can be right even if the assumptions they are based on are wrong (e.g., Friedman 1953).[2]

As-if models work well in many respects. But tests of the predictions that follow from as-if rational choice (as well as direct tests of axioms) have also established many empirical anomalies. Behavioral economics describes these regularities and suggests formal models to explain them (e.g., Camerer 2005). Debates between rational-choice models and behavioral models usually revolve around psychological constructs, such as loss aversion (Kahneman and Tversky 1979) and a preference for immediate rewards, which have not been observed directly. But technology now allows us to open the black box of the mind and observe brain activity directly. The use of data like these to constrain and inspire economic theories and make sense of empirical anomalies is called "neuroeconomics" (Camerer, Loewenstein, and Prelec 2005; Chorvat and McCabe 2005; Zak 2004). It is important to note that neuroeconomists fully appreciate that the revealed-preference approach does not endorse the idea of measuring utilities directly (Gul and Pesendorfer 2005). The neuroeconomic view does not misunderstand the revealed preference approach to economics; it simply takes a different approach. Furthermore, the presumption is that creating more realistic assumptions will lead to better predictions. Friedman's view was that (1) theories should be judged by accuracy of predictions, and (2) false assumptions could lead to accurate predictions. Neuroeconomics shares the emphasis on accuracy in principle 1, but also bets on the possibility that improving the accuracy of assumptions will lead to more accurate predictions.

An analogy to organizational economics illustrates the potential of neuroeconomics. Until the 1970s, the "theory of the firm" was basically a reduced-form model of how capital and labor combine to create a production function as the basis for an industry supply curve. Contract theory opened up the black box of the firm and modeled the details of the nexus of contracts between shareholders, workers, and managers (which is what a firm is). The new theory of the firm replaces the (still-useful) fiction of a profit-maximizing firm that has a single goal with a more detailed account of how components of the firm interact and communicate to determine firm behavior. Neuroeconomics proposes to do the same by treating an agent like a firm: replace the (useful) fiction of a utility-maximizing agent who has a single goal with a more detailed account of how components of the agent's brain interact and communicate to determine agent behavior.

Much of the potential of neuroeconomics comes from recent improvements in technology for measuring brain activity. For example, fMRI (functional magnetic resonance imaging) measures oxygenated blood flow in the brain (which is correlated with neural activity on the scale of a couple of seconds and a few millimeters). The behavior of animals and patients who have localized lesions in specific brain areas can help us determine if the damaged area is necessary for certain behaviors. At an even more detailed level, one can record activity in a single neuron at a time (single-unit recording), generally from primates but occasionally from neurosurgical patients. Older tools like electroencephalogram (EEG), the recording of very rapid electrical activity from outer brain areas, and psychophysiological recording (skin conductance and pupil dilation, for example), continue to be useful, often as complements corroborating interpretations from other methods.

All these tools give clues about a detailed theory of how decision making actually works. The success of the rational actor model in as-if applications shows that this level of detail is not necessary for certain sorts of analysis, especially those that deal with populations of decision makers instead of individuals. (For example, neuroeconomics will never displace the powerful concepts of supply and demand or market equilibrium.) However, a deeper understanding of the mechanics of decision making will help us better understand deviations from the rational model. Knowing the process of decision making should allow us to understand not only the limits of our abilities to calculate optimal decisions, but also the heuristics we use to overcome these limits.

Furthermore, in most areas of behavioral economics there is more than one alternative theory. Often there are many theories that are conceptually different but difficult to separate using current data. To the extent that some of these theories commit to neural interpretations, the brain evidence can help sort out which theories are on the right track and can also suggest new theories. The study of ambiguity aversion detailed in section 5.3 is intended in this chapter as a case study of how two types of brain evidence (fMRI and lesion patient behavior) can adjudicate a long-standing debate in decision theory about whether ambiguity aversion exists and where it comes from.

The ability to use these neuroscientific technologies to establish neural circuitry depends on the fact that the brain is largely modular in structure. A lot is known about which general areas of the brain deal with vision, hearing, and other sensory information, and these areas are consistently activated across people. While the degree of modular specialization is sometimes surprising (e.g., there is a "facial fusiform area" apparently devoted to face recognition), most higher-order processing requires a "circuit" or collaboration among many component processes, which are in turn parts of different modules. Less is known about higher processing than about specific sensory processing, but neuroscientists have a general idea of where certain types of emotional and rational processing occurs, and empirical regularity is accumulating very rapidly.

5.1 Neuroeconomic Brain Imaging Experiments

Brain imaging, or scanning, is the neuroscientific tool now getting the most attention. Functional (fMRI) imaging uses the same magnetic resonance (MR) scanner that has been used for medical purposes for decades. The innovation in fMRI, which began only about ten years ago, is that it scans the brain much more rapidly to detect differing levels of oxygenated blood in the brain while subjects are performing some task. Most brain imaging involves a comparison of brain activity when a subject performs an experimental task and a control task. The difference between images taken while the subject is performing the two tasks provides a picture of brain regions that are differentially activated by the experimental task. The modular nature of the brain allows us to interpret these activations in the context of other evidence about what tasks activate the same areas.

Imaging is increasingly popular for two reasons. First, it is noninvasive, unlike single neuron recording, which implants electrodes directly into the brain, or transcranial magnetic stimulation (TMS), which stimulates brain areas to create temporary lesions. Second, fMRI provides relatively good temporal and spatial resolution, even for areas deep in the brain (which cannot be measured by EEG). Images are taken every few seconds and data are recorded from voxels that are 3–4 millimeters on a side. Scanning is expensive, but usually modest sample sizes (10–20 subjects) are enough to establish suggestive regularity if studies are well-designed.

There have already been several prominent studies of economic decision making using fMRI and PET (positron emission tomography), another form of scanning technology.[3] We mention a few to show how imaging can address the kinds of questions economists care about. All these results are tentative; more will be learned rapidly in the next few years.

5.1.1   Game Theory and Social Emotions

Experiments have proved very useful in testing game theory because game theory often depends on subtle details of moves and information, which can be easily controlled in an experiment (and difficult to measure in many field applications (Camerer 2003)). Neuroeconomics experiments enable a similar attention to the details of how equilibration results from cognition and how social preferences influence strategic behavior.

In an early study, McCabe et al. (2001) compared brain activity when subjects played trust games against other humans to activity when playing against randomized opponents. Among players who did not cooperate very often, there were no differences in activity between the two conditions. But among high cooperators there was additional activity in frontal cortex when playing other humans. McCabe et al. interpret this activity as evidence of a specialized "theory of mind" circuitry used to form beliefs about what other human players will do. Gallagher et al. (2002) find a similar result when analyzing play of a mixed-strategy game (rock, paper, scissors) against a randomized opponent. In one condition the subject was told that the opponent was a computer, and in the other the subject was told that the opponent was human. In both cases subjects were simply playing against the Nash equilibrium strategy that randomizes between all three strategies, but in the condition where they were told they were playing another human being there were significant activations in the anterior paracingulate cortex. These studies show neurally that forming beliefs about another player's moves is fundamentally different than forming beliefs about "nature's" moves, even when these are empirically identical.

In the ultimatum game, one player, the proposer, offers a take-it-or-leave-it share x of an amount, say \$10, to another player, the responder. If the responder takes the offer they earn $\$10 - x$ and x, respectively. If the responder rejects the offer they both get nothing and the game is over. This game has been studied in hundreds of experiments. The typical result is that players offer around 40 percent of the pie (often half), and offers below 20 percent are rejected in most societies (e.g., Camerer 2003, chapter 2).[4]

Sanfey et al. (2003), using fMRI, studied the behavior of responders who received offers in ultimatum games. They found that when offers were unfair as compared to fair, three areas were active: the dorsolateral prefrontal cortex (DLPFC), the anterior cingulate (ACC), and the insula. The insula is an area active in registering body discomfort. It is activated when people feel, among other things, social exclusion (Eisenberger, Lieberman, and Williams 2003) and disgust (Calder et al. 2000). Their interpretation is that neurons in the insula are activated by unfairness, the DLPFC is processing the future reward from keeping the money, and the ACC is an arbiter that weighs these two conflicting inputs to make a decision. Whether players reject unfair offers or not can be predicted rather reliably (a correlation of 0.45) by the level of their insula activity.

One controversy in behavioral economics is the nature of social preferences expressed in games like the ultimatum game, trust games, and their kin, which are used to study reciprocity. Consider punishment—the willingness of A to punish B if A believes B has treated her badly. If the players play only once, A has no direct or reputational incentive to punish B at all. So what is A thinking or feeling when she punishes B?

This question was studied using PET imaging by de Quervain et al. (2004). In their study, two players, A and B, played a trust game in which A invested money, which grew in value, and the "trustee" player B could repay or keep the money (Weigelt and Camerer 1988; Berg, Dickhaut, and McCabe 1995). The subject A whose behavior was imaged was asked, after play, whether she wanted to punish the trustee or not. The price of punishment was also varied so that during some conditions A punished at a direct cost to herself.

When players punished, de Quervain et al. found activity in the nucleus accumbens (part of the striatum), a region known for processing rewards derived from actions (O'Doherty et al. 2004). Thus, punishment appears to generate an internal sense of reward, just as receiving money does. They also found activity in the frontal cortex when the price of punishment was being weighted. To an economist, this provides a simple way to modify the self-interest mathematically: a preference-based theory in which punishment motives and money-earning motives are neurally similar and respond to prices in a thoughtful way.

fMRI has also been used to help understand the neural basis of the concept of equilibrium in games. In game theory, players are in equilibrium when they all best respond to accurate beliefs about what other players will do. But this concept of equilibrium is focused on a static situation; it says nothing about how players reach equilibrium. One neuroscientific hypothesis of equilibrium is that an equilibrium choice requires that the player uses similar circuitry to make her own choice and to form her beliefs about the other player, perhaps simulating the other player's choice in order to make an accurate guess. Put differently, if a player is using a simple decision rule like "one-step reasoning" (pick the strategy with the highest average payoff, as if the other players' choices are all equally likely), then more reasoning will be evident in calculating the optimal choice than in guessing what others will do (because the guess is a simple diffuse prior which requires little thought).

These considerations suggest that when activity during the act of making a choice and activity when making a guess overlap sufficiently, equilibrium choices are more likely—that is, equilibrium is a state of mind revealed by a high degree of mental overlap in choosing and guessing. Indeed, Bhatt and Camerer (2005) found a sharp difference between differential activity in choosing and reporting beliefs when trials were in equilibrium (beliefs were accurate and choices were optimal given guesses) and out of equilibrium.

In equilibrium trials there is only a small difference in activity between choosing and reporting beliefs. This difference is in the ventral striatum, an area known to encode anticipated reward. This area may imply that players expect larger rewards from making choices (since the payment schemes were not identical across the two tasks of choosing and guessing), or that players have a kind of internal cash register that senses when they have made an accurate equilibrium choice, even though the games were played without feedback.

In out-of-equilibrium trials, there was differing activity in many areas between the tasks of choosing a strategy and guessing what others will choose. These areas include the DLPFC (observed by Sanfey et al. 2003), and paracingulate cortex (observed by Gallagher et al. 2002). This is consistent with the idea that many players have a rather shallow way of forming beliefs that requires little processing, consistent with some behavioral models of limited "levels of thinking" (Camerer, Ho, and Chong 2004).

Bhatt and Camerer (2005) also studied what happens when players generate second-order beliefs—that is, what do they think the other player thinks they will do? (These complex judgments are important in successful deception and in creating social emotions like shame[5]). There are two ways to generate a second-order belief: (1) apply some general circuitry for forming a belief, but take the other player's perspective, or (2) figure out what you plan to choose, and then ask whether the other player is likely to guess your choice. Two facts support the second explanation: choices and second-order beliefs match surprisingly often, and there is more overlap in neural activity during the choice and second-order belief tasks than between those tasks and the belief task. Furthermore, players who were more self-focused, in the sense of equating their choice and their second-order belief (differentially activating the anterior insula), actually earned less in the game.

5.1.2 Intertemporal Choice

The problem of intertemporal choice has been studied at length in economics and psychology. One apparent empirical fact is that people display a preference for immediacy. When faced with two decisions about future payoffs, one later than the other, they act as if they are very patient (i.e., they possess a relatively high discount factor). When these same subjects are given the choice between an immediate reward and a future payoff they show a strong tendency to choose the immediate reward, implying a much lower discount factor (Laibson 1997; O'Donaghue and Rabin 1999). Fitting discount factor functions to data from rewards at different points in time across many animal species (including humans) generally shows a hyperbolic form, $d(t) = 1/(1 + kt)$, rather than an exponential $d(t) = d^t$. For modeling purposes, a good approximation of the hyperbolic form is a two-piece quasi-hyperbolic function, which weights current rewards by 1 and future rewards at time t by $\beta\delta^t$(50). When $\beta = 1$ the function reduces to an exponential. The parameter β captures the preference for immediacy, and δ expresses the relative preference for rewards at different future points.

This two-piece function is a natural candidate for study in fMRI because the two systems can be isolated by comparing different types of choices. Indeed, McClure et al. (2004) find that when people choose between an immediate reward and a future reward (with presumed weights of 1 and $\beta\delta$) relative to two distant rewards (with relative weights of δ^t and δ^{t+1}), areas with projections from the limbic regions are active. When weighing any two choices many areas are active, but only prefrontal and anterior cingulate areas seem to be involved in the δ system.

5.2 Finding Circuitry

Finding areas of differential brain activity using fMRI is not actually the main goal of these studies. The real goal is to use the observed brain activity to hypothesize a circuit of different brain regions that interact to generate a behavior (such as a decision). To understand the circuit, we need to know which areas are active *and* how they interact. Using scanning evidence, the neural circuitry of decisions must be largely inferred from what we know of neurophysiology and the time series of activations in various parts of the brain. Even so, scanning evidence is only sufficient to show that the activated regions are correlated with the decision task. More evidence is necessary to establish any causal link between brain areas and decisions.

One way to determine whether a region is a necessary part of a circuit is to observe patients who have local lesions in that region. These patients are generally victims of strokes, encephalitis, other brain injuries, or neurosurgical interventions. An ideal lesion patient has a localized lesion, preferably bilateral (on both sides of the brain), which overlaps a specialized functional or neuroanatomical area of the brain. If the patient with damage to region X is reasonably normal in most cognitive functions (like IQ and memory), and if the patient does not do a task normally, we can infer that region X is a necessary part of the circuit for that task. Other methods of establishing necessity include creating temporary lesions using TMS. But even these techniques only establish that the regions are necessary for a task, not that they are sufficient. There is also some research being done on the role of different neurotransmitters, rather than specific brain areas, in certain decision-making processes. These studies can actually demonstrate the sufficiency of different neurotransmitters for certain behaviors. For example Kosfeld et al. (2005) found that you can increase the level of trust in a person by administering a dose of oxytocin.

Lesion patients show startling dissociations between tasks that seem remarkably similar. For example, there are lesion patients who can write well, but can't read. Patients with permanent anterograde amnesia—the awful inability to form new memories—do not form conscious declarative explicit memories for emotions or physical procedures. However, these patients actually do form such memories implicitly; that is, they know information but don't know that they know it. This dissociation indicates that declarative memories and meta-knowledge are stored separately.[6]

The study described in section 5.3 uses a combination of fMRI scanning evidence and behavioral data from lesion patients to examine the circuitry of choice under uncertainty. Lesions in the same areas activated in a scanning study can help us understand the interactions of the regions and establish whether a lesioned area is a necessary part of a hypothesized circuit.

Another important tool that will prove valuable in neuro-economics is what neuroscientists call "computational models" (which economists would call a "calibration exercise"). In computational models, a detailed numerical specification of a neural circuit is suggested. Given those details, simulated input to the circuit leads to a predicted output (typically depending on the values of some free parameters). The model is calibrated by finding parameter values that maximize the fit of predicted output to actual data. Compared to models in economics, these specifications are often incredibly detailed and clearly motivated by what is known about neuroanatomical connections between areas (e.g., Kim and Whalen 2004). As in economic theory, computational models are valuable because they force the modeler to be perfectly clear about how the components of a circuit are linked and because the hypothesized circuit is subjected to empirical scrutiny.

5.3   Ambiguity Aversion

The study described in this section uses a combination of fMRI scanning evidence and behavioral experiments with lesion patients to examine the circuitry of choice under uncertainty. It is meant as a detailed illustration of how fMRI can be used to do neuroeconomics with more detail than is typically permitted in neuroscience journals.

In the theories of choice under uncertainty used in social sciences and behavioral ecology, the only variables that should influence an uncertain choice are the judged probabilities of possible outcomes and the evaluation of those outcomes. But confidence in judged probability can vary widely. In some choices, such as gambling on a roulette wheel, probability can be confidently judged from relative frequencies, event histories, or from an accepted theory. At the other extreme, such as the chance of a terrorist attack, probabilities are based on meager or conflicting evidence where important information is clearly missing. The two types of uncertain events are often called risky and ambiguous, respectively. In subjective expected utility theory (SEU), the probabilities of outcomes should influence choices but confidence about those probabilities should not. But many experiments show that many people are more willing to bet on risky outcomes than on ambiguous ones, holding judged probability of outcomes constant (Camerer and Weber

1992). This empirical aversion to ambiguity motivates a search for neural distinctions between risk and ambiguity, as in other studies on neuroeconomics that explored the neural foundations of economic decision (Glimcher and Rustichini 2004; Camerer, Loewenstein, and Prelec 2005; McClure et al. 2004).

5.3.1   Background

5.3.1.1   The Ellsberg paradox   The difference between risky and ambiguous uncertainty is illustrated by the Ellsberg paradox (Ellsburg 1961). Imagine one deck of twenty cards composed of ten red and ten blue cards (the risky deck). Another deck has twenty red or blue cards, but the composition of red and blue cards is completely unknown (the ambiguous deck). A bet on a color pays a fixed sum (e.g., $10) if a card with the chosen color is drawn, and zero otherwise (see figure 5.1).

In experiments with these choices, many people would rather bet on a red draw from the risky deck than a red draw from the ambiguous deck, and similarly for blue (Becker and Brownson 1964; MacCrimmon 1968). If betting preferences are determined only by probabilities, this pattern is a paradox. In theory, disliking the bet on a red draw from the ambiguous deck implies that its subjective probability is lower $(p_{amb}(red) < p_{risk}(red))$. The same aversion for the blue bets implies $p_{amb}(blue) < p_{risk}(blue)$. But these inequalities, and the fact that the probabilities of red and blue must add to one for each deck, imply that $1 = p_{amb}(red) + p_{amb}(blue) < p_{risk}(red) + p_{risk}(blue) = 1$, a contradiction. The paradox can be resolved by allowing choices to depend on both subjective probabilities of events and on the ambiguity of those events. For example, if ambiguous probabilities are subadditive, then $1 - p_{amb}(red) - p_{amb}(blue)$ represents reserved belief and indexes the degree of aversion to ambiguity (Schmeidler 1989). Other models assume additive but set-valued probabilities; in other words, people believe there is a range of possible probabilities, and ambiguity aversion is the result of people pessimistically assuming the worst probability. This model and others are silent about possible neural circuitry. Ambiguity aversion suggests that choices can depend on how much relevant information is missing, or how ignorant people feel compared to others (Frisch and Baron 1988; Fox and Tversky 1995).

5.3.1.2   Ambiguity Aversion in Economics and Social Science
Aversion to taking action in ambiguous situations has been studied in

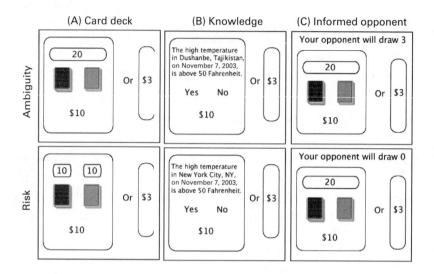

Figure 5.1
Sample screens from the experiment. The top-panel conditions are called ambiguous because the subject is missing relevant information available in the risk conditions (bottom
panel). Subjects always choose between betting on one of the two options on the left side
or taking the certain payoff on the right. (A) Card deck treatment: ambiguity is not knowing the exact proportion, risk is knowing the number of cards (indicated by numbers
above each deck). (B) Knowledge treatment: ambiguity is knowing less about the uncertain events (e.g., Tajikistan) relative to risk (e.g., New York City). (C) Hostile opponent
treatment: ambiguity is betting against an opponent who has more information (who
drew a three-card sample from the deck) than risk (where the opponent drew no cards
from the deck). Bets win if the subject chooses the realized color and opponent chooses
the opposite color; if both players choose the same color they take the sure payoff.

economics and politics (Mukerji and Tallon 2004), including macroeconomic policy making (Sargent and Hansen 2003), wage setting and
contracting (Bewley 2002; Mukerji 1998), strategic thinking (Lo 1999;
Camerer and Karjalainen 1994), voting (Ghirardato and Katz 2000),
and financial investment (Dow and da Costa Werlang 1992; Epstein
and Wang 1994). We illustrate with two examples from law and
finance.

Law provides an interesting example illustrating the psychology
of ambiguity aversion. In Scottish law there are three verdicts—guilty,
not guilty, and not proven. The third is an unusual verdict in legal systems.[7] According to Peter Duff (1999), the difference between "not
guilty" and "not proven" is that the verdict of "not guilty" means the
accused definitely did not commit the crime—that is, it is a positive
declaration of innocence—whereas the verdict of "not proven" (193) is

thought to imply solely that the accused's guilt has not been conclusively demonstrated. The "not proven" and "not guilty" verdicts have the same legal implication because both prohibit retrial even in the face of new evidence. "Not proven" verdicts are returned in about a third of jury trials, typically when the jury thinks the defendant is actually guilty but cannot legally convict because of a lack of corroborating evidence, which is required by Scottish law. For example, these verdicts are common in sexual assault trials where the only witness to the crime is the accusing victim and the jury believes the defendant is guilty, but cannot convict based on the weight of available evidence.[8]

Turning to finance, "home bias" in investment is an important economic pattern that might be due to ambiguity aversion. Home bias is the tendency for investors to invest in stocks that are literally closer to home. For example, investors in most countries tend to invest heavily in stocks from their home country and very little in stocks from foreign countries. In 1989, American, Japanese, and British investors held 94 percent, 98 percent, and 82 percent of their investments in home-country stocks (Dow and da Costa Werlang 1992) even though the latter two markets account for only a modest fraction of the world portfolio. International home bias is shrinking, however (Amadi 2004), as more investors buy global index funds and overseas stocks.

Unless investors have private information about their home stocks, home bias is a mistake because it leads to highly undiversified portfolios (especially for investors who do not live in the United States or Japan). Using 1989 data, French and Poterba (1991) estimate that given the apparent trade-off between risk (stock return variation) and return (average percentage returns), the extra risk due to the reluctance to hold foreign stocks amounts to a sacrifice in annual percentage return of 1–2 percent per year. Assuming an average unbiased return of 7 percent (Siegel 1998), a typical historical estimate, a person with home bias who invests a lump sum at age twenty-five will end up with only half as much money at age sixty-five as an investor who is unbiased and holds a worldwide index fund.

Interestingly, home bias exists at many levels besides the international one: portfolio managers prefer to invest in companies with headquarters nearby, United States investors preferred their own regional "Baby Bell" companies after the breakup of AT&T, workers invest too heavily in the stock of the companies they work for, and investors in many countries prefer to invest in nearby companies or in those whose managers speak the same language they do (Graham, Harvey, and Huang 2005).

There are basically four explanations[9] of home bias: (1) higher transaction costs of buying foreign stocks; (2) inside information about local stocks; (3) optimism about relative returns of local stocks (Strong and Xu 2003); and (4) aversion to ambiguity (usually called a "taste for familiarity" in finance research). The transaction cost and inside information explanations (1 and 2) do not explain patterns like investment in the Baby Bell spinoff stocks. If investors are optimistic about local stocks and pessimistic about nonlocal stocks (explanation (3)), they should short-sell the latter, but rarely do. (An investor who is ambiguity-averse toward nonlocal stocks will not want to buy them, and won't want to sell them short either.) Therefore, the familiarity explanation (4) holds up rather well across all the documented levels of home bias. This explanation is consistent with the idea that investors have a pure distaste for betting on either side of a proposition that they lack knowledge of or familiarity with, which is very much like the knowledge treatment in our experiments.

5.3.1.3 Theory Individuals, including economists, have a hard time understanding their own inconsistency with regard to ambiguity. Ellsberg wrote:

There are those who do not violate the axioms, or say they won't, even in these situations...; such subjects tend to apply the axioms rather their intuition, and when in doubt, to apply some form of the Principle of Insufficient Reason. Some violate the axioms cheerfully, even with gusto...; others sadly but persistently, having looked into their hearts, found conflicts with the axioms and decided, in Samuelson's phrase, to satisfy their preferences and let the axioms satisfy themselves. Still others... tend, intuitively, to violate the axioms but feel guilty about it and go back into further analysis. (1961, 655)

The standard way to think about choice under uncertainty is to assume that a person's value for a gamble is simply the average of the possible outcomes, weighted by the probabilities that the outcome will occur. Specifically assume that there is a set of possible states of the world $e \in E$, each occurring with some probability (or with some probability distribution function if E is continuous), $p(e)$ and a set of actions $f \in L$, which yield some outcome with utility $f(e)$ if e occurs. Expected utility theory states that the utility of some action $f \in L$ is equal to $\sum_{e \in E} p(e)f(e)$ (or the corresponding integral for continuous E). The existence of this sort of representation depends on the independence axiom, stated here.

Axiom 5.3.1   Independence axiom $\forall f, g, h \in L$, where L is the set of possible actions, $f \succ g \Leftrightarrow \alpha f + (1 - \alpha)h \succ \alpha g + (1 - \alpha)h \; \forall \alpha \in (0, 1)$.

Behavioral experiments have found many counterexamples to this axiom, even in unambiguous situations. Maurice Allais first challenged this axiom in 1953 with a thought experiment. Consider four lotteries:

A   100 with certainty

B   0 with 1 percent chance, 100 with 89 percent chance and 500 with 10 percent

C   0 with 89 percent 100 with 11 percent chance

D   0 with 90 percent chance and 500 with 10 percent chance

Expected utility theory implies that $A \succ B \Leftrightarrow C \succ D$, but in fact, most people would tend to choose A and over B, but D to C (Allais 1953).

Most alternatives to SEU focus on modifying this axiom to varying degrees. Several of these fall under the general rubric of maxmin expected utility (MEU) (Gilboa and Schmeidler 1989). In these models decision makers have a convex set of priors (a set of possible probability distributions over possible "states of nature") and act as if the worst case is realized.[10] The model uses a weakened version of the independence axiom, called "certainty independence."

Axiom 5.3.2   Certainty independence $\forall f, g \in L$ and $h \in L_c$, where L_c is the set of constant acts, and $\forall \alpha \in (0, 1)$, $f \succ g \Leftrightarrow \alpha f + (1 - \alpha)h \succ \alpha g + (1 - \alpha)h$.

The standard independence axiom is stronger than certainty independence in that it allows h to be any act in L rather than restricting it to constant acts L_c, but both of these axioms explicitly deal with the reduction of compound lotteries, since this is at the center of how we represent ambiguity mathematically. Namely, there is some set of possible probability distributions over the states of nature: in the first stage of the compound lottery one of these distributions is chosen and in the second stage the actual state of nature is chosen. Under SEU this is equivalent to a one-stage lottery where the possible distributions are linearly combined (in the discrete case the probability that some state

$e \in E$ occurs is simply $\sum_P Ł(P)P(s)$ where P is a possible distribution and $Ł(P)$ is the likelihood with which it occurs).

In addition, Gilboa and Schmeidler included an uncertainty aversion axiom, which states that decision makers prefer a mixture of acts with objective probabilities over the acts themselves:

$\forall f, g \in L$ and $\alpha \in (0, 1), f \sim g$ implies $\alpha f + (1 - \alpha)g \succeq f$.

Under standard conditions with the aforementioned changes, the preference relation is represented by a function $J(f)$ up to a unique affine transformation:

$$J(f) = \min\left\{ \int uof \, dP \mid P \in C \right\}$$

where f is an act, u is a von Neumann-Morgenstern utility function over outcomes, and C is a closed and convex set of finitely additive probability measures on the states of nature.

In these models pessimism can be measured by the size of the set of priors. Larger sets of priors[11] will generally include worse possibilities and imply more pessimism. These models explain the Ellsberg paradox by allowing the probabilities assigned to each outcome (red or black) to depend on the bet that is made. In other words, there is a set of possible values from $p(R)$ ranging from p_* to p^*. When betting on red, the "worst" prior out of the decision maker's set is the one with the lowest odds on red, $p(R) = p_*$, so the expected utility of the red bet is low. When betting on black, the worst prior out of the set is the one with the lowest odds on black, $p(R) = p^*$ so $p(B) = 1 - p^*$, so the expected utility of the black bet is low. In this account, the subadditivity of the revealed subjective probabilities in the paradox is due to the fact that *different* priors are used to evaluate the expected utility of each bet. This effect is like Murphy's Law: if something can go wrong, it will.

Other models treat ambiguity as a two-stage lottery where the actual probabilities are chosen in a first stage (Segal 1987). Here the explanation for ambiguity aversion comes from a violation of the reduction of compound lotteries. Nonexpected utility is used to explain the Ellsberg paradox.

Finally, some models take the stance that ambiguity aversion is an overgeneralization of a rational aversion to asymmetry in information (Frisch and Baron 1988). These models argue that since many people confront incomplete information when facing a better-informed opponent, they treat the Ellsberg paradox as if there is asymmetric information (i.e., they act as if they are playing a game against a malevolent experimenter who is trying to trick them). We examine this "hostile opponent" hypothesis with the third treatment in our study, where subjects actually play against a better-informed opponent.

At some point in the future, economic theories might specify not only the link between unobservable factors and observed choices (such as beliefs and bet choices), but also a claim about neural circuitry that implements observed choices. Reviewing the many theoretical papers on ambiguity, we found only one suggestion about neural activity, in Raiffa (1961). He writes: "But if certain uncertainties in the problem were in cloudy or fuzzy form, then very often there was a shifting of gears and no effort at all was made to think deliberately and reflectively about the problem. Systematic decomposition of the problem was shunned and an over-all 'seat of the pants' judgment was made which graphically reflected the temperament of the decision maker" (691). Raiffa's suggestion seems to be that under ambiguity, deliberation and reflection (thought to be activities in the prefrontal cortex) are limited, and a temperamental "seat of the pants" judgment takes over. Unfortunately the seat of the pants is not a brain area, but we could interpret him more broadly as suggesting there is a rapid emotional reaction to ambiguity. Thus we translate Raiffa's observation, in neural terms, as implying a more rapid emotional reaction to ambiguous choices than to risky ones.

5.3.2   Experimental Design

We explored the neural differences with varying levels of uncertainty by using a combination of fMRI data and behavioral data from lesion patients. The fMRI study used three experimental treatments: bets on card decks (based on the Ellsberg example above), bets on high- and low-knowledge world events, and bets against an informed or uninformed opponent (see figure 5.1).

The card deck treatment is a baseline pitting pure risk, where probabilities are known with certainty, against pure ambiguity. The knowledge treatment uses choices about events and facts, which fall along a spectrum of uncertainty from risk to ambiguity. From the perspective of the MEU model, the high-knowledge questions correspond to smaller sets of priors than do the low-knowledge questions.

The hostile opponent's treatment offers bets against another person, who is either better-informed than or equally informed as the subject about the contents of an ambiguous deck. In this condition the "opponent" draws a sample of cards from an ambiguous deck before making his bet. The subject has the option of making a simultaneous bet, but this will only count if the subject bets on the *opposite* of the color the informed opponent chose. Since the opponent should always bet on the majority color from his sample, the subject's bet will only count when it is on the minority color from a random sample in the deck; in other words, when the subject is more likely to lose than win. This implies that the subject's expected value from winning is lower when the opponent is informed.[12]

Notice that all three treatments have one condition where the subjects are missing some relevant information relative to the other. We call all these treatments the ambiguous conditions and the other treatments the risky conditions. Subjects made twenty-four choices in each treatment between certain amounts of money and bets on events. The amount of the certain payoff and the amount of the bet varied across trials.

In these experiments we allow 6–8 seconds between trials. This break was necessary to allow the activations caused by the previous trial to dissipate. We also randomize the length of these intertrial intervals, because using a fixed interval can create anticipation effects in the seconds just before the new trial is presented; these effects are diminished by having a random intertrial interval length.

For each treatment, we estimated a general linear model (GLM) using standard regression techniques. Two primary regressors were used in the GLM, one for the ambiguity trials and one for the risky trials. The regressors were constructed in the following way: first we created a boxcar regressor (dummy variable) that was 1 during the risky (ambiguous) trial and 0 elsewhere. These regressors were then convolved with a "hemodynamic response function." This function allows us to take into account the fact that the increase in oxygenated blood to an area of the brain is lagged and the time series has a distinctive shape. Maximum likelihood estimation was used to fit:

$$B_t = \beta_{amb} A_t + \beta_{risk} R_t + \beta_0$$

where $\{B_t\}$ is the time series for some voxel in the brain.[13] Voxels with regression coefficients significantly different from 0 can be said to covary with either risk or ambiguity. We are mostly interested in which voxels are differentially activated by ambiguity with respect to risk—in other words, voxels where β_{amb} is significantly different from

β_{risk}. As the experiment was self-paced, the length of the trials varied.[14] To find areas differentially activated by ambiguity and risk across all three treatments, a one-way analysis of variance (ANOVA) of the three conditions was performed, correcting for nonsphericity and excluding areas significantly different between the three treatments.

The regressors were anchored to stimulus presentation, meaning that the original dummy variable turns "on" when the stimulus is presented as opposed to when a decision is made, based on the hypothesis that the reaction to uncertainty would occur before the decision. We also analyzed the time courses of activation anchored at both the stimulus onset and the decision time but did not find anything interesting when compared to the stimulus-to-decision period.

5.3.3   Results

5.3.3.1   fMRI Study   Areas that were more active during the ambiguous condition relative to the risk condition are listed in table 5.1. These included the orbitofrontal cortex (OFC) and the amygdala (figure 5.2a, b). Critchley, Mathias, and Dolan (2001) found OFC activation as subjects anticipated information about a financial gain or loss. Our study shows activity in this area even though there is no feedback during the experiment. More subtly, the OFC appears to be involved in *integrating* emotional and cognitive information. OFC lesion patients often behave inappropriately in social situations despite knowledge of what proper behavior entails (Berthoz et al. 2002). So the OFC may be active generally in emotional integration over a wide spectrum of situations.

The amygdala has been specifically implicated in processing information related to fear, for example, recognizing frightened faces (Bechara, Damasio, and Damasio 2003; Adolphs 2002; Critchley et al. 2000). We hypothesized that this area would be important for processing uncertain events since risk and ambiguity aversion could be interpreted as fear of the unknown.[15] In addition, the role of the amygdala in reacting to missing information is consistent with evidence of its involvement in interpersonal evaluations with missing social information, where familiarity modulates amygdala response. Showing unfamiliar black faces to white subjects elicits amygdala activation, which correlates with the strength of implicit associations between black names and negatively valenced words (Phelps et al. 2000). This correlation disappears when the black faces are familiar (e.g., Bill Cosby),

Table 5.1
Ambiguity > risk: Local maxima of clusters, $p < 0.001$ uncorrected, clusters with fewer than 10 voxels not shown

Cluster			Voxel				X	Y	Z	Regions	
p_{cor}	k_E	p_{unc}	p_{FWE}	p_{FDR}	T	Z				Laterality	Region
0.01	82	0.001	0.011	0.007	5.96	5.04	51	33	−6	Right	Lateral orbitofrontal cortex
0	109	0	0.897	0.017	3.92	3.6	54	18	−21	Right	
			0.052	0.007	5.38	4.67	−54	−60	42	Left	Inferior parietal lobule
0	112	0	0.1	0.007	5.13	4.5	−45	−54	33	Left	
			0.06	0.007	5.33	4.63	−9	48	39	Left	Dorsomedial prefrontal cortex
0	119	0	0.306	0.008	4.66	4.16	−12	63	21	Left	
			0.072	0.007	5.26	4.59	54	−54	36	Right	Supramarginal gyrus
			0.599	0.01	4.3	3.89	54	−63	30	Right	
0	226	0	0.162	0.007	4.94	4.36	18	54	18	Right	Dorsomedial prefrontal cortex
0.06	52	0.007	0.229	0.008	4.79	4.26	12	54	30	Right	
			0.379	0.009	4.56	4.09	12	27	57	Right	
0	154	0	0.201	0.008	4.85	4.3	36	18	42	Right	Middle frontal gyrus
			0.884	0.016	3.94	3.62	42	9	45	Right	
			0.22	0.008	4.81	4.27	60	−36	−3	Right	Middle temporal gyrus
			0.485	0.009	4.43	3.99	63	−27	−6	Right	
			0.626	0.01	4.27	3.87	51	−24	−9	Right	
0.44	21	0.066	0.302	0.008	4.67	4.17	−39	−9	−15	Left	Sub-gyral
0.13	40	0.015	0.331	0.009	4.63	4.14	39	6	−27	Right	Frontoinsular cortex

0.41	22		0.951	0.019	3.8	3.5	42	15	−24	Right	Lateral orbitofrontal cortex
		0.061	0.547	0.01	4.36	3.94	54	27	6	Right	Lateral orbitofrontal cortex
0.26	29	0.034	0.584	0.01	4.32	3.91	−54	36	−6	Left	Lateral orbitofrontal cortex
0.74	12	0.154	0.75	0.013	4.13	3.76	−15	−15	−15	Left	Amygdala/Parahippocampal gyrus
			0.993	0.026	3.57	3.32	−21	−6	−18	Left	Amygdala
0.41	22	0.061	0.825	0.014	4.03	3.69	33	−6	−27	Right	Amygdala/Parahippocampal gyrus

Note: All local maxima uncorrected p-values are significant to three significant figures, and are omitted from the table.

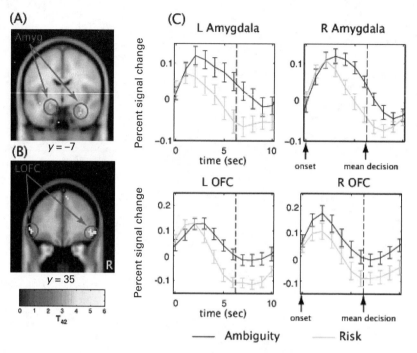

Figure 5.2
Regions showing greater activation to ambiguity than risk: random effects analysis of all three treatments revealed regions that are differentially activated in decision making under ambiguity relative to risk (at $p < 0.001$, uncorrected). These regions include (A) left amygdala and right amygdala/parahippocampal gyrus, (B) bilateral OFC, and bilateral inferior parietal lobule, (C) mean time courses of amygdala and OFC (time synched to trial onset, dashed vertical lines are mean decision times, error bars are SEM, $n = 16$). Time courses are plotted using the most significant voxel in each cluster.

which suggests the amygdala may be partly reacting to ambiguity in the social evaluation of faces; the activity dissipates when faces are familiar and more like risky gambles, which have less missing social information. Similarity of activity in all three fMRI treatments also suggests that aversion to betting on ambiguous events may be an overgeneralization of a rational aversion to betting against other agents who are better-informed.

Areas activated during the risk condition relative to ambiguity are listed in table 5.2. These include the dorsal striatum (caudate nucleus) (figure 5.3a), an area that has been implicated in reward prediction. (67; 58; 48) One earlier study (62) also found differential activation in the caudate during risk relative to ambiguity using PET.[16]

Table 5.2
Risk > ambiguity: Local maxima of clusters, $p < 0.001$ uncorrected, clusters with fewer than 10 voxels not shown

Cluster			Voxel				X	Y	Z	Regions	
p_{cor}	k_E	p_{unc}	p_{FWE}	p_{FDR}	T	Z				Laterality	Region
0.06	52	0.007	0.063	0.012	5.31	4.62	0	−6	6	Middle	Caudate
			0.993	0.033	3.57	3.32	9	6	6	Right	
			0.952	0.023	3.79	3.5	−12	6	0	Left	
0	641	0	0.07	0.012	5.27	4.59	12	−60	−3	Right	Culmen
			0.119	0.012	5.07	4.45	9	−78	3	Right	Lingual gyrus
			0.162	0.012	4.94	4.36	−12	−75	15	Left	Cuneus
0.01	81	0.001	0.295	0.012	4.68	4.18	−15	−72	51	Left	Precuneus
0.26	29	0.034	0.338	0.012	4.62	4.13	−3	9	45	Left	Precentral gyrus
0.12	41	0.014	0.569	0.012	4.33	3.92	12	−75	51	Right	Precuneus
			0.906	0.02	3.9	3.58	21	−84	39	Right	
0.74	12	0.154	0.923	0.021	3.87	3.56	−42	−75	30	Left	Angular gyrus

Note: All local maxima uncorrected p-values are significant to three significant figures, and are omitted from the table.

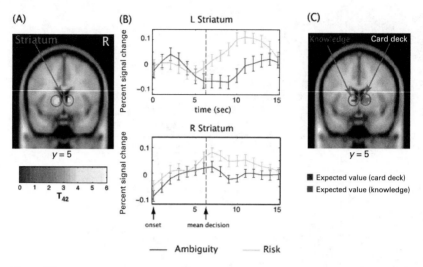

Figure 5.3
Regions showing greater activation under risk than ambiguity: random effects analysis of all three treatments revealed brain regions that are differentially activated in decision making under risk. These regions include (A) dorsal striatum, and also precuneus and premotor cortex, and (B) Mean time courses for risk areas (time synched to trial onset, dashed vertical lines are mean decision times, error bars are SEM, $n = 16$), (C) These dorsal striatal areas were significantly correlated with the expected value of the subjects' choices in the risk condition of the card deck treatment (red, right), and both risk and ambiguity conditions of the knowledge treatment (blue, left), $p < 0.005$. The laterality of these activations is consistent with the fact that language processing tends to occur in the left brain, while more abstract mathematical processing tends to occur in the right brain.

Time courses also showed different patterns of activation in the ambiguity > risk and risk > ambiguity regions, indicating two distinct systems at work. Whereas the amygdala and OFC reacted rapidly at the onset of the trial (figure 5.2c), the dorsal striatum activity built more slowly and peaks after the decision time (figure 5.3b). Furthermore, these activations are present in all three experimental treatments[17] (see figures 5.4 and 5.5).

One simplified way of interpreting this data is to hypothesize that there are two interacting systems: (1) a vigilance system in the amygdala and OFC that responds more rapidly to the stimuli, and (2) a reward-anticipation system in the striatum that is farther downstream. The overall activity differences in the contrasts indicate that system 2 is more active during risky decisions, which make sense since in these situations subjects have the information necessary for accurate reward prediction. Conversely, during ambiguous conditions, the first

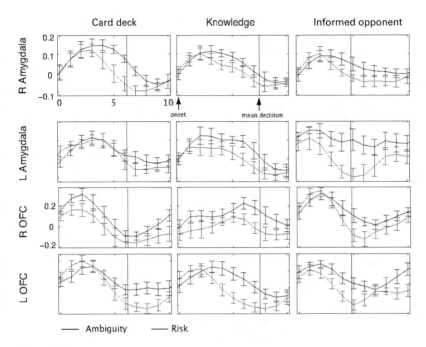

Figure 5.4
Time courses of percentage signal change in brain regions that are differentially activated in decision making under ambiguity in card deck, knowledge, and informed opponent conditions. Note that the qualitative aspects of the activation differences between ambiguity and risk are preserved between the pooled time courses in figure 5.2.

rapid system 1 appears to be more active, indicating that it may be reacting to the level of information available (less information during the ambiguous situations leads to greater vigilance, in the form of higher activation levels, in the amygdala and OFC). Both systems are active to varying degrees during risky and ambiguous trials. The difference is one of degree: as the level of information available to the decision maker rises, activity in system 1 declines relative to more ambiguous situations; the converse is true of system 2.

We measure the degree of ambiguity aversion for each subject and see if this correlates with brain activity in a between-subjects analysis. The subjects' utility functions for money are assumed to follow a power function $u(x, \rho) = x^\rho$, which is conveniently characterized by one parameter and widely used in empirical estimations of this sort. Subjects are assumed to weight probabilities according to the function $\pi(p, \gamma) = p^\gamma$. The ρ parameter is interpreted as the risk aversion

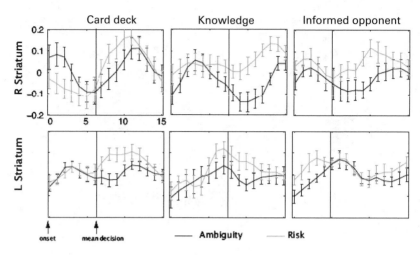

Figure 5.5
Time courses of percentage signal change in brain regions that are differentially activated in decision making under risk in card deck, knowledge, and informed opponent conditions. Note once again that the qualitative patterns are preserved in the pooled time courses in figure 5.3.

coefficient; in other words, the curvature of the utility function. The γ parameter is interpreted as the ambiguity aversion coefficient; meaning the amount people over or under-weight probabilities because they are not confident in their judgments. If subjects over-weight ambiguous probabilities ($\gamma < 1$), we characterize them as ambiguity-preferring. If they under-weight ambiguous probabilities ($\gamma > 1$, as in the nonadditive prior view), we characterize them as ambiguity-averse. If subjects weight probabilities linearly ($p = 1$), we characterize them as ambiguity-neutral. We assume subjects combine these weighted probabilities and utilities linearly, so that their weighted subjective expected utility is $U(p, x, \gamma, \rho) = \pi(p, \gamma)u(x, \rho)$.

The tasks are all binary choices in which subjects either choose a gamble to win x (with probability p) or 0, or a certain payoff c. For the risky deck, the ratios of the cards are the probabilities. For the ambiguous decks and all knowledge questions, we assumed $p = 1/2$. If subjective p is different than $1/2$ (e.g., because a subject happens to know a lot about fall temperatures in New York), then subjective probabilities are not held constant across the knowledge trials. This possibility biases our analysis against finding common regions of activation across treatments, so it would imply that the results described in the text are conservative about the true extent and commonality of ambiguity and risk-specific regions. We constrain $\gamma = 1$ in all risk conditions and estimate p from behavioral data in the ambiguity conditions.

The probability that the subject chooses the gamble rather than the sure amount c is given by the logit or softmax formula, $P(p, x, c, \gamma, \rho, \lambda) = 1/(1 + \exp\{-\lambda(U(p, x\rho) - u(c, \rho))\})$. The parameter λ is the sensitivity of choice probability to the utility difference (the degree of inflection), or the amount of "randomness" in the subject's choices ($\lambda = 0$ means choices are random; as λ increases, the function is more steeply inflected at 0).

Denote the choice of the subject in trial i by y_i, where $y_i = 1$ if subject chooses the gamble, and 0 if the subject chooses the certain payoff. We fit the data using maximum likelihood, with the log likelihood function

$$\sum_{y_i} [y_i \log(P(p, x, c, \gamma, \rho, \lambda)) + (1 - y_i) \log(1 - P(p, x, c, \gamma, \rho, \lambda))].$$

This analysis gives us a value of γ^j for each subject in the fMRI experiment. The γ^j estimated from the knowledge rounds positively correlates with brain activity across subjects as measured by the contrast values, $\beta^j_{amb} - \beta^j_{risk}$, between ambiguity and risk (averaged over the three treatments) in the right OFC ($r = .55$, $p < 0.02$, one-tailed), and left OFC ($r = 0.37$, $p < 0.1$, one-tailed) (figure 5.6a). This means that the subjects who exhibited more ambiguity aversion revealed by choice also show greater neural differences between risk and ambiguity in the OFC.[18]

5.3.4   Lesion Data

To validate the fMRI results and establish a necessary role for the OFC, we conducted behavioral experiments similar to the card deck task using a lesion method. Twelve neurological subjects with focal brain lesions were partitioned into those whose lesions included the focus of OFC activation revealed in our fMRI study ($n = 5$), and a comparison group whose temporal lobe lesions did not overlap with any of our fMRI foci ($n = 7$). The two groups had equivalent IQs, mathematical abilities, and performances on other background tasks as well as decision tasks. This excludes these factors as possible explanations for the differences in risk and ambiguity aversion between the two groups.

As noted earlier, behavioral data was collected from twelve patients with focal lesions to determine the necessity of OFC activation

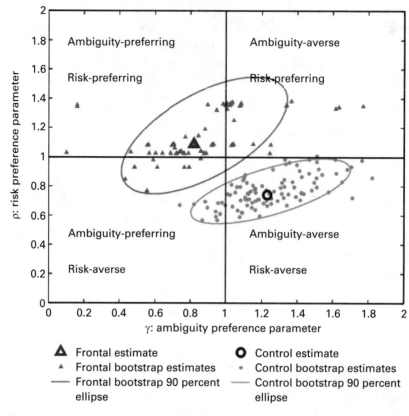

Figure 5.6
(A) Regression of right OFC contrast values on the behavioral measure of ambiguity γ (calibrated from knowledge questions). (B) Measures of risk (ρ) and ambiguity (γ) preferences of OFC ($n = 5$) and control group ($n = 7$). The risk-neutral line ($\gamma = 1$) and the ambiguity-neutral line ($\rho = 1$) demarcate four quadrants as labeled. Open symbols plot ML estimates of a group-level stochastic choice model (frontals: ($\gamma = 0.82$, $\rho = 1.09$); lesion controls: ($\gamma = 1.23$, $\rho = 0.74$)). Solid symbols represent 100 bootstrapped (γ, ρ) estimates. Ellipses are two-dimensional 90 percent confidence intervals around the bootstrapped data. Angle of the ellipse reflects correlation between ρ and γ (0.42 for frontal, 0.31 for control).

Table 5.3
Proportion of patients choosing certain payoffs instead of a gamble with the possible reward of 100 points. Risky decks were all half red and half black

Lesion	Certain Amt.	Ambiguity	Risk
Control	15	0.29	0
	25	0.29	0.14
	30	0.57	0.29
	40	0.71	0.57
	60	0.71	0.86
OFC	15	0	0
	25	0	0
	30	0	0
	40	0.20	0.20
	60	0.40	0.60

for ambiguity aversion. In the ambiguity condition, patients were shown an actual card deck with twenty cards, in some mixture of red and black they could not see. They were given a series of choices between certain amounts of points (15, 60, 30, 40, and 25, in that order) and bets on the color of their choice from the card deck for 100 points. In the risky condition they were shown a deck with exactly ten red and ten black cards whose colors they could see. They made choices between a bet on the color of their choice from the deck for 100 points, or certain amounts of 30, 60, 15, 40, and 25 (in that order; see table 5.3).[19].

We could estimate p and γ for each individual in the fMRI study. We were, however, forced to pool data within each patient group because there are not enough data points to estimate each patient's parameter. The behavioral data were pooled and a bootstrap procedure was used to create one hundred pseudosamples with corresponding (γ, p) pairs. Two-dimensional confidence interval analysis of these pairs (figure 5.6b) shows that frontal patients are risk-and ambiguity-neutral (i.e., the hypothesis that $\gamma = p = 1$ cannot be rejected). This behavior of frontal patients was significantly different than the damage control group, who were averse to both risk and ambiguity. The OFC-lesioned group was therefore abnormally neutral toward ambiguity (which is, ironically, a hallmark of rationality under SEU).

The parameter γ enables us to link the fMRI and lesion studies. Assume that the frontal patients would have a right OFC (ROFC) contrast value of zero if they were imaged during these tasks (since all have ROFC damage). Then we can guess what value of γ the OFC patients might exhibit behaviorally by extrapolating correlation between ROFC activity and γ in figure 5.6a to the case where there is zero activity in ROFC. This extrapolation gives a predicted $\gamma = 0.85$. The actual value estimated from the OFC patients' behavioral choices is $\gamma = 0.82$, which is reasonably close to the extrapolated prediction.

5.3.5 Discussion

The two hypothesized systems, amygdala/OFC and striatum, are active in both ambiguity and risk; the differences in activation between the two are driven by the level of uncertainty in the different conditions. The fact that we see similar activation patterns for the real-world treatment as the card deck treatment supports the hypothesis that risk and ambiguity are in fact points on a spectrum of uncertainty rather than two completely different entities. The reaction of the amygdala and OFC seems to be tied to the level of perceived uncertainty. That these areas are also activated by the hostile-opponent treatment indicates that the reaction to uncertainty is an instance of a more general vigilance reaction to possibly dangerous situations.

An interesting implication of this study is that models of risk and ambiguity that treat the two as quantitatively instead of qualitatively different may be more neurally, and therefore behaviorally, accurate. The current models of risk aversion relying solely on the curvature of the utility function do not allow for this. The implication that both types of aversion are the result of a direct dampening of activity in the dorsal striatum, which may well be the internal representation of utility in the brain, could help resolve some of the paradoxes of risk aversion as well as ambiguity aversion; for example, the vastly different expressions of risk over small versus large bets.

The regions implicated in our fMRI experiments and confirmed by behavioral experiments with lesion patients have been observed in previous studies using different tasks. The striatum-amygdala-OFC network is well-established in animal and human studies as a system for reward learning, including probabilistic learning (Critchley, Mathias, and Dolan 2001). The OFC is highly interconnected with the basolateral amygdala. These interconnections appear to play vital roles in learning and reversal learning in rats (Schoenbaum, Chiba, and Gallagher 2000).

Lateral OFC, in particular, appears to be necessary to change existing associations (O'Doherty et al. 2003). Our findings that the OFC is activated as a function of ambiguity, and that its damage reduces sensitivity to ambiguity, suggest that this structure is a necessary component for reacting to gradations of uncertainty. The idea that ambiguity aversion in card deck and knowledge choices is related to the rational aversion to betting against a better-informed opponent (the hostile opponent hypothesis) is supported by similarities in time courses in the amygdala, OFC, and striatum between all three treatments.

We present evidence that the human brain responds to varying levels of uncertainty, contrary to many decision theories that regard choices under risk and under ambiguity as equivalent. fMRI data suggests that uncertainty is represented in a system that includes the amygdala and OFC.

Both the amygdala and OFC are known to receive rapid multimodal sensory input; both are bidirectionally connected and known to function together in evaluating the value of stimuli (Gaffan, Murray, and Fabre-Thorpe 1993); and both are likely involved in the detection of salient, relevant, and ambiguous stimuli. The latter function has been hypothesized especially for the amygdala (Whalen 1998; Adams et al. 2003). Critically, such a function also provides a reward-related signal that can motivate behavior by virtue of the known connections between the amygdala/OFC and the striatum (Amaral et al. 1992). Under ambiguity, the brain is alerted to the fact that information is missing, that choices based on the information available therefore carry more unknown (and potentially dangerous) consequences, and that cognitive and behavioral resources must be mobilized to seek out additional information from the environment.

Understanding the neural basis of choice under uncertainty, in the broader sense including both risk and ambiguity, is important because it is a fundamental activity at every societal level, from retirement savings to insurance pricing to determining international military policy. These choices vary not only because of the presence of uncertainty, but the perceived *level* of uncertainty. Our results suggest that we pursue a unified model of uncertainty, which would treat risk and ambiguity as points on a larger continuous scale. The knowledge treatment of the experiment further implies that the relevant level of uncertainty might be a function of mathematically unrelated factors, such as familiarity with related but irrelevant information.

Finally, economists should care about understanding the neural basis of decision only if the extra level of detail helps us make predictions that standard economic theories would not make. For example, the evidence in this chapter suggests that the amygdala and OFC participate in evaluating the degree of uncertainty, generating an aversion to ambiguity and also signaling a larger anticipated reward from risky bets to the striatum. Knowing that these particular areas are part of a candidate circuit is most useful for economics if we know something special about their properties and other functions they perform. Fortunately, a lot is known about the amygdala's structure and function. It is rapidly activated by exposure to fearful stimuli (as briefly as 5–15 milliseconds of exposure to a fearful face (Whalen 1998)). Furthermore, it is possible that if there are competing stimuli influencing the amygdala, then the OFC cannot disentangle which stimulus generates the influence. These two properties lead to the following prediction: suppose the amygdala is stimulated by some fear-inducing stimulus that is independent of an ambiguous bet, such as anticipation of an impending electric shock a few seconds later. While waiting for the potential shock, the subject chooses between a sure amount or an ambiguous bet. If the OFC mistakes the amygdala activity from the shock anticipation for a fear of betting under ambiguity, then the subject may be more averse to ambiguous bets when a shock is anticipated (compared to control conditions when there is no shock anticipation). We do not know if this experiment will work; if the OFC can separate the influence of shock-anticipation fear from ambiguity-aversion-driven fear then the experiment will not work. But if the experiment does show an effect, then we have a very powerful challenge to the standard economic idea of stable preferences. Adding the shock anticipation will have essentially changed the expressed preference, not because we have truly changed the degree of aversion to ambiguous bets, but because we used our knowledge of the components of circuitry to trick the OFC into thinking the amygdala was afraid of the bet rather than afraid of the shock.

This phenomenon could even be incorporated into a theoretical model using standard parts from the economic theory hardware store. Suppose the amygdala is activated by various state variables (shock anticipation, fearful faces, ambiguous bets, etc.). The amygdala observes a state variable and sends a signal to the OFC. (This is like an infant who is crying, but the crying itself does not signal to a concerned parent what condition—hunger, pain, fatigue—caused the crying.) The OFC gets the signal but does not observe the state variable. The OFC must then make a decision, such as pricing an ambiguous gamble. Since the OFC does not know the source of fear, it implements more aversion to ambiguity.

5.4   Conclusion

The goal of neuroeconomics is to ground economic theory in details of how the brain works in decision making, strategic thinking, and exchange. One way to achieve this is to observe processes and constructs typically considered unobservable in order to decide between many theories of behavioral anomalies like risk aversion, altruistic punishment, and reciprocity. Another likely outcome is that thinking about brain details will provide a new way of understanding concepts that have been traditionally left out of economic analysis, like emotion, willpower, habit, and the biological basis of demand. No one neuroeconomic study will be able to conclusively do either of these things, but by combining experiments and types of data we may gain insights into behavior that we cannot arrive at by introspection of behavioral observation.

The study discussed in this chapter illustrates both of these goals to varying degrees. First, it allows us to use neural evidence to discount models of ambiguity that treat it as merely a two-stage lottery by showing that there may be two interacting systems determining the experienced utility of an option, one responding to the level of information in general and one using input from this system to discount the reward of the possible results. Second, it suggests a substantially different way to look at risk aversion. Considering a more general uncertainty aversion that dampens the utility of a gamble allows us to consider careful models of risk where the context of the gamble is important, something that is very difficult if we only consider a single universal utility function.

Notes

1. However, Colander (2005, 20) notes that Ramsey, Edgeworth, and Fisher all speculated about measuring utility directly before the neoclassical revolution declared utility to be inherently unobservable and only revealed by observable choices. Ramsey and Edgeworth speculated about a "psychogalvanometer" and a "hedonimeter," respectively, which sound remarkably like modern tools. Would these economists be neuroeconomists if they were reincarnated today?

2. The most charitable way to interpret Friedman's "F-twist" is that theories of market equilibrium based on utility maximization of consumers are equivalent, at the market level, to unspecified other theories that allow violations of utility maximization but include some institutional repairs or corrections for those violations. That is, the theory states $U \rightarrow M$, but even if U is false, there is an alternative theory $[(not - U) \ and \ R] \rightarrow M$,

in which a "repair condition" R suffices in place of assumption U to yield the same prediction M. If so, the focus of attention should be on specifying the repair condition R.

3. For PET, subjects are injected with a small amount of radioactive solution (often glucose with a radioactive marker) and the scanner simply localizes where the radioactive material goes during different tasks. The advantage of this method over fMRI is that PET measures glucose metabolism, a more direct correlate to neural activity than the blood oxygenation level dependent (BOLD) signal. The major disadvantage is that it has a much lower temporal resolution (on the order of minutes rather than seconds).

4. There are interesting variations between average offers across societies, however, which are correlated with the degree of market integration and production of public goods in those societies (Henrich et al. 2005). From a neural point of view, we believe differing social norms of fairness in these societies probably generate different activity in insula, which generate different offer and rejection patterns. Just as the food and social habits people find disgusting can vary across cultures, so can norms of what offers are "disgustingly unfair."

5. Dufwenberg and Gneezy (2000) measured second-order beliefs in trust games similar to those studied by McCabe et al. (2001). In their games, each investor was asked how much they thought the trustee would repay (call this guess $E_{investor}(y)$), and the trustee was asked to guess the investor's guess about repayment (i.e., $E_{trustee}(E_{investor}(y))$). The second-order guess was correlated (.44) with the trustee's actual repayment y. This correlation suggests the trustees' feel a sense of moral obligation to live up to the investor's expectations, so their second-order belief about what that investor's expectation might be is an important driver of their decision.

6. For example, if you show anterograde amnesiacs a chess board and ask "Do you know how to play?" they will often say no even if they've been taught the rules before. But if you force them to play—"Let's just start"—they will play chess according to the rules. They know the rules, they just don't know that they know them. This syndrome was illustrated effectively in the popular 2002 movie *Memento* (Bayley, Frascino, and Squire 2005).

7. "Not proven" is a vestige of an earlier time when juries just decided whether facts were proven or not proven, and judges decided guilt based on those factual judgments.

8. In the recent (2004–2005) trial of former pop star Michael Jackson for child molestation, some jurors said they believed he was guilty but the evidence wasn't sufficient to prove his guilt (Jackson was acquitted). In Scotland they might have delivered a "not proven" verdict.

9. A fifth explanation springs from the observation that patriotism across countries, measured by the World Values Survey, is correlated across countries with the extent of countrywide home bias (Morse and Shive 2004). This is the national equivalent of preferring to bet on your home team in sports, but it does not seem to explain all the other levels of home bias.

10. Returning to the Ellsberg example, a prior is simply the vector $(p, 1 - p)$ where p is the probability that the state is red. As you can see, the set of overall possible priors is the line segment in the real plane going between the points $(0, 1)$-definitely black, to $(1, 0)$-definitely red. A decision maker's set of priors in this example is taken to be an unbroken segment of this line.

11. In the Ellsberg example larger intervals for possible p.

12. For example, assume that the subject has prior knowledge that the deck will either contain five red cards and fifteen blue cards, or fifteen red cards and five blue cards. Assume that the opponent draws one card before choosing how to bet, and the opponent always bets on the color that he drew. The subject, having no information about the deck, will bet randomly on red or blue. Suppose the subject chooses to bet on red (without loss of generality). When the deck has five red cards and fifteen blue cards, the opponent will draw a blue with probability $3/4$. As a result, the subject will end up betting against the opponent's blue draw 75 percent of the time, and winning that bet only one-fourth of the time. One-quarter of the time, the opponent draws a red card and bets red, in which case the subject's red bet does not count (and the subject earns the sure amount c). Therefore, the subject's expected value, conditional on the deck having fifteen blue cards, is $3/4$ $1/4x + 1/4c$. The expected value, conditional on the deck having fifteen red cards, is $3/4c + 1/4$ $3/4x$. Since each of these conditional expected values is equally likely, the overall expected value is $c/2 + 3/16x$. When the informed opponent does not have better information, then both subjects bet randomly and the subject's expected value is $c/2 + x/4$ (since half the time their colors match and they earn c, and half the time they bet and the subject wins that bet half the time). Comparing the two expected values, there is a small drop in expected value ($x/4 - 3/16x = x/16$) when betting against the informed opponent. This drop leads to a stricter constraint on when it is rational to take the gamble ($x > 8/3c$ instead of $x > 2c$).

13. The time series B_t for each voxel went through a high-pass filter and an AR(1) (or autoregressive model of 1) correction.

14. Mean response times were 6.39 seconds (ambiguity) and 6.16 seconds (risk), and were not significantly different.

15. The amygdala is also involved in emotional learning and conditioning, both of which should be relevant in dealing with ambiguous situations (Phelps et al. 2004).

16. See the RC-AC image at ⟨http://www.econ.umn.edu/_arust/neuroecon.html⟩.

17. Note that it is rational in the hostile opponent's treatment to discount some of the payoff in the gamble, as the gamble only wins if the better-informed opponent chose the wrong color. The hostile opponent hypothesis is that bets on ambiguous card decks and low-knowledge events, while normatively different than bets against the hostile opponent, are generated by similar neural circuitry. The time courses in the amygdala, OFC, and striatum are similar across all three treatments, consistent with this hypothesis.

18. We also analyzed activations based on actual decisions: trials where people gambled versus trials where they chose the sure payoffs. We found some interesting activations in these subtractions, but there does not appear to be any interaction between these decision conditions and the ambiguity versus risk conditions. This implies that the differences we see in the ambiguity/risk comparisons are purely a reaction to the level of uncertainty the subject is exposed to. While these reactions are almost certainly then an input into the actual decision, the areas we see appear to be involved in evaluating the situation rather than determining choice.

19. There are three small differences in this task and the card deck treatment in the fMRI experiment: (1) there were fewer choices in the lesion experiment, due to time constraints in conducting experiments with lesion patients and the need for multiple trials to extract fMRI signal; (2) there was wider range of certain point amounts in the lesion task (in case patients were extremely risk- and ambiguity-averse or -preferring); and (3) due to human

subjects restrictions, the lesion task choices were not conducted for actual monetary payments.

References

Adams, R., H. Gordon, A. Baird, N. Ambady, and R. Kleck. 2003. "Effects of Gaze on Amygdala Sensitivity to Anger and Fear Faces." *Science* 300, no. 5625 (June): 1536.

Adolphs, R. 2002. "Neural Systems for Recognizing Emotion." *Current Opinion in Neurobiology* 12: 169–177.

Allais, M. 1953. "Le Comportement de l'Homme Rationnel Devant le Risque: Critique des Postulats et Axiomes de l'école Américaine." *Econometrica* 21: 503–546.

Amadi, A. 2004. "Equity Home Bias: A Disappearing Phenomenon." Working Paper, University of California at Davis. Available at http://ssrn.com/abstract=540662.

Amaral, D., J. Price, A. Pitkanen, and S. Carmichael. 1992. "Anatomical Organization of the Primate Amygdaloid Complex." In *The Amygdala: Neurobiological Aspects of Emotion, Memory, and Mental Dysfunction*, ed. J. P. Aggleton, 1–66. Wiley, New York.

Bayley, P. J., J. C. Frascino, and L. R. Squire. 2005. "Robust Habit Learning in the Absence of Awareness and Independent of the Medial Temporal Lobe." *Nature* 436: 550–553.

Bechara, A., H. Damasio, and A. Damasio. 2003. "Role of the Amygdala in Decision-Making." *Annals of the New York Academy of Sciences* 985: 356–369.

Becker, S., and F. Brownson. 1964. "What Price Ambiguity? On the Role of Ambiguity in Decision Making." *Journal of Political Economy* 72: 62–73.

Berg, J., J. Dickhaut, and K. McCabe. 1995. "Trust, Reciprocity and Social History." *Games and Economic Behavior* 10, no. 1: 122–142.

Berthoz, S., J. Armony, R. Blair, and R. Dolan. 2002. "An fMRI Study of Intentional and Unintentional (Embarrassing) Violations of Social Norms." *Brain* 125: 1696–1708.

Bewley, T. 2002. "Knightian Decision Theory, Part I." *Decisions in Economics and Finance* 25: 79–110.

Bhatt, M., and C. F. Camerer. 2005. "Self-referential Thinking and Equilibrium as States of Mind in Games: fMRI Evidence." *Games and Economic Behavior* 52, no. 2: 424–459.

Bruni, L., and R. Sugden. 2007. "The Road Not Taken: Two Debates about the Role of Psychology in Economics." *Economic Journal* 117, no. 516.

Busino, G. 1964. "Note Bibliographique Sur le cours." In Epstolario, Vilfredo Pareto, 1165–1172. Rome: Accademia Nazionale dei Lincei.

Calder, A. J., J. Keane, F. Manes, N. Antoun, and A. W. Young. 2000. "Impaired Recognition and Experience of Disgust Following Brain Injury." *Nature Neuroscience* 3: 1077–1078.

Camerer, C. F. 2003. *Behavioral Game Theory: Experiments in Strategic Interaction*. Princeton University Press, Princeton.

Camerer, C. F. 2005. "Behavioral economics. Paper Prepared for the World Congress of the Econometric Society. Available at www.hss.caltech.edu/~camerer.

Camerer, C. F., T.-H. Ho, and J. K. Chong. 2004. "A Cognitive Hierarchy Theory of One-Shot Games." *Quarterly Journal of Economics* 119: 861–898.

Camerer, C., and R. Karjalainen. 1994. "Ambiguity-Aversion and Non-Additive Beliefs in Non-Cooperative Games: Experimental Evidence." In *Models and Experiments on Risk and Rationality*, ed. B. Munier and M. Machina, 325–358. Dordrecht: Kluwer Academic Publishers.

Camerer, C., G. Loewenstein, and D. Prelec. 2005. "Neuroeconomics: How Neuroscience Can Inform Economics." *Journal of Economic Literature* 43: 9–63.

Camerer, C., and M. Weber. 1992. "Recent Developments in Modeling Preferences: Uncertainty and Ambiguity." *Journal of Risk and Uncertainty* 5: 325–370.

Chorvat, T., and K. McCabe. 2005. "Neuroeconomics and Rationality." *Chicago-Kent Law Review* 80: 101.

Colander, D. 2005. "Neuroeconomics, the Hedonimeter, and Utility: Some Historical Links." Working Paper, Middlebury College.

Critchley, H., R. Elliot, C. Mathias, and R. Dolan. 2000. "Neural Activity Relating to Generation and Representation of Galvanic Skin Conductance Responses: A Functional Magnetic Resonance Imaging Study." *Journal of Neuroscience* 20: 3033–3040.

Critchley, H., C. Mathias, and R. Dolan. 2001. "Neural Activity in the Human Brain Relating to Uncertainty and Arousal During Anticipation." *Neuron* 29: 537–545.

de Quervain, D. J.-F., U. Fischbacher, V. Treyer, M. Schellhammer, U. Schnyder, A. Buck, and E. Fehr. 2004. "The Neural Basis of Altruistic Punishment." *Science* 305: 1254–1258.

Dow, J., and S. R. da Costa Werlang. 1992. "Uncertainty Aversion, Risk Aversion and Optimal Choice of Portfolio." *Econometrica* 60: 197–204.

Duff, P. 1999. "The Scottish Criminal Jury: A Very Peculiar Institution." *Law and Contemporary Problems* 62: 173.

Dufwenberg, M., and U. Gneezy. 2000. "Measuring Beliefs in an Experimental Lost Wallet Game." *Games and Economic Behavior* 30: 163–182.

Eisenberger, N. I., M. D. Lieberman, and K. Williams. 2003. "Does Rejection Hurt? An fMRI Study of Social Exclusion." *Science* 302: 290–292.

Ellsberg, D. 1961. "Risk, Ambiguity, and the Savage Axioms." *Quarterly Journal of Economics* 75, no. 4: 643–669.

Epstein, L., and T. Wang. 1994. "Intertemporal Asset-Pricing under Knightian Uncertainty." *Econometrica* 62: 283–322.

Fox, C., and A. Tversky. 1995. "Ambiguity Aversion and Comparative Ignorance." *Quarterly Journal of Economics* 110: 585–603.

French, K., and J. Poterba. 1991. "Investor Diversifcation and International Equity Markets." *American Economic Review* 81: 222–226.

Friedman, M. 1953. *Essays in Positive Economics*. Chicago: University of Chicago Press.

Frisch, D., and J. Baron. 1988. "Ambiguity and Rationality." *Journal of Behavioral Decision Making* 1: 149–157.

Gaffan, D., E. A. Murray, and M. Fabre-Thorpe. 1993. "Interaction of the Amygdala with the Frontal Lobe in Reward Memory." *European Journal of Neuroscience* 5, no. 7: 968–975.

Gallagher, H. L., A. I. Jack, A. Rrepstorff, and C. D. Frith. 2002. "Imaging the Intentional Stance in a Competitive Game." *NeuroImage* 16: 814–821.

Ghirardato, P., and J. Katz. 2000. Indecision Theory: Explaining Selective Abstention in Multiple Elections. Working Paper No. 1106, California Institute of Technology.

Gilboa, I., and D. Schmeidler. 1989. "Maxmin Expected Utility with Non-Unique Prior." *Journal of Mathematical Economics* 18: 141–153.

Glimcher, P., and A. Rustichini. 2004. "Neuroeconomics: The Concilience of Brain and Decision." *Science* 306: 447–452.

Graham, J. R., C. R. Harvey, and H. Huang. 2005. "Investor Competence, Trading Frequency, and Home Bias." Working Paper No. 11426, National Bureau of Economic Research.

Gul, F., and W. Pesendorfer. 2005. "The Case for Mindless Economics." Working Paper, Princeton University.

Henrich, J., et al. 2005. "'Economic Man' in Cross-Cultural Perspective: Ethnography and Experiments from 15 Small-Scale Societies." *Behavioral and Brain Sciences* 28: 795–855.

Jevons, W. S. 1871. *The Theory of Political Economy*. London: Penguin.

Kahneman, D., and A. Tversky. 1979. "Prospect Theory: An Analysis of Decision under Risk." *Econometrica* 42: 263–292.

Kim, H., and P. J. Whalen. 2004. "A Computational Model of Amygdala-Basal Forebrain-Prefrontal Cortex Interaction in the Detection and Resolution of Predictive Uncertainty." Doctoral Thesis, University of Wisconsin-Madison.

Kosfeld, M., M. Heinrichs, P. Zak, U. Fischbacher, and E. Fehr. 2005. "Oxytocin Increases Trust in Humans." *Nature* 435: 673–676.

Laibson, D. 1997. "Golded Eggs and Hyperbolic Discounting." *Quarterly Journal of Economics* 112, no. 2: 443–477.

Lo, K. C. 1999. "Extensive Form Games with Uncertainty Averse Players." *Games and Economic Behavior* 28: 256–270.

MacCrimmon, K. 1968. "Descriptive and Normative Implications of the Decision-Theory Postulates." In *Risk and Uncertainty*, ed. K. Borch and J. Mossin, 3–32. London: MacMillan.

McCabe, K., D. Houser, L. Ryan, V. Smith, and T. Trouard. 2001. "A Functional Imaging Study of Cooperation in Two-Person Reciprocal Exchange." *Proceedings of the National Academy of Sciences* 98: 11832–11835.

McClure, S. M., D. Laibson, G. Loewenstein, and J. D. Cohen. 2004. "Separate Neural Systems Value Immediate and Delayed Monetary Rewards." *Science* 306: 503–507.

Morse, Adair, and Sophie Shive. 2004. "Patriotism in Your Portfolio." Annual Meeting Paper, European Financial Managent Association, Basel.

Mukerji, S. 1998. "Ambiguity Aversion and Incompleteness of Information." *American Economic Review* 88: 1207–1231.

Mukerji, S., and J.-M. Tallon. 2004. "An Overview of Economic Applications of David Schmeidler's Models of Decision Making under Uncertainty." In *Uncertainty in Economic Theory: A Collection of Essays in Honor of David Schmeidler's 65th Birthday*, ed. I. Gilboa, 283–302. Oxford: Routledge.

O'Doherty, J., H. Critchley, R. Deichmann, and R. Dolan. 2003. "Dissociating Valence of Outcome from Response Switching in Human Orbital and Ventral Prefrontal Cortices." *Neuroscience* 23: 7931–7939.

O'Doherty, J., P. Dayan, J. Schults, R. Deichmann, K. Friston, and R. Dolan. 2004. "Dissociable Roles of Ventral and Dorsal Striatum in Instrumental Conditioning." *Science* 304: 452–454.

O'Donoghue, T., and M. Rabin. 1999. "Doing It Now or Later." *American Economic Review* 89, no. 1: 103–124.

Phelps, E., M. Delgado, K. Nearing, and J. Ledoux. 2004. "Extinction Learning in Humans: Role of the Amygdala and VMPFC." *Neuron* 43: 897–905.

Phelps, E., K. O'Connor, W. Cunningham, E. Funayama, J. Gatenby, J. Gore, and M. Banaji. 2000. "Performance on Indirect Measures of Race Evaluation Predicts Amygdala Activation." *Journal of Cognitive Neuroscience* 12: 729–738.

Raiffa, H. 1961. "Risk, Ambiguity and the Savage Axioms: Comment." *The Quarterly Journal of Economics* 75: 690–694.

Sanfey, A. G., J. K. Rilling, J. A. Aronson, L. E. Nystrom, and J. D. Cohen. 2003. "The Neural Basis of Economic Decision-Making in the Ultimatum Game." *Science* 300: 1755–1758.

Sargent, T., and L. Hansen. 2003. *Robust Control and Economic Model Uncertainty*. Unpublished Monograph.

Schmeidler, D. 1989. "Subjective Probability and Expected Utility without Additivity." *Econometrica* 57: 571–587.

Schoenbaum, G., A. Chiba, and M. Gallagher. 2000. "Changes in Functional Connectivity in Orbitofrontal Cortex and Basolateral Amygdala during Learning and Reversal Training." *Neuroscience* 20: 5179–5189.

Segal, U. 1987. "The Ellsberg Paradox and Risk Aversion: An Anticipated Utility Approach." *International Economic Review* 28, no. 1: 175–202.

Siegel, J. 1998. *Stocks for the Long Run*, 2nd ed. New York: Irwin.

Strong, N., and X. Xu. 2003. "Understanding the Equity of Home Bias: Evidence from Survey Data." *Review of Economics and Statistics* 85: 307–312.

Weigelt, K., and C. F. Camerer. 1988. "Reputation and Corporate Strategy: A Review of Recent Theory and Implications." *Strategic Management Journal* 9: 443–454.

Whalen, P. J. 1998. "Fear, Vigilance and Ambiguity: Initial Neuroimaging Studies of the Human Amygdala." *Current Directions in Psychological Science* 7, no. 6: 177–188.

Zak, P. 2004. "Neuroeconomics." *Philosophical Transactions of the Royal Society of Biology* 7: 13–21.

IV   Economics and Happiness

6   Happiness and Public Policy: A Challenge to the Profession

Richard Layard

The theory behind public economics needs radical reform. It fails to explain the recent history of human welfare, and it ignores some of the key findings of modern psychology. Indeed these two failings are intimately linked: it is because the theory ignores psychology that it is unable to explain the facts.

The fact is that, despite massive increases in purchasing power, people in the West are no happier than they were fifty years ago. We know this from population surveys and other supporting evidence that I review in this chapter.

The most obvious explanations come from three standard findings of the new psychology of happiness.[1] First, a person's happiness is negatively affected by the incomes of others (a negative externality). Second, a person's happiness adapts quite rapidly to higher levels of income (a phenomenon of addiction). And third, our tastes are not given—the happiness we get from what we have is largely culturally determined.

These findings provide a challenge to the theory and conclusions of public economics as set out, for example, in Atkinson and Stiglitz (1980). The challenge to public economics is to incorporate the findings of modern psychology while retaining the rigor of the cost-benefit framework that is the strength and glory of our subject.[2] In this chapter I first review the measurement of happiness. Then I take the three findings that I discussed one by one and pursue the policy implications of each of them. I end with some overall reflections.

6.1   Measuring Happiness

In the United States the General Social Survey asks people, "Taking things all together, how would you say you are these days—would

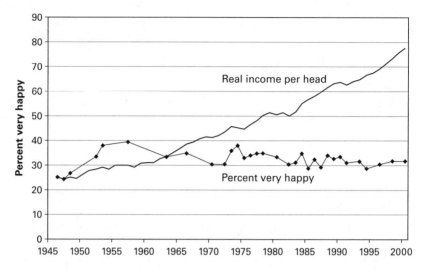

Figure 6.1
Income and happiness in the United States.

you say you are very happy, pretty happy, or not too happy?" As figure 6.1 shows, there has been no increase in happiness since the 1950s—nor any significant decrease in unhappiness. Similar findings apply in Japan and the United Kingdom and in most European countries (where the series began in 1975).

You might reasonably question whether such remarks mean anything, but significant new evidence from neuroscience suggests that they do.[3] Richard Davidson of the University of Wisconsin has identified areas in the prefrontal cortex where the level of electrical activity is highly correlated with self-reported happiness (both across people, and within people over time). Moreover, even if the use of words has changed over time between cohorts, one would not expect it to change within a cohort—yet each cohort experienced a stable level of happiness since the 1950s despite huge increases in their purchasing power.

There is also the cross-sectional evidence across countries—among industrialized countries with incomes over $20,000 per head there is no relation between average income and average happiness. These intercountry differences do have real information content, since John Helliwell can explain 80 percent of the variance across fifty countries with only six variables.[4] Finally, reverting to time series, there is the clear fact of increased criminal behavior and the likelihood that depression has increased—no one thinks it has fallen.

In due course we should have better time series on the happiness of people, including neurological measurements, and clearer evidence on where are the real areas of unhappiness in our society. But from what we already know, we can conclude that over the last fifty years happiness in the West has not risen, though it almost certainly has in the Third World, where income has a much greater impact on happiness at both the individual and societal level.

The finding about the West is contrary to standard economic theory. For simplicity we can write standard theory as

$$u = u(y, h) \qquad (u_1 > 0; u_2 < 0),$$

where u is (cardinal) utility, y is real income (which has risen), and h is hours (which have fallen for most people). Clearly we need an expanded model of happiness if we are to explain what is happening. We need to incorporate the standard findings of modern psychology.

6.2 Social Comparisons

The most obvious of these is the fact that we compare our incomes with those of others.[5] If others become richer, this reduces our satisfaction with whatever we have. The conventional wisdom is that people compare themselves mainly with people who are close to themselves in the income distribution, but if the income distribution is reasonably stable the income of this reference group will be proportional to average income $(\bar{y})$.[6] So an expanded theory could be for simplicity

$$u = u(y - \alpha\bar{y}, h).$$

In every study of happiness that I have seen average income $(\bar{y})$ attracts a large and significant negative coefficient. This is so whether we use cross-sections of states or neighborhoods or time series (with time dummies). In some studies the negative effect of average income is almost as large as the positive effect of own income. There is also, I should add, no evidence that people compare their leisure with other people's and some evidence that they do not.[7] The preceding model helps explain the paradox that individuals seek higher income and get happiness from it (the correlation is about 0.15), while societies gain less from higher income than the isolated individual does.

Many small pieces of evidence corroborate the validity of this analysis. For example, the U.S. General Social Survey provides data on how the individual perceives his relative income. If we regress happiness on own actual income and on perceived relative income, the latter explains more than the former. Similarly, in Switzerland happiness is explained by income relative to income aspirations, and the average income in the local community increases a person's aspirations.

6.2.1   Policy Implications

This is a case of negative externality. To focus on the efficiency aspect of the problem, we can assume there are n people who are identical, with the same happiness function and the same hourly wage of unity. The socially optimal level of individual work effort (h) is now given by

$$u_1 - nu_1\alpha\frac{1}{n} + u_2 = 0.$$

Here the second term reflects the external disbenefit that comes from the rise in average income, which adversely affects the happiness of all n people. Another way to think about this optimality condition is to ask: if everyone agreed with everyone else about how hard one should work in order to short-circuit the rat race, how hard would one work? Clearly the answer is given by

$$u_1(1 - \alpha) + u_2 = 0.$$

One way to coordinate this outcome is through a linear income tax with marginal rate t. The individual will work until

$$u_1(1 - t) + u_2 = 0.$$

So the marginal rate t that leads us to the social optimum is

$$t = \alpha.$$

It equals the cost to society expressed as a fraction of the gain to the individual. According to the studies I have quoted, this rate might be quite substantial. This does not necessarily mean that taxes should be higher than they are now. It does mean that they should be higher than they ought to be if there were no negative externality to be considered.

   We are talking here of a corrective tax—one that will reduce work effort to a level where the fruitless incentive to raise your relative income has been fully offset: the external cost has been fully internalized. This means that we need to rethink the measures of "excess burden" we use in cost-benefit analysis. The excess burden is normally calculated on the basis that any tax wedge of whatever size is distorting and reduces work effort below its efficient level. But we now know that people would work too hard if taxes were zero. So taxes only become distorting if they are levied above the optimum level to correct for the negative externality. To assert otherwise is to fly in the face of a central and well-established fact of human nature.

Libertarians object to this whole line of argument on the grounds that it panders to envy. They do not apparently mind pandering to greed. We should of course try to educate people away from both envy and greed, since neither is conducive to happiness. But at the same time we should set our other policy instruments at whatever level is optimal for the state of mind that currently prevails. (We could never completely eliminate the drive for status since it is hardwired into our biology, as studies of male monkeys show: when a monkey is moved between groups so that his status rises, there is an increase in his serotonin, a neurotransmitter associated with happiness.[8] The reverse happens when his status falls.)

6.3   Adaptation

A second key finding of psychology is adaptation. All living organisms respond to external changes in ways that restore their internal balance. This does not mean that for given genes there is a set point of happiness that can only be temporarily disturbed—the clear evidence of explainable differences in happiness between societies refutes this. So does the clear evidence of long-term changes in the happiness of individuals.[9] But adaptation does make it harder to secure permanent increases in happiness through increases in income.

Survey evidence shows clearly that a rise in income raises happiness more initially than it does in the long run.[10] This is because income is in part addictive. Having once experienced a higher standard of living, we cannot revert to where we were before and feel the same as we did then. To allow for this effect, we can add lagged income to the happiness function, with a negative effect. Assume for simplicity that

$$u = u(y - \beta y_{-1}, h).$$

Empirical work strongly supports this formulation, both in studies of happiness and of job satisfaction. In the U.S. General Social Survey the change in income has more effect on happiness than does its level: in other words, $\beta > 0.5$. In the Swiss study I mentioned earlier lagged income is a major influence on income aspirations, and this has been confirmed by numerous studies by Van Praag and Frijters (1999). By contrast, there is no evidence that people become habituated to good personal relationships, but there is less time for these when people work more.

6.3.1   Policy Implications

Habituation to income is only a problem for public policy if this effect is unforeseen. But there is substantial evidence that people over-estimate the extra happiness they will get from extra possessions.[11] For simplicity, assume there is no foresight: individuals do not realize that their current consumption will reduce their future happiness. Robert Frank has called this a negative internality. The result is that people will work too hard and consume too much. To be rigorous, redefine y in the previous equation to mean consumption. Then if the rate of discount (d) for utility equals the interest rate, and if real wages are constant, the efficient corrective tax rate is

$$t = \beta(1 - d).$$

It is the same type of correction as for an externality, except that the damage comes one period later.[12] The required correction is toward lower work effort and thus lower consumption. But there is no required correction toward higher saving. This only becomes necessary to the extent that real wages are rising.

   To the extent that addiction is foreseen, the need for tax is less. But much of the addiction to general spending, like the addiction to smoking, is not foreseen. If we are willing to tax addictive substances, we should also be willing to tax other forms of addiction.

6.3.2   Loss Aversion

At this point we need to introduce a quite different consideration: loss aversion. In the account we have given so far,

$$u = u((1 - \beta)y + \beta\Delta y, h),$$

whatever the sign of Δy. But important research by Kahneman and his colleagues shows that the effect on happiness of one unit of Δy is typically twice as great when Δy is negative as when it is positive.[13] This means that the utility of income function is kinked at the previous period's income, reflecting a status quo bias or endowment effect. And it is this kink which makes people so risk-averse. This is a fortunate finding, for as Rabin (2000) has shown, without this finding it would be impossible to explain why the same people can be risk-averse to small risks yet willing to undertake very large ones if the expected gain is high enough. Given the simplicity of this explanation of risk behavior, it is time that the textbooks and the theory of finance stopped using an incorrect explanation. Clearly it is loss aversion which makes stabilization policy so important. If Lucas (2003) had used Kahneman's estimates of this, he would have come to rather large estimates of the cost of fluctuations.[14]

6.3.3   Adaptation and Poverty

Let me add one further comment on adaptation. It clearly means that the function relating happiness to income is flatter in the long run than in the short run. Existing studies support the idea that the marginal utility of income diminishes with income, both within societies and across societies.[15] But the curvature is probably less in the long run than the short run. If so, the optimum degree of equality is less than if we focused on the short-run relationships.

Some on the left object to taking adaptation into account, just as some on the right object to taking social comparisons into account. Both arguments seem contrary to a humane philosophy, which should both seek to modify human nature but also work with human nature as it is. If there are some experiences that are totally impossible to adapt to, like mental illness, and some like poverty to which there is partial adaptation, that information is relevant to policy and we should use it in determining our priorities for public expenditure. At present our policies are based far too much on policy makers' judgments about how they would feel in a given situation, rather than on detailed studies of how people actually feel.[16]

6.4   Tastes

Economics normally assumes that tastes are given. This is clearly false in two senses. First, social factors can affect our ordinal preferences—our indifference curves. But second, they may also affect the cardinal happiness we get from a given consumption bundle, even if they have no effect on our indifference curves. Thus, as we have argued, average community income affects our happiness, as does our own lagged income. But there are many other taste variables, which I shall call T, so that now we are looking at

$u = u(y, h, T)$.

Good tastes are those which increase happiness, and vice versa.

How far can public economics take into account the formation of tastes? If it aims to provide a general framework for policy, it must do so. I will give only three examples.

The most obvious is advertising. Though advertising can provide information, it almost always makes us feel we need more money than we should otherwise have felt we needed. For example, the U.S. General Social Survey provides data on how a person perceives their position in the income distribution. If we regress this estimate on a person's actual income and the hours he watches television, we find that watching TV makes a person feel poorer,[17] and thus less happy. The problem of advertising is greatest in relation to children, which explains why Sweden bans advertising directed at children.

Another example is performance-related pay (PRP). The theory in favor of this is blindingly obvious to most economists: we must align the interests of the agent with those of the principal. He must therefore be directly and rapidly rewarded for his performance. The more we do this, the more we add to his motivation.

But can we assume that his tastes will remain constant? Probably not. Psychologists have done many experiments to examine the effect on a person's inner motivation of increasing the external motivating factors. Most of these studies show that extra financial rewards reduce internal motivation and can even reduce total motivation unless they are very large.[18] It is easy to understand why—if someone pays you to do something, you may cease to feel that you ought to do it anyway. A simple example comes from an Israeli childcare center. To encourage people to pick up their children on time they fined parents who were late. The result was that more people were late—they felt it was acceptable to be late since now they paid for it.

However, PRP is often a good idea when there is an unambiguous measure of performance. But usually there is no such measure and individuals have to be ranked against their colleagues. Often the rankings by different colleagues are poorly correlated. The effect of all this is to raise the salience of rank order comparisons in the utility function. Relationships between colleagues become more strained as people try harder to climb above each other on a ladder where the total number of places is fixed. Since the extra pay is usually small, this additional stress can generally be justified only if shareholders or customers gain.

But, as I have suggested, these gains are uncertain. Economists should therefore be more humble before relying on the simple rationality postulate and recommending performance-related pay: they may well be changing tastes at the same time.

Finally, let me address the most global aspect of our tastes—our feelings about what our life is about. Economists offer a fairly clear view, if we leave aside the rare studies of altruism. We say that each person seeks to be as happy as possible and the question of what makes him happy is unimportant. For example, it is not important whether it makes him happy to help other people or not. (We then, according to Atkinson and Stiglitz, seek the optimum pattern of taxes and spending to maximize the social welfare function—always taking the individual utility function as given.)

This is not, of course, how most people feel. They think people's values matter. That is one reason why we have compulsory education—because the utility functions of other people's children put such obvious constraints on our own utility.

I am not suggesting that economists should become moralists. But in some ways they already are, and their individualistic view of the world has gained increasing influence as belief has waned in conventional religion and in socialism. Crudely, the view which the public absorbs from economists is this: don't expect people to be interested in anybody else beyond the family. But don't let that worry you, because the outcome will be as good as it could be, provided we establish the rule of law and the right tax/expenditure plan.[19] Given that, let's have the maximum of competition between firms and individuals.

This involves a major confusion. We do want the maximum of competition between firms, but not between individuals. We want a lot of cooperation between individuals, for one reason above all—that life is more enjoyable that way. Cooperation may also improve final output, but in many cases it will not—competition can be a formidable spur. But the final output is only justified by its contribution to happiness. A world where everyone else appears as a threat is unlikely to generate much happiness, even if it generates massive output.

6.5   Conclusion

I conclude that economics uses exactly the right framework for thinking about public policy. Policy instruments are set so as to maximize

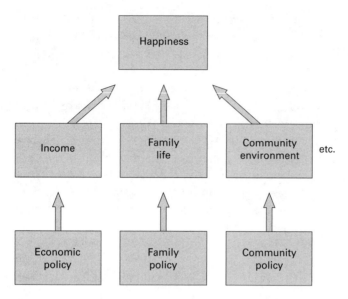

Figure 6.2
The policy maker's ideal world.

the sum of (cardinal) utilities, with additional weight given to those whose utility is low. What is wrong is the account we use of what makes people happy. Broadly, economics says that utility increases with the opportunities for voluntary exchange. This overlooks the huge importance of involuntary interactions between people—of how others affect our norms, our aspirations, our feelings of what is important, and our experience of whether the world is friendly or threatening.

One might wish to say that these things are the province of other social sciences. It would be convenient if life worked that way, as illustrated in figure 6.2. But it does not. We have already given important examples of this. Take mobility policy, illustrated in figure 6.3. More mobility certainly increases income, but it also affects the quality of relationships in the community and in families.[20] Economists should not advocate more mobility without also considering these effects.

This requires collaboration between economists and other social scientists, especially psychologists. In my view, the prime purpose of social science should be to discover what helps and what hinders happiness. Economists could play a lead role in promoting this approach: there is so much that could readily be studied and has not been.

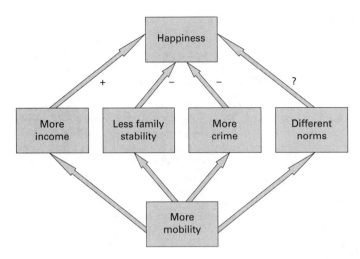

Figure 6.3
Reality.

Economists have much to contribute, especially cost-benefit analysis. Perhaps eventually costs and benefits could be expressed in utils. But for the present the money equivalent of a util will do fine, provided it is specified as the extra money that would in the long run secure for the average person an extra util of happiness.

Thirty years ago population surveys revolutionized labor economics. A similar revolution will soon revolutionize public economics, when psychological data on happiness are at last combined with the insights of revealed preference. This will lead to better theory, and to better policies.

Notes

This chapter draws heavily on Layard 2005a, 2005b, 1980.

1. I do not include inconsistent behavior that has been widely discussed (e.g., by Rabin 1998) but is probably less important than the three findings discussed here.

2. By public economics I mean the broad range of issues covered by Atkinson and Stiglitz (1980).

3. On this paragraph see Layard (2005a), chapter 3.

4. Helliwell (2003). The variables are the divorce rate, the unemployment rate, the percentage of citizens who say that "most people can be trusted," membership in non-religious organizations, the percentage of citizens who "believe in God," and the quality of government (an index based on four subindices).

5. For much evidence on this section see Layard (2005a), annex 4.1.

6. This whole issue needs more study. For example, if people only compared their incomes with incomes above their own, the optimum tax would be more progressive than otherwise. It is also sometimes suggested that people are more concerned with their rank order in the income distribution than with their relative income. Experiments with the U.S. General Social Survey suggest otherwise, but the case for corrective taxation would be similar whether people cared about rank or relative income (Layard 1980, 740). A third issue is the distinction between income and spending. Frank (1999) concentrates on relative consumption, and makes a further distinction between conspicuous and inconspicuous consumption. However, the comparisons people make do also focus on income, and we do not yet have enough information to distinguish between these variants.

7. Solnick and Hemenway (1998).

8. Brammer, Raleigh, and McGuire (1994).

9. Lucas et al. (2004).

10. On this section see Layard (2005a), annex 4.1.

11. See Loewenstein and Schkade (1999), Loewenstein, O'Donoghue, and Rabin (2003), Frey and Stutzer (2003) and Gilbert and Watson (2001).

12. See Layard (2005b), annex B, which assumes an infinite time horizon. See also Loewenstein et al. (2003).

13. Kahneman and Tversky (2000), 58.

14. Lucas (2003).

15. Helliwell (2003).

16. Similar criticisms apply to Quality-Adjusted Life Years (QALYs), which in the UK are based mainly on healthy people's judgments about how they would feel if ill rather than on studies of how ill people actually feel. A group of us are hoping to remedy this.

17. Layard (2005a), annex 6.1. This result is unlikely to reflect only omitted variables.

18. See Frey and Stutzer (2002) and Gneezy and Rustichini (2000).

19. Economists rarely suggest that businessmen should think directly about the interests of consumers as well as shareholders, on the implausible ground that if a firm did not maximize profits it would go bankrupt.

20. For evidence, see Layard (2005a), 179–180 and accompanying reference.

References

Atkinson, A., and J. Stiglitz. 1980. *Lectures in Public Economics*. London: McGraw-Hill.

Brammer, G., M. Raleigh, and M. McGuire. 1994. "Neurotransmitters and Social Status." In *Social Stratification and Socioeconomic Inequality* vol. 2, ed. L. Ellis, 75–91. Westport, CT: Greenwood.

Frank, R. 1999. *Luxury Fever: Money and Happiness in an Era of Excess*. New York: Free Press.

Frey, B., and A. Stutzer. 2002. *Happiness and Economics: How the Economy and Institutions Affect Well-Being*. Princeton, NJ: Princeton University Press.

Frey, B., and A. Stutzer. 2003. "Economic Consequences of Mispredicting Utility." Working Paper, Institute for Empirical Research in Economics, University of Zurich.

Gilbert, D., and T. Watson. 2001. "Miswanting: Some Problems in the Forecasting of Future Affective States." In *Feeling and Thinking*, ed. J. Forgas, 178–200. Cambridge: Cambridge University Press.

Gneezy, U., and A. Rustichini. 2000. "A Fine is a Price." *Journal of Legal Studies* 29: 1–18.

Helliwell, J. 2003. "How's Life? Combining Individual and National Variables to Explain Subjective Well-Being." *Economic Modelling* 20: 331–360.

Kahneman, D. and A. Tversky, eds. 2000. *Choices, Values and Frames*. New York: Cambridge University Press.

Layard, R. 1980. "Human Satisfactions and Public Policy." *Economic Journal* 90: 737–750.

Layard, R. 2005a. *Happiness: Lessons From a New Science*. New York: Penguin.

Layard, R. 2005b. "Rethinking Public Economics: The Implications of Rivalry and Habit." In *Economics and Happiness: Reality and Paradoxes*, ed. L. Bruni and P. L. Porta, 147–169. Oxford: Oxford University Press.

Loewenstein, G., and D. Schkade. 1999. "Wouldn't It Be Nice? Predicting Future Feelings." In *Well-Being: The Foundations of Hedonic Psychology*, ed. D. Kahneman, E. Diener, and N. Schwarz, 85–108. New York: Russell Sage Foundation.

Loewenstein, G., T. O'Donoghue, and M. Rabin. 2003. "Projection Bias in Predicting Future Utility." *Quarterly Journal of Economics* 118: 1209–1248.

Lucas, R. 2003. "Macroeconomic Priorities." *American Economic Review* 93: 1–14.

Lucas, R., A. Clark, Y. Georgellis, and E. Diener. 2004. "Unemployment Alters the Set-Point for Life Satisfaction." *Psychological Science* 15: 8–13.

Rabin, M. 1998. "Psychology and Economics." *Journal of Economic Literature* 36: 11–46.

Rabin, M. 2000. "Diminishing Marginal Utility of Wealth Cannot Explain Risk Aversion." In *Choices, Values and Frames*, ed. D. Kahneman and A. Tversky, 202–208. New York: Cambridge University Press.

Solnick, S. and D. Hemenway. 1998. "Is More Always Better? A Survey on Positional Concerns." *Journal of Economic Behavior and Organization* 37: 373–383.

Van Praag, M. S. Bernard, and Paul Frijters. 1999. "The Measurement of Welfare and Well-Being: The Leydon Approach." In *Well-Being: The Foundations of Hedonic Psychology*, ed. Daniel Kahnemann, Ed Diener, and Norbest Schwarz, 413–433. New York: Russell Sage Foundation.

7

What Happiness Research Can Tell Us about Self-Control Problems and Utility Misprediction

Alois Stutzer and Bruno S. Frey

7.1 Happiness Research Challenges the Rational Consumer Hypothesis

Neoclassical economic theory relies on revealed behavior to evaluate the utility generated by the option chosen in a particular decision. This procedure assumes that individuals are perfectly informed about what brings how much utility and that they are perfectly capable of maximizing that utility. These assumptions imply that people do not make any systematic mistakes when making decisions. They may, however, commit random errors, but these errors cancel each other out in the aggregate and can therefore be disregarded. These assumptions are extreme and far-reaching. Few noneconomists would share the conviction that individuals cannot systematically err.

This chapter takes a step beyond standard neoclassical economics: (1) systematic errors in consumption are taken seriously, and (2) a strategy is proposed to test the assumption that individuals do not commit any systematic mistakes when consuming, and that they therefore reach the highest achievable utility level given the constraints they face.[1]

A recent revolution in economics—happiness research—has made it possible to approximate individuals' utility in a satisfactory way for many questions (see Kahnemanm, Diener, and Schwarz 1999; Frey and Stutzer 2002a, 2002b; Layard 2005). The consumption *decision* can therefore be separated from the *utility* thereby produced. The research results discussed in this chapter suggest that specific consumption decisions taken by particular individuals are not utility-maximizing, according to the individuals' *own* evaluation.

The empirical challenge of standard economic theory put forward in this chapter discusses concrete consumption decisions—it does not remain at an abstract level. The focus is on smoking and eating habits, watching television, and commuting choice. Thereby we draw strongly on empirical research in which the *dependent* variable is reported subjective well-being or life satisfaction and consumption behavior serves as the main *explanatory* variable. This approach is promising, as it puts forward a proxy for utility to evaluate choice behavior. However, the approach is subject to the same econometric difficulties faced by studies that examine the determinants of behavior, namely, the possibility of omitted variables and endogeneity bias.

Our contribution is structured as follows: section 7.2 discusses the potential of happiness research to explore time-inconsistent consumption behavior due to problems of self-control. Section 7.3 expands the analysis to the misprediction of utility in general. Section 7.4 offers concluding remarks.

7.2   Limited Self-Control and Individual Well-Being

Consumer choice is considered to be the result of rational utility maximization in most micro- and macroeconomic analyses. This view is, however, challenged by research in economics and psychology that reports a large number of different anomalies in a real-life decision-making context. Anomalies are understood in the sense of individual behavior violating certain axioms underlying the rational consumer hypothesis (Kahneman, Knetsch, and Thaler 1991). Two of the most challenging deviations from utility-maximizing consumption choice are due to people having time-inconsistent preferences and mispredicting utility.

Standard economics assumes that people have no self-control problems, but that they are able to make decisions according to their long-term preferences. Viewed this way, consuming goods and pursuing activities that some people consider addictive, or at least bad habits, such as smoking cigarettes, taking cocaine, watching TV, or driving expensive cars, are considered a rational act. Contrary to this view, many people judge their own and other people's consumption behavior as irrational in that they think they would be better off if they consumed fewer goods and cared more for their future well-being. Such self-control problems involve two aspects: myopia and procrastination. In both cases, the present is emphasized at the expense of the long term. When affected by myopia, people focus on consuming in the present and lack discernment or long-range perspective in their thinking and planning, thus undermining their well-being over time. In this respect, generally goods offering immediate benefits at negligible immediate marginal costs are tempting. Procrastination focuses on putting off or delaying an onerous activity more than a person would have liked when evaluating it beforehand. In economics, this inconsistent time preference is most prominently formulated in models of hyperbolic discounting (see, e.g., Laibson 1997). A low discount factor (i.e., a discount factor decreased by β, $\beta \in (0,1)$) is applied between the present and some point in time in the near future, and a constant discount factor δ is applied thereafter. An excellent account of the recent extensive empirical and theoretical literature on time-inconsistent preferences is provided in Frederick, Loewenstein, and O'Donoghue (2002).

Based on revealed preference, it is difficult, if not impossible, to discriminate between the view of consumers as rational actors and consumers mispredicting utility or facing self-control problems. Two extensions of the traditional emphasis on ex ante evaluation and observed decision are insightful. First, the standard economic concept of decision utility is complemented with the concept of experienced utility (Kahneman, Wakker, and Sarin 1997). The latter refers to an individual's evaluation of actual experiences in terms of positive and negative affects or satisfaction. This separation of concepts makes it possible that orderings of experiences systematically diverge from orderings of options derived from observed behavior. The second extension is closely related to the first, and emphasizes ex post evaluations as a valuable source of information about the possibility of bounded rationality in people's decision making. How do people fare after they have made decisions? If anomalies interfere in people's decision making, there might well be a gap between what individuals want and what individuals like.

This opens the question of how the (normative) standard is ascertained and whether seemingly irrational behavior should be judged welfare-reducing because it violates certain time-consistency criteria. While there is an extended debate on this issue (see, e.g., Bernheim and Rangel 2007), we use people's own evaluation as a standard when they are not confronted with a particular decision. The empirical approach proposed in the following section, based on individuals' judgments of their current subjective well-being, corresponds precisely with that point of view.

7.2.1   Methodological Approach: Ex Post Evaluation Based on Experienced Utility

Recent advances in psychology on the measurement of subjective well-being and the adoption of these measures in large surveys allow for a new way of approaching the issue of irrational consumption behavior. With such a proxy measure for utility at hand, it becomes possible to discriminate between competing theories that make the same predictions concerning individual behavior, but differ in what they put forward as individual utility levels. This kind of test is a powerful tool in challenging theories that proved resistant to a multitude of observed behavior patterns.

We discuss and illustrate the new methodological approach for three specific issues, namely smoking, obesity, and TV viewing. First results based on the approach are consistent with complementary evidence, suggesting self-control problems are involved in all three issues.

7.2.2   Smoking

Economic models can make systematically different predictions for the effect of excise taxes on people's utility, while they may all predict reduced consumption of the good that is taxed. People suffer a loss when a normal good is taxed, but experience increased utility when the tax helps to overcome a bad habit. Depending on whether systematic errors in consumption are assumed for particular forms of consumption, like smoking or drinking alcoholic beverages, people might advocate sin taxes to encourage individuals to improve their lot, or oppose them as being discriminatory against particular pleasures in life. In a nutshell, the standard economic model predicts that recent increases in cigarette taxes and restrictions on smoking both reduce smoking and make individuals worse off. A model incorporating self-control problems, however, predicts that smoking is reduced while individual utility is increased.

Research on happiness can contribute to this debate and directly study the effect of, say, tobacco taxes on people's subjective well-being. In two longitudinal analyses across the U.S. and Canadian states, Gruber and Mullainathan (2005) perform such a test with data from the General Social Survey. They analyze the effect of changes in state tobacco taxes on the reported happiness of people who are predicted to smoke at the prevailing tobacco tax. They arrive at the result that a real cigarette tax of 50 cents[2] significantly reduces the likelihood of being unhappy among those with a propensity to be smokers. In fact, they would, with a 50-cent tax, be just as likely to report being unhappy as those not predicted to be smokers (i.e., the proportion of smokers in the lowest happiness category would fall by 7.5 percentage points). This result favors models of time-inconsistent smoking behavior, in which people have problems with self-control.[3] Moreover, the result shows that price increases can serve as a self-commitment device.

Problems of self-control with smoking also arise due to temptation (Bernheim and Rangel 2004). Alternative tests would relate the happiness of potential smokers to clean air laws. These tests would capture exogenous changes in cues or moments of temptation. A comparison of results would allow the assessment of the boundaries of prices as a means of affecting self-regulation.

Research findings on subjective well-being with regard to self-control problems with smoking complement other evidence suggesting self-control problems in a systematic way. There is a large market offering all kinds of drugs and therapies to people who want to stop smoking. In fact, eight out of ten smokers would like to quit smoking and try it every eight and a half months on average (Gruber and Koszegi 2001).

7.2.3 Obesity

The marked increase in people being either overweight or obese has been the epidemiological landslide of the last two decades in many Western countries.[4] In many European countries, the prevalence of obesity has risen threefold or more since the 1980s (World Health Organization Europe 2005). People in Europe have now, on average, a BMI of almost 26.5. The percentage of obese adults varies between 7.7 percent in Switzerland and 22.4 percent in the United Kingdom and the Slovak Republic (see figure 7.1). Being overweight accounts for 10–13 percent of deaths and 8–15 percent of healthy days lost due to disability and premature mortality in the European Region (World Health Organization 2002). In the United States, adult obesity rates have more than doubled since the 1980s. In the year 2000, three in ten adults were classified as obese (Flegal et al. 2002).

A debate has started about the economic causes of this phenomenon, as well as its consequences (see, e.g., Cutler, Glaeser, and Shapiro 2003; Finkelstein, Ruhm, and Kosa 2005). Increased obesity has been explained by the relationship of energy expenditure to energy intake. Energy expenditure is lower nowadays because manual labor has been

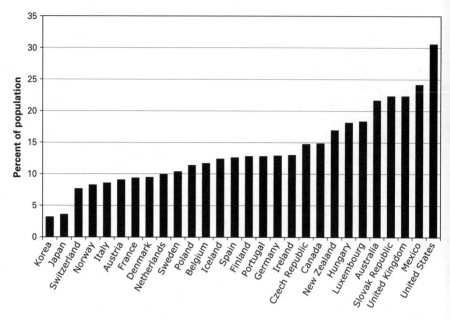

Figure 7.1
Obesity across countries. Percentage of population aged 15 and over with a BMI greater
than 30 (2003 or latest available year). *Source*: OECD (2005).

replaced by more sedentary work, due to technological changes (Lakdawalla and Philipson 2002). However, this trend started long before
the obesity epidemic took off. The increase in calories consumed fits
the obesity pattern better and is of sufficient magnitude to account for
its increased prevalence (Putnum and Allshouse 1999). In particular,
higher snack calories are responsible for higher energy intake for men
and even more so for women (Cutler, Glaeser, and Shapiro 2003).

What is the economic rationale behind the shifting energy household? Looking at relative prices suggests that, since the early 1980s,
they decreased for calorie-dense foods and drinks relative to fruits and
vegetables, which are less energy-dense (Finkelstein, Ruhm, and Kosa
2005). These price reductions were made possible by new technologies
in food production, in particular for prepackaged and prepared food.
People have reacted by eating more frequently (snacking), eating big-
ger portions, spending less time on food preparation, and thus gaining
weight.

This brings up the question of how these increases in body weight,
causing considerable harm to people's health, are to be evaluated. Do

people eat too much? What is the standard for "too much" if people have free choice about when and how much they want to eat? Traditional economics advises us to resort to consumer sovereignty under such conditions. "Even with full information about the benefits of physical activity, the nutrient content of food, and the health consequences of obesity, some fraction of the population will optimally choose to engage in a lifestyle that leads to weight gain because the costs (in terms of time, money, and opportunity costs) of not doing so are just too high" (Finkelstein, Ruhm, and Kosa 2005, 252). This might apply all the more because health insurance and taxpayers finance a large amount of the monetary costs of obesity.

However, the possibility of individually consuming "too much" food is excluded by assumption in the revealed preference approach.[5] In order to uphold this view, one would have to reconcile the prevalence of obesity with other behavioral regularities, like people spending large sums of money on diets and health clubs, or people's weight yo-yoing as they go from one diet to the next. An alternative approach accepts that people might face self-control problems when exposed to the temptation of immediate gratification from food when they are hungry or have a craving for something sweet, fatty, or salty.[6] Evidence on subjective well-being can contribute to a broader understanding of obesity, as it provides information about people's evaluation of their situation *after* they have decided about their food and beverage consumption. If technical progress in producing fatty food is indeed a major driving force behind obesity, the standard economic model predicts that individuals will become heavier and happier. However, if individuals have self-control problems, we would expect them to become heavier and less happy.

In a first step, it can be studied whether obese people are less satisfied. According to an empirical investigation for roughly eight thousand young women, obesity is related to lower satisfaction with work, family relationships, partner relationships, and social activities (but not satisfaction with friendships) (Ball, Crawford, and Kenardy 2004). Other studies report correlations between obesity and symptoms of depression, whereby the risk of depression is higher for obese women than obese men (e.g., McElroy et al. 2004; Needham and Crosnoe 2005). These findings, however, provide only limited insights, as the correlations can be due to third variables affecting both eating behavior and subjective well-being, or because low life satisfaction and stress can lead to obesity. The latter has been studied in a longitudinal analysis for 5,867 pairs of twins (Korkeila et al. 1998). It is found that high levels of stress and low levels of life satisfaction are both predictors of weight gain over six years and for certain groups of people over fifteen years of age. Another panel study addresses the reverse relationship. Taking baseline mental health into account, it analyzes the long-term consequences of obesity, finding an increased risk for depression (Roberts et al. 2002). These results are valuable in assessing the relevance of the phenomenon, but they have to be supplemented with further evidence to identify the contribution of self-control problems to the link between obesity and subjective well-being.

Alternatively, it is possible to characterize conditions where attempts to recapture self-control are encouraged. It is to be expected that those people who stand to lose a lot from being obese, or who have access to resources, are more successful in controlling their behavior. For example, obese women seem to suffer a salary and promotion penalty (see the references in Finkelstein, Ruhm, and Kosa 2005). They have strong incentives to control their body weight and might suffer the most when their lack of willpower leads to failure. Consistent with this point of view, people in the top income quintile, or in professions with a low prevalence of obesity, report the largest well-being costs of obesity (Felton and Graham 2005).

There are two related open questions stemming from these approaches. The first is regarding the nature of limited self-control. People are exposed to many opportunities with low immediate marginal costs but high marginal benefits. The question arises whether people with a self-control problem make myopic decisions when faced with all, or most, of these opportunities, or whether they can control some challenges to self-control, but find it too difficult to control all of them. The latter view fits in with the idea that there is a limited capacity for self-regulation. Resisting one temptation may result in poorer regulation of a concurrent desire for immediate gratification, or vice versa (Muraven, Tice, and Baumeister 1998).[7] This mechanism might be relevant in understanding the interplay between obesity and smoking (Gruber and Frakes 2006).

The second, closely related question, is whether reduced willpower as such, rather than its consequences, is responsible for lower well-being. People who experience self-control problems might suffer reduced self-esteem, and thus lower subjective well-being. Related empirical evidence is found in a community sample of two thousand adults (Greeno et al. 1998). In addition to a higher BMI, the lack of perceived eating control was also associated with lower satisfaction with life. For men, it was only the lack of eating control that was correlated with reported subjective well-being.

7.2.4 TV Viewing

The rational consumer spends the optimal amount of time watching TV. This time seems to constitute a substantial amount of people's leisure time. In many countries, the overall population watches as many hours of TV as it devotes to paid work (Corneo 2005). The largest number of heavy TV viewers[8] in Europe is found in Greece. As much as 36.8 percent of the population (age fifteen and older) reports that they spend three hours a day or more watching TV. At the other end of the ranking, only 8.4 percent of Switzerland's population are heavy TV viewers (see figure 7.2). In contrast to the rational choice point of view, the same extent of TV viewing might also be observed when viewers have difficulty switching off their TV set, and would actually have preferred to watch less TV if asked ex post, or for some, even ex ante. The

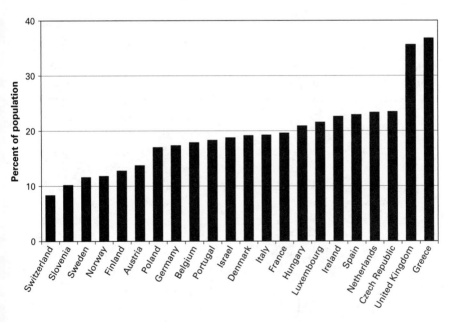

Figure 7.2
Percentage of heavy TV viewers across Europe. Percentage of population aged 15 and over who spend more than three hours watching TV during a normal weekday. *Source:* Frey, Benesch, and Stutzer (2005), based on the first wave of the European Social Survey 2002–2003.

two views lead to systematically different evaluations of the large expansion of cable TV in the 1990s. The standard economic model predicts an increase in individual well-being with more TV viewing. In contrast, a model based on individuals with self-control problems predicts more TV viewing, but reduced happiness.

The reason why TV may lend itself to overconsumption is mainly due to the immediate benefits and the negligible immediate marginal cost of engaging in this activity. One just has to push a button. In contrast to going to the cinema, the theater, or any outdoor activity, there is no need to be appropriately dressed before leaving the house and no need to buy a ticket or to reserve a seat in advance. Watching TV does not require any special physical or cognitive abilities (Kubey and Csikszentmihalyi 1990, 173). Unlike other leisure activities, TV viewing does not need to be coordinated with other persons. It is quite possible to sit alone in front of the TV, while other leisure activities, such as tennis or golf, require a partner with similar time availability and similar preferences. As a consequence, watching TV has, compared to other leisure activities, an exceedingly low or nonexistent entry barrier. At the same time, it offers entertainment value and is considered to be one of the best ways of reducing stress. Moreover, while watching TV, immediate marginal costs are even lower and having a remote control is an invitation to ultra short-term optimization (zapping). Many of the costs resulting from such consumption behavior are not experienced immediately, or not predicted at all. The negative effects of not enough sleep, for example, only arise the next day, and the consequences of underinvestment in social contacts, education, or career take much longer to appear. An increase in one's material aspirations, due to the rich, famous, and beautiful being overrepresented on the screen, might not be foreseen at all. These characteristics of the consumption good induce many individuals to fall prey to excessive TV viewing.[9]

In this chapter, the role of self-control problems in TV viewing is addressed with regard to consumers' utility. It is hypothesized that, for people facing similar restrictions, heavy TV viewing indicates impeded self-control rather than a love of TV. Accordingly, heavy TV consumption is expected to result in lower utility. In addition, similar to the argument on smoking in section 7.2.2, an increase in the price of TV viewing would be expected to increase the well-being of TV viewers with a self-control problem.

For most consumers, however, the price of viewing an additional hour of TV is zero. It is thus not easy to pursue the approach proposed by Gruber and Mullainathan (2005) to test the rational consumer hypothesis (at least as long as pay-per-view is not more common). An interesting alternative might be the extreme case of no TV. While it is definitely not optimal, it might be compared to unrestrained consumption. The introduction of TV would represent a situation for a possible comparison. However, in most countries, this technological innovation gained ground too early in the last century to be able to match it with data on reported subjective well-being.

There are, however, some natural experiments about access to TV that provide insights as to the consequences of TV for factors closely related to individual well-being. A certain Canadian city was unable to receive any TV signals up until 1973 because of its location in a steep valley. Otherwise it was similar to two cities in the vicinity used as control cases. A study by Williams (1986) suggests that the introduction of TV crowded out other activities, in particular those outside the home, such as taking part in sports activities or attending clubs. It also reduced the reading abilities and creative thinking of children and fostered more aggressive behavior and stereotyped ideas about gender roles. TV also reduced the problem-solving capacities of adults. Another study by Hennigan et al. (1982), based on a natural experiment, takes a look at the advent of TV in the United States, which, due to technical reasons, took place at different times in different places. Petty crime, but not violent crime, increased. Observing the same time period, Gentzkow (2006) finds that the advent of TV reduced voter turnout.

So far, we are therefore restricted to studying the subjective well-being of heavy TV viewers, controlling for many individual characteristics. Such an approach is followed in a large study on TV viewing and life satisfaction for twenty-two European countries in 2002 and 2003 (Frey, Benesch, and Stutzer 2007). It is found that the more people spend time watching TV, the lower is their reported satisfaction with life, ceteris paribus. The result of the econometric analysis is consistent with the hypothesis that heavy TV viewers suffer significant reductions in their utility because they are unable to fully control their TV consumption: they watch too much, even according to their own evaluation.

Where do the costs of the misallocation of time come from? There are lost alternatives in the present, such as engaging in more stimulating activities or socializing. It is found, for example, that people watching a lot of TV spend less time with family and friends and invest less in relational goods in general (Bruni and Stanca 2007). But there are additional future costs. One might be tired the next morning because of a lack of sleep. Seen long-term, people might change their beliefs about the world and about the sources of well-being. In particular, the exposure to the healthy, wealthy, and good-looking people on TV is expected to increase people's aspirations with regard to their own body, but also with regard to their consumption standard. There is substantial research on the relationship between TV viewing and materialism, (e.g., Kasser 2002) and TV viewing and financial satisfaction (Bruni and Stanca 2006; Layard 2005). Most studies find a positive correlation between extensive TV consumption and those outcomes related to lower subjective well-being. In the study for twenty-two European countries mentioned earlier (Frey, Benesch, and Stutzer 2007), half of the correlation between TV consumption and life satisfaction can be attributed to heavy TV viewers having lower financial satisfaction, attributing more importance to being rich, feeling less safe, trusting other people less, and thinking that they are involved less in social activities than are their peers.[10] Because these costs are not experienced immediately, individuals with time-inconsistent preferences are unable to adhere to the amount of TV viewing they planned or that, in retrospect, they would consider optimal for themselves. This tendency is aggravated when people mispredict future costs because they underestimate utility from socializing and neglect changes in preference due to TV consumption.

7.3   The Misprediction of Utility or Overvalued Choice Options

Standard economics assumes that people can successfully predict future utility; at least, no systematic deviations are expected. If there were any, individuals would correct them in the long run by learning. Scitovsky (1976) criticized this view as "unscientific" because "it seemed to rule out—as a logical impossibility—any conflict between what man chooses to get and what will best satisfy him" (4). In many careful experiments and surveys, psychologists have studied people's success in forecasting the utility they were about to experience (for reviews, see Loewenstein and Schkade 1999; Wilson and Gilbert 2003). While they find that people accurately predict whether an emotional experience primarily elicits good or bad feelings, people often hold incorrect intuitive theories about the determinants of happiness. For instance, they overestimate the impact of specific life events on their experienced well-being with regard to intensity, as well as with regard to duration.

The standard economic model of consumer decisions is probably appropriate for most goods and activities and for most situations. It is also appropriate when individuals make random prediction errors. There are, however, situations in which people have to make a tradeoff and decide among different activities, goods, or options that systematically differ in the extent to which their future utility can be correctly predicted. There are options, or attributes of options, that are more salient than others when making a decision, and are thus relatively overvalued. If people choose options according to this evaluation, their experienced utility is lower than what they expected and lower than what they could have experienced if they would not have mispredicted their utility. Moreover, they consume different goods with different attributes and pursue different activities than in a situation where no option in the choice set would have special salience.

7.3.1   Why Are Some Options Overvalued?

We see four major sources for systematic over- and undervaluation of choice options. For all of them, we derive predictions with regard to the actual goods and activities that receive too much or too little emphasis when people make decisions.

7.3.1.1   Adaptation Is Underestimated   Research on affective forecasting shows that people overestimate their reactions to specific events because they are embedded within other daily life events they are not currently aware of. For instance, seeing one's favorite soccer team winning is experienced simultaneously with other events occurring in the environment. Another example of errors in predicting emotions is that people underestimate their ability to successfully cope with negative events. Young academics might be particularly worried about life after a negative tenure decision. Gilbert et al. (1998) asked assistant professors to predict how happy they would be after a positive and a negative tenure decision. The answers were compared with the reported subjective well-being of academics affected by a tenure decision made five or fewer years previously. Although assistants predicted they would be less happy during the first five years after being turned down, there was no statistically significant difference between those who had and had not received tenure. Similarly, assistants also overestimated the positive impact of receiving tenure on their subjective well-being. The general insight is that people usually have biased expectations about the intensity and duration of emotions, in the sense that the emotional impact is often lower than predicted because people adapt more than they foresee. Options are thus overvalued to the extent that adaptation is neglected. Overvaluation of an opportunity is at a maximum if full adaptation occurs, but adaptation is neglected. In contrast, overvaluation is at a minimum, or nil, if there is no adaptation or adaptation is perfectly foreseen. Because of people's tendency to neglect adaptation, misprediction is, in general, at a maximum for options providing stimuli that fade away when repeatedly experienced. While there is considerable evidence for adaptation (for a survey, see Frederick and Loewenstein 1999), there is no systematic understanding of the extent to which people can adapt to different stimuli and the extent to which they can foresee it. The emerging picture suggests, however, that adaptation is more likely to be underestimated for goods and options serving extrinsic material desires than for those satisfying intrinsic and social needs.

7.3.1.2   Distorted Memory of Past Experiences   When individuals make decisions about future consumption or allocation of time in the absence of information about their current experience, they have to resort to their respective experiences in the past. People reflect on specific moments from the past or access generalizations about likely emotions in a particular type of situation (for a discussion, see Robinson and Clore 2002). The specific information available has priority in people's judgment. Therefore, the more memorable moments of an experience disproportionately affect retrospective assessments of feelings (Kahneman 1999). What counts as "more memorable" tends to be the most intense moment (peak) and the most recent moment (end) of an emotional incident. This peak-end rule, or duration neglect, has been established in many experimental tests (Kahneman 2003). Accordingly, there is the potential for systematic misprediction if people base their judgments on retrospection. Goods and activities related to short-term experiences—in particular, peak emotions—are overvalued relative to those providing long-term experiences of moderate but enduring positive feelings.

7.3.1.3   Rationalization of Decisions   Individuals have a strong urge to justify their decisions, both to themselves and to other persons (for predecision justification, see Shafir, Simonson, and Tversky 1993). It is not only predicted consumption utility that, for example, affects the decision to buy something, but also whether people think they are getting a bargain (Thaler 1999). There is a general tendency to resist affective influences and to take rationalistic attributes into account when making decisions. Hsee et al. (2003) call this reason-based choice "lay rationalism." In experiments they find, for example, that people focus their decisions on absolute economic payoffs and play down noneconomic concerns. Other experiments find that people emphasize aspects of events that are easy to articulate and neglect aspects that are important for experience when they are asked to give reasons during the decision-making phase (e.g., Wilson and Schooler 1991). Similarly, people seem to base their choices on rules and principles and bypass predictions on the experiential consequences of their choices (e.g., Prelec and Herrnstein 1991). These arguments imply, however, that people do not optimally consider various attributes of different options so that utility would be maximized. In sum, choice options for which it is easy to provide rationalistic justifications are overvalued relative to options that lack a handy rationale.

7.3.1.4 Intuitive Theories about the Sources of Future Utility   So far, the reasons for misprediction link the systematic overvaluation of some goods relative to others to the characteristics of these goods with regard to adaptation, memorability, and rationalization. In addition, there is a reason for misprediction that builds directly on people's beliefs. People have very diverse intuitive theories about what makes them happy (for a discussion, see Loewenstein and Schkade 1999). These beliefs have a direct influence on people predicting future utility and can cause them to overvalue some options compared to others. Moreover, these beliefs play a role because they shape the reconstruction of past emotions and make them consistent with current self-conceptions or beliefs (Ross 1989). Thus, intuitive theories interact with the three previously discussed sources of misprediction. In predicting utility, they can accentuate biases that lie in the nature of the goods. However, they can also counteract people's tendency to overvalue some goods relative to others. The fourth source of misprediction is thus the least specified.

An important belief refers to acquisition and possession as central goals on the path to happiness; in other words, to materialism (e.g., see Tatzel 2002 for a discussion in economics). It has been empirically studied whether people who pursue this belief are in fact correctly guided and enjoy a higher well-being than those following other beliefs. It is found that people with material life goals report lower self-esteem and life satisfaction than people with non-material life goals (e.g., Sirgy 1998; Kasser 2002). This correlation is probably partly due to confounding unobserved personality traits and reversed causality due to a compensatory reaction of people with low subjective well-being. However, it might also indicate that people who believe intuitively in materialism are prone to mispredict future utility.

Based on the four sources affecting the valuation of choice options when people make decisions, two propositions can be derived:

1. When faced with a decision, individuals *overconsume* goods and activities with overvalued attributes relative to those goods and activities lacking salient attributes.

2. The systematic distortions in allocation due to utility misprediction *reduce individuals' experienced utility* according to their *own* best interests.

7.3.2   Related Phenomena

The hypothesis that people systematically mispredict utility when faced with some tradeoffs links up to various strands of literature where similar phenomena have been identified.

The aspect of underestimated adaptation to new situations has been neatly introduced in a theoretical model of intertemporal decision making by Loewenstein, O'Donoghue, and Rabin (2003). Based on their model of projection bias, various phenomena can be modeled, like the misguided purchase of durable goods or consumption profiles with too much consumption early on in life. Misprediction of utility thus provides an alternative to seemingly irrational saving behavior that is usually addressed in a framework of self-control problems.

It has been argued that the "work-life balance" of individuals today is distorted. People are induced to work too much and to disregard other aspects of life. This proposition has been forcefully put forward for the United States, where individuals are said to be "overworked" (Schor 1991). This is consistent with misprediction of utility, whereby it is argued that people overvalue income relative to leisure.

Competing for status involves negative externalities and therefore too much effort is invested in gaining status and acquiring "positional goods" (Frank 1985, 1999). Misprediction of utility magnifies the distortions of competing for status in consumption if utility from consumption is overvalued.

Mispredicting utility might also explain people's behavior in court. It has been empirically shown (Tyler, Huo, and Lind 1999) that, when it comes to making decisions, individuals tend to prefer institutions promising favorable outcomes. But ex post they state that they would have preferred an institution that put more emphasis on (just) procedures. This finding suggests that people tend to overvalue outcome relative to procedural utility. Procedural utility is the satisfaction derived from the process itself rather than from its outcome (see the survey by Frey, Benz, and Stutzer 2004).

There is a long tradition in economics arguing that individuals tend to focus too much on material goods and disregard goods providing nonmaterial benefits (Lane 1991; Lebergott 1993). Most important, Scitovsky (1976) claimed that "comfort goods" are overconsumed compared to goods providing "stimulation." The former are described as defensive activities, providing protection from negative affect. They consist of the consumer goods achieved through rapid productivity growth. In contrast, stimulation comes from creative activities providing novelty, surprise, variety, and complexity. These aspects emphasize the renewal of pleasurable experiences. According to Scitovsky, stimulation is at a competitive disadvantage relative to comfort goods because it has a higher cost of access and because consumers are myopic about the future benefits derived from stimulating activities. The argument about systematic errors in consumption, however, also fits in with a framework of mispredicting utility.

7.3.3 Empirical Approaches and Findings
The misprediction of future utility can be related to macrophenomena like overconsumption, outcome orientation (relative to procedural considerations), and overworking. However, whether misprediction of utility is involved in these phenomena is very difficult to assess from observed behavior alone. How can we judge whether the costs of running a big car are due to an overvaluation of the pleasure of driving a vehicle that will not even fit on most parking lots?

We propose to study data on reported subjective well-being in order to better understand consumers' behavior and difficulties in decision making. So far, empirical research on people mispredicting utility is very scattered. While there is evidence for mistakes in affective forecasting, we are not aware of any evaluation on whether there are systematic differences in over- and undervaluation of some goods and activities. We briefly describe some research designs and report some results that provide initial insights.

First, people's difficulties in predicting the intensity and duration of emotions are well documented in research on affective forecasting (see, e.g., Loewenstein and Adler 1995; Wilson and Gilbert 2003). Standard research designs are prospective longitudinal studies about self-reported emotions. People are asked how happy they expect themselves to be after some event has happened or some option has been chosen. These predictions are then compared with reported subjective well-being when actually experiencing the new situation. There are several limits to this design. (1) Usually only predictions for changes in the near future are assessed. (2) The way in which scales of measurement are interpreted can change over time, for example, due to maturation or a change in the anchor. (3) Predictions might also affect actual feelings or even become self-fulfilling prophecies. Some of these problems can be eliminated by conducting studies between subjects, where one group's predictions are contrasted with a different group's actual reports (see, e.g., Gilbert et al. 1998).

A second approach is based on individual welfare functions, a concept developed by van Praag (1968). A cardinal relationship between income and welfare is established by asking individuals to add income intervals to a number of verbally described income levels.[11] When answering this "income evaluation question," respondents should take into account their own situation with respect to family and job. Up to nine verbal descriptions ranging from "excellent" to "very bad" are grouped along an interval scale between 0 and 1. The bounded scale reflects that the individual welfare function measures relative welfare as perceived only by the individual. Each individual evaluates his or her income by comparing it with the worst possible position and a position of complete satiation. Thus, the translation of the verbal qualifications results in a sequence of points $(y_i, U(y_i))$ for each respondent, where y_i is the income level and $U(y_i)$ is the number in the $[0, 1]$-interval. It can be shown (van Praag 1968) that the individual evaluations of income $U(y)$ correspond closely to a lognormal distribution function

$$U(y) = \int_0^y \frac{1}{\sigma\sqrt{2\pi}} \cdot \frac{1}{t} \exp\left[-\frac{1}{2}\left(\frac{\ln(t) - \mu}{\sigma}\right)^2\right] dt$$

$$\equiv L(y; \mu, \sigma) \equiv N[\ln(y); \mu, \sigma],$$

with $L(y; \mu, \sigma)$ the lognormal distribution function with parameters μ and σ and $N[\ln(y); \mu, \sigma]$ the normal distribution function with average μ and variance σ^2.

For each individual, the parameters can be econometrically esti-
mated. The psychological interpretation of μ and σ is as follows: $\exp(\mu)$
is the median value of the lognormal distribution, meaning it fixes the
income level corresponding to an evaluation of 0.5. For a high "want
parameter" μ, and therefore $\exp(\mu)$, an individual requires a high
income to reach a welfare evaluation of 0.5. σ reflects the "welfare
sensitivity;" it determines the slope of the individual welfare function
around the median value $\exp(\mu)$. An individual with a high σ evaluates a broad range of incomes differently from zero and one and thus
does not react sensitively to ex ante income changes.

Individual welfare functions have been estimated for several countries with good results, particularly for the Netherlands and Belgium
(see, e.g., van Herwaarden, Kapteyn, and van Praag 1977). A particularly interesting aspect is the connection established between the want
parameter μ and income y, $\mu = \alpha_0 + \alpha_1 \ln(y)$, which measures the
"preference drift" due to a change in income. A positive coefficient for
income ($\alpha_1 > 0$) suggests that the ex post evaluation of a higher income
is smaller than its ex ante evaluation. In other words, rich people evaluate a higher income as being just "sufficient" than do poor people.
Empirical estimates for the Netherlands and Belgium yield a positive
value for α_1. Its magnitude of between 0.55 and 0.65 suggests that
more than half of an ex ante expected welfare increase of higher
income evaporates when higher income is reached. This can be interpreted as adaptation to a higher income standard that is *not*
anticipated.

In a study for Switzerland, the framework is extended and linked to
reported life satisfaction (Stutzer 2004). Individuals' income evaluations are used as a proxy for income aspirations. It is found that the
positive effect on life satisfaction generated by a higher income level of
a particular percentage is entirely offset if income aspirations are of the
same higher magnitude. Thus, it is the discrepancy between income
and income aspirations that is correlated with individuals' reported
subjective well-being. The positive effects of higher income are overestimated, as found in the study by van Herwaarden, Kapteyn, and
van Praag (1977) mentioned earlier. Income rated as sufficient (as a
proxy for income aspirations) increases, ceteris paribus, by 4.2 percent
for a 10 percent increase in income.

Third, in order to get an idea of any systematic asymmetries in adaptation, the findings for income (or consumption) can be compared to
the goods and activities that are often involved when people make

trade-offs involving a higher material standard of living. It has been found that individuals do not adapt their utility evaluation in the case of undesirable experiences that inhibit intrinsic need satisfaction. In particular, severe health problems, like chronic illness, or illness that gets progressively worse, reduce autonomy and lead to lasting reductions in reported subjective well-being (e.g., Easterlin 2005). Widowers suffer, on average, for years from their lot (e.g., Stroebe, Stroebe, and Hansson 1993). Having a job includes many aspects that provide flow experiences and satisfy intrinsic needs, like being in the company of workmates, applying expertise, and experiencing autonomy. Accordingly, being unemployed is repeatedly found to have high negative nonpecuniary effects on people's subjective well-being, with little habituation (Clark 2002). By way of contrast, having a job with a high degree of autonomy, as in the case of self-employed people, is related to high job satisfaction. Frey and Benz (2003), for example, show that the self-employed derive more utility from their work than people employed by an organization, if controlled for income earned or hours worked. Moreover, they can explain this difference using people's evaluation of the use of initiative at their workplace and their satisfaction with the actual work itself (25). Intrinsic attributes also characterize the work of volunteers. In fact, it is found that people doing volunteer work are more satisfied with their life in general, even when taking the possibility of reverse causality into account (Meier and Stutzer 2007).

Fourth, a comprehensive approach is proposed by Frey and Stutzer (2004) for a set of individual choices, all involving a tradeoff with commuting. In an empirical test of people mispredicting utility, people's decision to commute for longer or shorter hours is analyzed. The commuting decision involves the trade-off between salary or housing quality on the one hand, and commuting time on the other. Rational utility maximizers only commute when they are compensated. However, when people overestimate utility from goods serving extrinsic desires, they are expected to opt for too much commuting and suffer lower utility. It is found that commuting is far from being fully compensated and, on average, people who commute one hour one way would need an additional 40 percent of their monthly salary to be as satisfied with their life as people who do not commute. There is, however, significant variation between people. Incomplete compensation is much stronger for people with strong extrinsic life goals.

Based on the previous findings, we think that for many people there is a tension when they have to trade off material and nonmaterial or social goods and activities. Misprediction of utility is quite likely across these option categories. When people make trade-offs, material factors get more attention and are overvalued due to the neglect of adaptation, to rationalization, and to memory biases. There are consequences with regard to behavior—material goods are overconsumed—and with regard to individual well-being—people are less well off than they could be without mispredicting utility.

7.4   Concluding Remarks

Standard neoclassical economic theory assumes that individuals do not commit any systematic errors in their consumption decisions because they know their own preferences best and are able to make the consequent decisions. The main message of this chapter is that it is necessary to go beyond this narrow approach. One should take into account the methodological advances made possible by happiness research. They allow us to empirically test whether individuals do or do not make errors, rather than simply assuming that they do not, as is the case in revealed preference theory. The possibility to proxy utility in a satisfactory way using life satisfaction or happiness enables economists to empirically study the difference between decisions made and the satisfaction produced. We see a large potential in using this approach to study many areas of consumption choice, and to refine the initial findings on smoking, eating, TV viewing, and commuting.

It should be noted that this analysis is not a normative evaluation from the point of view of a benevolent social planner. Rather, the focus is on the mistakes in consumption that individuals commit according to their own perception, placing people in a less favorable position in terms of their own utility evaluation.

The systematic errors in consumption identified and discussed for four specific areas are no cause for immediate government intervention. It is very likely that individuals are quite capable of making satisfactory consumption decisions for most of the goods most of the time. Moreover, it is doubtful whether the government is able to make better decisions in the interests of the persons concerned (Frey and Stutzer 2006). Nevertheless, our results raise the question of whether activities, typically subject to excess consumption, should be subsidized by the public, and whether taxes in fact produce the extent of dead weight losses claimed in standard public economics. With regard to subsidies, this applies in particular to public TV and commuting, which in many countries are highly subsidized by the government. With regard to taxes, tobacco taxes are a case in point, as they may not only serve as a means to generate revenue to finance health care, but may also help to overcome problems of self-control. We think, however, that a more effective way to deal with individual errors in consumption is to help individuals make more reasoned decisions, enabling them to get a clearer picture of the future utility of particular consumption goods and services. In some cases, a "cooling-down period" may be beneficial. In other cases, people could be informed about self-control mechanisms.

Notes

We are grateful for helpful remarks from Christine Benesch, Matthias Benz, Andrew Clark, Lorenz Goette, Bart Golsteyn, John Komlos, and Bernard van Praag.

1. We are aware that there are specific situations in which the standard economic model rules out certain types of behavior and mere observation of a certain action rejects the standard economic model. Studies successfully pursuing this approach are very rare, however. Two important exceptions documenting such behavior are DellaVigna and Malmendier (2006), who examine gym attendance under different contracts, and Skiba and Tobacman (2005), who show that certain types of payday loans would always be rejected by time-consistent individuals.

2. The average real (in 1999 US$) cigarette tax in the United States is 31.6 cents in the sample (Gruber and Mullainathan 2005, 5).

3. In another study, the negative internality from suffering a self-control problem and being a smoker is assessed (Jürges 2004). The monthly compensation required to make a smoker as well off as a nonsmoker is estimated to be approximately 500 euros. However, the effects of smoking on life satisfaction were not identified, based on changes in exogenous conditions restricting the possibilities to smoke.

4. Overweight and obese are defined relative to people's weight to height ratio in metric units, as captured in the body mass index BMI: BMI = kg/m2. Adults with a BMI $\geq$ 30 kg/m2 are classified as obese and those with a BMI $\geq$ 25 kg/m2 as overweight.

5. Other lines of argument within revealed preference emphasize the variation in individual discount rates for outcomes in the future as an explanation for increased obesity (e.g., Komlos, Smith, and Bogin 2004). In their empirical study, Borghans and Golsteyn (2006) conclude, however, that it is unlikely that BMI increased because of an increase in the time discount rate.

6. The self-control issue is explicitly addressed in Cutler, Glaeser, and Shapiro (2003), whereby its relevance in the assessment of consumers' welfare is discounted because it would require only some exercise on the part of overweight people to balance their energy household. Observed inactivity thus seems to indicate that overweight people do not suffer from their body mass. However, the trade-off is calculated assuming that people have self-control problems with eating, but not with taking physical exercise. This does not fit our casual observations.

7. People's ability to self-regulate in a certain domain may not only depend on the effort they invest in other domains, but also on effort invested in the successful performance of tasks in daily work and family life (if they involve self-regulatory exertion of effort). This line of argument might be pursued to explore the relation between increased demands on women at home and on the job on the one hand, and female obesity on the other hand.

8. By "heavy TV viewers" we mean people who spend a great deal of time watching TV, and not TV viewers who are overweight (although watching a lot of TV is sedentary and invites people to snack, which can in turn lead to obesity).

9. Regarding television consumption, there is some (anecdotal) evidence that individuals may have self-control problems: 40 percent of U.S. adults and 70 percent of U.S. teenagers admit that they watch too much TV (Kubey and Czikszentmihalyi 2002).

10. While these correlations are suggestive, it has to be kept in mind that third factors could be driving differences in the different attitudes as well as in TV viewing.

11. For example, "Please try to indicate what you consider to be an appropriate amount for each of the following cases. Under my/our conditions, I would call a net household income per [month] of: about ____ very bad; . . . about ____ very good. Please enter an answer on each line" (van Praag 1993, 367).

References

Ball, Kylie, David Crawford, and Justin Kenardy. 2004. "Longitudinal Relationships among Overweight, Life Satisfaction, and Aspirations in Young Women." *Obesity Research* 12, no. 6: 1019–1030.

Bernheim, Douglas, and Antonio Rangel. 2004. Addiction and Cue-Triggered Decision Processes. *American Economic Review* 94, no. 5: 1558–1590.

Bernheim, Douglas, and Antonio Rangel. 2007. "Behavioral Public Economics: Welfare and Policy Analysis with Nonstandard Decision-Makers." Forthcoming in *Behavioral Economics and Its Applications*, ed. Peter A. Diamond and Hannu Vartiainen. Princeton, NJ: Princeton University Press.

Borghans, Lex, and Bart H. H. Golsteyn. 2006. "Time Discounting and the Body Mass Index: Evidence from the Netherlands." *Economics and Human Biology* 4, no. 1: 39–61.

Bruni, Luigino, and Luca Stanca. 2006. "Income Aspirations, Television and Happiness: Evidence from the World Values Surveys." *Kyklos* 59, no. 2: 209–225.

Bruni, Luigino, and Luca Stanca. 2007. "Watching Alone: Relational Goods, Television and Happiness." Forthcoming in *Journal of Economic Behavior and Organization*.

Clark, Andrew E. 2002. "A Note on Unhappiness and Unemployment Duration." Mimeo., DELTA, Paris.

Corneo, Giacomo. 2005. "Work and Television." *European Journal of Political Economy* 21, no. 1: 99–113.

Cutler, David M., Edward L. Glaeser, and Jesse M. Shapiro. 2003. "Why Have Americans Become More Obese?" *Journal of Economic Perspectives* 17, no. 3: 93–118.

DellaVigna, Stefano, and Ulrike Malmendier. 2006. "Paying Not to Go to the Gym." *American Economic Review* 96, no. 3: 694–719.

Easterlin, Richard A. 2005. "Building a Better Theory of Well-Being." In *Economics and Happiness: Framing the Analysis*, ed. Luigino Bruni and Pier Luigi Porta, 29–64. Oxford: Oxford University Press.

Felton, Andrew, and Carol Graham. 2005. "Variance in Obesity across Cohorts and Countries: A Norms-Based Explanation Using Happiness Surveys." Mimeo., The Brookings Institution.

Finkelstein, Eric A., Christopher J. Ruhm, and Katherine M. Kosa. 2005. "Economic Causes and Consequences of Obesity." *Annual Review of Public Health* 26: 239–257.

Flegal, Katherine M., Margaret D. Carroll, Cynthia L. Ogden, and Clifford L. Johnson. 2002. "Prevalence and Trends in Obesity among U.S. Adults, 1999–2000." *Journal of the American Medical Association* 288, no. 14: 1723–1727.

Frank, Robert H. 1985. *Choosing the Right Pond: Human Behavior and the Quest for Status*. New York: Oxford University Press.

Frank, Robert H. 1999. *Luxury Fever: Why Money Fails to Satisfy in an Era of Excess*. New York: Free Press.

Frederick, Shane, and George Loewenstein. 1999. "Hedonic Adaptation." In *Well-Being: The Foundation of Hedonic Psychology*, ed. Daniel Kahneman, Ed Diener, and Norbert Schwarz, 302–329. New York: Russell Sage Foundation.

Frederick, Shane, George Loewenstein, and Ted O'Donoghue. 2002. "Time Discounting and Time Preference: A Critical Review." *Journal of Economic Literature* 40, no. 2: 351–401.

Frey, Bruno S., Christine Benesch, and Alois Stutzer. 2007. "Does Watching TV Make Us Happy?" Forthcoming in the *Journal of Economic Psychology*.

Frey, Bruno S., and Matthias Benz. 2003. "Being Independent Is a Great Thing: Subjective Evaluations of Self-Employment and Hierarchy." IEW Working Paper No. 135, University of Zurich.

Frey, Bruno S., Matthias Benz, and Alois Stutzer. 2004. "Introducing Procedural Utility: Not Only What, but Also How Matters." *Journal of Institutional and Theoretical Economics* 160, no. 3: 377–401.

Frey, Bruno S., and Alois Stutzer. 2002a. *Happiness and Economics: How the Economy and Institutions Affect Well-Being*. Princeton, NJ: Princeton University Press.

Frey, Bruno S., and Alois Stutzer. 2002b. "What Can Economists Learn from Happiness Research?" *Journal of Economic Literature* 40, no. 2: 402–435.

Frey, Bruno S., and Alois Stutzer. 2004. "Economic Consequences of Mispredicting Utility." Institute for Empirical Research in Economics Working Paper No. 218, University of Zurich.

Frey, Bruno S., and Alois Stutzer. 2006. "Mispredicting Utility and the Political Process." In *Behavioral Public Finance*, ed. Edward J. McCaffery and Joel Slemrod, 113–140. New York: Russell Sage Foundation.

Gentzkow, Matthew. 2006. "Television and Voter Turnout." *Quarterly Journal of Economics* 121, no. 3: 931–972.

Gilbert, Daniel T., Elizabeth C. Pinel, Timothy D. Wilson, Stephen J. Blumberg, and Thalia P. Wheatley. 1998. "Immune Neglect: A Source of Durability Bias in Affective Forecasting." *Journal of Personality and Social Psychology* 75, no. 3: 617–638.

Greeno, Catherine G., Christine Jackson, Elizabeth L. Wiliams, and Stephen P. Fortmann. 1998. "The Effect of Perceived Control over Eating on the Life Satisfaction of Women and Men: Results from a Community Sample." *International Journal of Eating Disorders* 24, no. 4: 415–419.

Gruber, Jonathan H., and Michael Frakes. 2006. "Does Falling Smoking Lead to Rising Obesity?" *Journal of Health Economics* 25, no. 2: 183–197.

Gruber, Jonathan H., and Botond Koszegi. 2001. "Is Addiction 'Rational?' Theory and Evidence." *Quarterly Journal of Economics* 116, no. 4: 1261–1303.

Gruber, Jonathan H., and Sendhil Mullainathan. 2005. "Do Cigarette Taxes Make Smokers Happier." *Advances in Economic Analysis and Policy* 5, no. 1: 1–43.

Hennigan, Karen M., Linda Heath, J. D. Wharton, M. L. Delrosario, T. D. Cook, and B. J. Calder. 1982. "Impact of the Introduction of Television on Crime in the United States: Empirical Findings and Theoretical Implications." *Journal of Personality and Social Psychology* 42, no. 3: 461–477.

Hsee, Christopher K., Jiao Zhang, Fang Yu, and Yiheng H. Xi. 2003. "Lay Rationalism and Inconsistency between Predicted Experience and Decision." *Journal of Behavioral Decision Making* 16, no. 4: 257–272.

Jürges, Hendrik. 2004. "The Welfare Costs of Addiction." *Schmollers Jahrbuch* 124, no. 3: 327–353.

Kahneman, Daniel. 1999. "Objective Happiness." In *Well Being: The Foundations of Hedonic Psychology*, ed. Daniel Kahneman, Ed Diener, and Norbert Schwarz, 3–25. New York: Russell Sage Foundation.

Kahneman, Daniel. 2003. "Experienced Utility and Objective Happiness: A Moment-Based Approach." In *The Psychology of Economic Decisions*, vol. 1, ed. Isabelle Brocas and Juan D. Carillo, 187–208. Oxford: Oxford University Press.

Kahneman, Daniel, Ed Diener, and Norbert Schwarz, eds. 1999. *Well-Being: The Foundations of Hedonic Psychology*. New York: Russell Sage Foundation.

Kahneman, Daniel, Jack L. Knetsch, and Richard H. Thaler. 1991. "The Endowment Effect, Loss Aversion, and Status Quo Bias: Anomalies." *Journal of Economic Perspectives* 5, no. 1: 193–206.

Kahneman, Daniel, Peter P. Wakker, and Rakesh Sarin. 1997. "Back to Bentham? Explorations of Experienced Utility." *Quarterly Journal of Economics* 112, no. 2: 375–405.

Kasser, Tim. 2002. *The High Price of Materialism*. Cambridge, MA: MIT Press.

Komlos, John, Patricia K. Smith, and Barry Bogin. 2004. "Obesity and the Rate of Time Preference: Is There a Connection?" *Journal of Biosocial Science* 36, no. 2: 209–219.

Korkeila, M., J. Kaprio, A. Rissanen, M. Koskenvuo, and T. I. A. Sorensen. 1998. "Predictors of Major Weight Gain in Adult Finns: Stress, Life Satisfaction and Personality Traits." *International Journal of Obesity* 22, no. 10: 949–957.

Kubey, Robert, and Mihaly Csikszentmihalyi. 1990. *Television and the Quality of Life: How Viewing Shapes Everyday Experience*. Hillsdale, NJ: Lawrence Erlbaum Associates.

Kubey, Robert, and Mihaly Czikszentmihalyi. 2002. "Television Addiction Is No Mere Metaphor." *Scientific American* 286, no. 2: 74–80.

Laibson, David. 1997. "Golden Eggs and Hyperbolic Discounting." *Quarterly Journal of Economics* 112, no. 2: 443–477.

Lakdawalla, Darius, and Tomas Philipson 2002. "The Growth of Obesity and Technological Change: A Theoretical and Empirical Examination." Working Paper No. 8946, National Bureau of Economic Research.

Lane, Robert E. 1991. *The Market Experience.* Cambridge: Cambridge University Press.

Layard, Richard. 2005. *Happiness: Lessons from a New Science.* New York: Penguin.

Lebergott, Stanley. 1993. *Pursuing Happiness: American Consumers in the Twentieth Century.* Princeton, NJ: Princeton University Press.

Loewenstein, George, and Daniel Adler. 1995. "A Bias in the Prediction of Tastes." *Economic Journal* 105, no. 431: 929–937.

Loewenstein, George, Ted O'Donoghue, and Matthew Rabin. 2003. "Projection Bias in Predicting Future Utility." *Quarterly Journal of Economics* 118, no. 4: 1209–1248.

Loewenstein, George, and David A. Schkade. 1999. "Wouldn't It Be Nice? Predicting Future Feelings." In *Well-Being: The Foundation of Hedonic Psychology,* eds. Daniel Kahneman, Ed Diener, and Norbert Schwarz, 85–105. New York: Russell Sage Foundation.

McElroy, Susan L., Renu Kotwal, Shishuka Malhotra, Erik B. Nelson, Paul E. Keck, and Charles B. Nemeroff. 2004. "Are Mood Disorders and Obesity Related? A Review for the Mental Health Professional." *Journal of Clinical Psychiatry* 65, no. 5: 634–651.

Meier, Stephan, and Alois Stutzer. 2007. "Is Volunteering Rewarding in Itself?" Forthcoming in *Economica.*

Muraven, Mark, Dianne M. Tice, and Roy F. Baumeister. 1998. "Self-Control as Limited Resource: Regulatory Depletion Patterns." *Journal of Personality and Social Psychology* 74, no. 3: 774–789.

Needham, Belinda L., and Robert Crosnoe. 2005. "Overweight Status and Depressive Symptoms during Adolescence." *Journal of Adolescent Health* 36, no. 1: 48–55.

Organisation for Economic Co-operation and Development (OECD). 2005. *OECD Factbook 2005: Economic, Environmental and Social Statistics.* Paris: OECD.

Prelec, Drazen, and Richard J. Herrnstein. 1991. "Preferences or Principles: Alternative Guidelines for Choice." In *Strategy and Choice,* ed. Richard J. Zeckhauser, 319–341. Cambridge: MIT Press.

Putnam, Judith Jones, and Jane E. Allshouse. 1999. "Food Consumption, Prices, and Expenditures, 1970–1997." Economic Research Service, Statistical Bulletin No. 965, U.S. Department of Agriculture.

Roberts, Robert E., William J. Strawbridge, Stephane Deleger, and George A. Kaplan. 2002. "Are the Fat More Jolly?" *Annals of Behavioral Medicine* 24, no. 3: 169–180.

Robinson, Michael D., and Gerald L. Clore. 2002. "Belief and Feeling: Evidence for an Accessibility Model of Emotional Self-Report." *Psychological Bulletin* 128, no. 6: 934–960.

Ross, Michael. 1989. "Relation of Implicit Theories to the Construction of Personal Histories." *Psychological Review* 96, no. 2: 341–357.

Schor, Juliet B. 1991. *The Overworked American: The Unexpected Decline of Leisure*. New York: Basic Books.

Scitovsky, Tibor. 1976. *The Joyless Economy: An Inquiry into Human Satisfaction and Consumer Dissatisfaction*. New York: Oxford University Press.

Shafir, Eldar, Itamar Simonson, and Amos Tversky. 1993. "Reason-Based Choice." *Cognition* 49, nos. 1–2: 11–36.

Sirgy, M. Joseph. 1998. "Materialism and Quality of Life." *Social Indicators Research* 43, no. 3: 227–260.

Skiba, Paige, and Jeremy Tobacman. 2005. "Payday Loans, Consumption Shocks, and Discounting." Mimeo., University of California at Berkeley.

Stroebe, Margaret S., Wolfgang Stroebe, and Robert O. Hansson, eds. 1993. *Handbook of Bereavement: Theory, Research, and Intervention*. Cambridge: Cambridge University Press.

Stutzer, Alois. 2004. "The Role of Income Aspirations in Individual Happiness." *Journal of Economic Behavior and Organization* 54, no. 1: 89–109.

Tatzel, Miriam. 2002. "'Money Worlds' and Well-Being: An Integration of Money Dispositions, Materialism and Price-Related Behavior." *Journal of Economic Psychology* 23, no. 1: 103–126.

Thaler, Richard H. 1999. "Mental Accounting Matters." In *Choices, Values and Frames*, ed. Daniel Kahneman and Amos Tversky, 241–268. Cambridge: Cambridge University Press.

Tyler, Tom R., Yuen J. Huo, and Edgar Allan Lind. 1999. "The Two Psychologies of Conflict Resolution: Differing Antecedents of Pre-Experience Choices and Post-Experience Evaluations." *Group Processes and Intergroup Relations* 2, no. 2: 99–118.

van Herwaarden, Floor, Arie Kapteyn, and Bernard M. S. van Praag. 1977. "Twelve Thousand Individual Welfare Functions: A Comparison of Six Samples in Belgium and the Netherlands." *European Economic Review* 9, no. 3: 283–300.

van Praag, Bernard M. S. 1968. *Individual Welfare Functions and Consumer Behavior: A Theory of Rational Irrationality*. Amsterdam: North-Holland.

van Praag, Bernard M. S. 1993. "The Relativity of the Welfare Concept." In *The Quality of Life*, ed. Martha Nussbaum and Amartya Sen, 362–385. New York: Oxford University Press.

Williams, Tannis Macbeth, ed. 1986. *The Impact of Television: A Natural Experiment in Three Communities*. Orlando: Academic Press.

Wilson, Timothy D., and Daniel T. Gilbert. 2003. "Affective Forecasting." In *Advances in Experimental Social Psychology*, vol. 35, ed. M. Zanna, 345–411. New York: Elsevier.

Wilson, Timothy D., and Jonathan W. Schooler. 1991. "Thinking Too Much—Introspection Can Reduce the Quality of Preferences and Decisions." *Journal of Personality and Social Psychology* 60, no. 2: 181–192.

World Health Organization. 2002. *The World Health Report 2002*. Geneva: World Health Organization.

World Health Organization Europe. 2005. "The Challenge of Obesity in the WHO European Region." Fact sheet EURO/13/05.

V

Procedural Utility and Decision-Making Mechanisms

8   The Relevance of Procedural Utility for Economics

Matthias Benz

8.1   Introduction

Economic science is based on the view that people care about outcomes. Consider, for example, a situation where individuals are involved as litigants in an arbitration process. At the end of the arbitration procedure, people have to choose whether to accept a court-ordered but non-binding award, or rather to go on to have a formal trial. From an economic perspective, there is a clear-cut prediction how people will behave in such a situation. They will compare the two alternatives at hand and choose the one that offers the higher expected monetary payoff (e.g., Cooter and Ulen 2000, 377–381). Yet in reality, people seem to behave quite differently. In a seminal study on real-life arbitration procedures, Lind et al. (1993) showed that outcome considerations were only modestly important for individuals' decisions to accept a court-ordered award. Rather, what litigants seemed to judge as crucial was the fairness of the arbitration procedure applied. When individuals felt they were treated in a respectful, impartial, and trustworthy way by the court authorities and that they were given due voice in the arbitration process, they were much more likely to accept a court-ordered award, irrespective of monetary outcomes involving sums of up to US$ 800,000.

In this chapter, I argue that procedural utility, similar to that involved in the arbitration example, emerges in many areas of economic and social life, and as a consequence, should be incorporated more widely into economic theory and empirical research. The general concept of procedural utility means that people not only care about outcomes, but also value the processes and conditions leading to outcomes. People often do not only care about the "what," but also about the "how." Or in yet other words, they value the means beyond the ends.

Procedural utility represents a quite different approach to human well-being and behavior than the standard approach applied in economics. But there is a considerable body of empirical evidence indicating that individuals care about processes in their own right. I discuss eight areas relevant for economics: consumption, work and employment, political participation, public good provision, taxes, inequality and redistribution, organizations, and the law. In each area, individuals have been found to derive direct utility from the institutions and procedures applied beyond considerations for material outcomes.

This chapter extends and complements an earlier survey article by Frey, Benz, and Stutzer (2004) that set out to introduce the concept of procedural utility into economics. In comparison to the earlier work, this paper more thoroughly details the concept of procedural utility and discusses how the concept differs from other related approaches in economics, such as outcome utility, inequality aversion (outcome fairness), or intentions. Moreover, the paper presents additional novel evidence on the role of procedural utility in several areas of the economy, polity, and society. Section 8.2 begins by outlining the psychological foundations of the concept of procedural utility and shows its differences from other economic approaches. Moreover, the main sources of procedural utility are presented; namely, institutions at the level of society (the decision-making mechanisms of the market, hierarchy, and democracy) and, on a smaller scale, fair procedures applied in social relationships. In section 8.3, I apply the concept to eight areas relevant for economics and present novel empirical evidence on the existence of procedural utility in these areas. Section 8.4 concludes the paper by discussing how the concept of procedural utility can be fruitfully integrated into the traditional economic approach.

8.2   The Concept of Procedural Utility

8.2.1   Beyond Outcomes
When economists apply economic theory to concrete problems and questions, they typically assume that human utility consists of outcomes only, as showcased by the arbitration example described in the introduction. Three additional examples shall illustrate the outcome orientation of the economic approach, two relating to the field of institutional economics and one relating to organizational economics.

Consider first a situation where a group of people, for example, a minority group, is granted the *democratic right* to vote. In economics, it is typically assumed that people value this voting right because it allows them to change the outcomes of the political process in their favor. The minority group, for example, can alter the scope or composition of public goods provided or it can vote for redistributive measures benefiting the group (e.g., Mueller 2003, 79–84). While such outcome aspects are without doubt important, a procedural view focuses more on the direct utility people may get from the voting right. Individuals might attach a high value to democratic rights simply because they give them a sense of inclusion, identity, and self-determination. This procedural utility can persist even if the voting right does not substantially affect political outcomes.

Imagine, as a second example, people subject to *hierarchical decision making*. Individuals working within a hierarchy often have different degrees of autonomy over their work content and how they can do their work. Economists typically assume that employees value such decision-making authority if it leads to better outcomes—for example, in the form of a higher income (e.g., Williamson 1975, 39; Aghion and Tirole 1997; Baker, Gibbons, and Murphy 1999). The concept of procedural utility, conversely, suggests that people may have a preference for autonomy in itself. Increased autonomy may be seen as a good decision-making procedure because it provides individuals with a direct utility from having control over their work.

Third, envisage firms planning to undertake *nominal wage cuts* in times of recession. Economic models predict that workers often resist such wage cuts, either because they individually constitute a bad outcome or because workers see them as unacceptable in terms of outcome fairness vis-à-vis the firm (e.g., Bewley 1999; Fehr and Götte 2005). A procedural perspective, in contrast, emphasizes the processes by which pay cuts are announced and undertaken. Employees' reactions to pay cuts may be less averse if they happen through fair processes; for example, when management thoroughly and sensitively explains the basis for the pay cuts (Greenberg 1990a). As a result, procedural aspects can have real consequences, as they may help to avoid unnecessary layoffs and lower the rate of unemployment at the economy level.

The three examples illustrate the outcome orientation of the economic approach. When economic theory is applied to concrete problems and questions, human utility is often reduced to outcome

considerations. This may in part reflect that important theoretical cor-
nerstones of economics, such as expected utility theory or game theory,
generally define preferences over monetary payoffs (Harsanyi 1993).
But in many respects, this restraint is odd. Economics, in principle, is a
science that is deliberately vague about what human preferences are
defined over. During the positivistic movement of the 1930s, economists just gave up the idea that utility could be observed directly and
adopted the view that the only way to infer utility was from revealed
behavior. But in principle, what individuals value could be anything.
Economics is thus potentially open to the integration of many forms
of human needs and desires. Some nonmaterial human motives that
have received attention recently in economics include identity (e.g.,
Akerlof and Kranton 2000, 2004), status (e.g., Frank 1985) or respect,
self-esteem, and pride (e.g., Khalil 1996; Köszegi 2002a, 2002b). In principle, economics is also open to the notion that individuals enjoy procedural utility. So far, only a few economists have argued against the
economic tendency to see outcomes as the only source of utility and
the only driving force behind behavior. Most prominently, Sen (1995,
1997) has repeatedly stressed that economic choice models should
combine preferences for outcome with those for processes (but see also
Anand 2001; Le Menestrel 2001; Sandbu 2004).

8.2.2 Psychological Foundations

As mentioned earlier, the general concept of procedural utility
means that individuals not only care about outcomes, but also value
the processes and conditions leading to outcomes. In order to reinte-
grate procedural utility into economics, the psychological foundations
of the concept have to be outlined. Procedural utility rests on three
building blocks that deviate in important respects from standard
economics, but are well-grounded in research in other social science
disciplines.

1. Procedural utility emphasizes utility as *well-being*. Utility is understood in a broad sense as pleasure and pain, positive and negative
affect, or life satisfaction.[1] This reinstates the original economic idea
that utility consists of everything that individuals value. Economists
have recently rediscovered well-being as a direct measure of human
utility, based on a substantial amount of research on reported subjective well-being or happiness strongly influenced by social psychology
(see Frey and Stutzer 2002a, 2002b; Diener et al. 1999; Oswald 1997 for
surveys).

2. Closely connected with this first point, procedural utility takes a broad view of the determinants of human utility. It posits that processes and institutions under which people live and act are *independent* sources of utility, apart from the outcomes that they also produce. People may judge an unfavorable outcome as acceptable if the procedure applied was "good," and a favorable outcome might provide them with little overall satisfaction if the procedure that brought it about was "bad." In this sense, procedures and decision-making mechanisms cannot only be judged in terms of outcomes, as is traditionally done in economics.

3. Procedural utility emerges because people have a *sense of self*. The way things are done provides individuals with important feedback information about how they have to perceive themselves and how they are perceived by others. In addition, different procedures and decision-making mechanisms allow people to live and act according to their own self-image to different extents. By focusing on people's sense of self, the concept of procedural utility reincorporates a central tenet of social psychology into economics (see, e.g., Baumeister 1998 for a survey). In recent decades, psychologists have developed a detailed understanding of the basic psychological needs of the human self, which is most stringently summarized in the "self-determination theory" of Deci and Ryan (2000).[2]

Three innate needs have been found to be essential: autonomy, competence, and relatedness. The desire for autonomy encompasses the experience to self-organize one's own actions or to be causal. The need for competence refers to the propensity to control the environment and to experience oneself as capable and effective. And the need for relatedness refers to the desire to feel connected to others in love and care, and to be treated as a respected group member within social groups. Different procedures can be expected to provide different procedural goods serving these innate needs. Importantly, procedures addressing innate psychological needs contribute to individual well-being *beyond outcomes* traditionally studied by economists. For example, self-determination theory stresses that procedures providing individuals with autonomy are not valued so much because they lead to better outcomes, but because having control over one's actions satisfies a basic psychological need of human beings.

Taken together, the three building blocks form a concept of procedural utility that can, in general, be applied to all situations where human action is shaped and constrained by procedures and institutions.

The psychological foundations of the concept permit the derivation of theoretical hypotheses on when procedural utility is expected to be more pronounced and when it is expected to be less important. This makes the concept falsifiable. In sum, procedural utility can be defined as the well-being people gain from living and acting under institutionalized processes as they contribute to a positive sense of self, addressing innate needs of autonomy, competence, and relatedness.

8.2.3   Sources of Procedural Utility

Procedural utility can emerge from different sources. These sources can be classified into two broad categories.

First, there is the procedural utility people get from *institutions*. At the societal level, the most important formal systems for reaching decisions are the price system (market), democracy, hierarchy, and bargaining (Dahl and Lindblom 1953). People may gain procedural utility from these institutions because they differently address innate needs of autonomy, competence, and relatedness, beyond shaping outcomes. The direct effects that institutions can have on individuals' well-being make procedural utility a particularly relevant concept for institutionally oriented social sciences, like institutional economics.

Second, procedural utility emerges in interactions between people. People evaluate actions toward them not only by their consequences, but also by how they feel they have been treated. This form of procedural utility has been extensively researched in the large literature on *procedural fairness* or *procedural justice* (see, e.g., Lind and Tyler 1988), which can be considered the best-investigated aspect of procedural utility. People have repeatedly been found to care about procedural fairness beyond outcomes, in particular when they deal with authorities in the public as well as private sphere.

Of course, a smooth transition often occurs between the two categories. Institutions, on the one hand, select and motivate people as to how to treat their fellow workers, citizens, and consumers. In a democracy, for example, politicians and public bureaucrats can be expected to treat citizens differently than in an autocracy. On the other hand, people who evaluate institutions, processes, or authorities usually base their judgment on the treatment experienced by the specific people involved. In this respect, the procedural utility effects of institutions will always be mediated to some extent by social interactions occurring within these institutions (see, e.g., Blader and Tyler 2003 on related evidence).

While the sources of procedural utility may sometimes be hard to distinguish, this does not mean that the concept could be applied arbitrarily. Whether procedural utility emerges from institutions like the market mechanism, democratic decision making, or hierarchy as such, or whether it stems from procedural differences on a smaller scale, for example, from procedural differences within an organization, a political system, or a legal framework, there is a common ground to all these channels of impact: individuals judge processes positively to the extent that they address innate needs of self-determination. Theoretical hypotheses are therefore possible.

With respect to procedural differences on a smaller scale, there is a clear understanding from the literature on "procedural fairness" about what constitutes a good procedure. As procedures on this level often involve how authority is exercised in organizations, public administrations, or legal contexts, innate needs are mainly affected by relational information that procedures convey, such as assessments of impartiality, trustworthiness of superiors and authorities, the extent to which individuals feel they are treated with dignity, and the extent to which individuals are given voice (see, e.g., Tyler et al. 1997). When institutions on a larger scale are considered, like democracy or hierarchy, one can derive similar hypotheses. This can be illustrated by the examples given at the outset of this section. For instance, democratic rights are expected to have positive procedural utility effects because they enhance individuals' perception of self-determination. Hierarchical decision making, in contrast, is likely to produce procedural disutility because it interferes with individuals' self-determination. Empirical results along these lines will be presented in section 8.3.

8.2.4   Differences to Other Approaches in Economics

While procedural utility has not been seriously integrated into economics so far, a few related approaches exist that have received some attention in the economic profession. In this subsection, I discuss how the procedural utility view distinguishes itself from these approaches. Apart from the distinction to traditional outcome utility already discussed, three seem most important: preferences for gambling, inequality aversion (outcomes fairness), and intentions.

First, the term "process utility" is sometimes used in the economic literature on *preferences for gambling*. Already Pascal (1670) considered the utility gained from gambling as an interesting phenomenon, and later Marschak (1950) and von Neumann and Morgenstern (1944) showed that it is incompatible with expected utility maximization. Recently, Le Menestrel (2001) established axioms for a model of rational decisions under risk and uncertainty that combines processes and consequences, explicitly using the term "process utility" to describe the utility people derive from acts like gambling. While gambling indeed may involve process aspects, there are important differences from the concept of procedural utility as proposed here. Gambling (in a non-pathological form) may also qualify as nontangible consumption, which is readily accessible using the standard economic approach. The important difference to the procedural utility concept proposed here is that gambling, like other forms of nontangible consumption, does typically not involve a "procedurally intense" environment. The concept of procedural utility stresses that a *comparative view* of different procedures and institutions should be undertaken with regard to how they address innate needs of self-determination. To the extent that procedures and institutions fulfill this role, they create procedural utility and affect human well-being beyond outcomes.

Second, economists have paid considerable attention recently to integrating *outcome fairness* into individual utility functions (e.g., Bolton and Ockenfels 2000; Fehr and Schmidt 1999; Konow 2003). What these theories have in common with the concept of procedural utility is that detailed considerations are made about what human utility consists of. However, there are also important differences. On the one hand, models of inequality aversion remain grounded in an outcome-oriented view traditional in economics, while procedural utility stresses that processes and institutions affect human utility beyond outcomes and also beyond outcome fairness. In the literature on procedural justice, this difference has been researched in detail and it has been repeatedly shown that people care about fair processes beyond aspects of individual outcomes, as well as of distributional fairness (e.g., Lind and Tyler 1988; Tyler and Blader 2000). On the other hand, the procedural utility concept employs a comparative institutional view typically absent from the literature on inequality aversion. For example, from the point of view of outcome fairness, it should make no difference to people's well-being in a country whether a given income distribution was brought about by a democratic or a dictatorial regime. The procedural utility perspective suggests that people might well judge the two situations differently, because they attach a value to institutions in their own right (see also Sen 1995 on this point, and the evidence discussed in section 8.3.6).

Third, the approach most closely related to procedural utility in economics is the notion that *intentions* matter for human well-being and behavior. Theories of intentions assume that people care about how they are treated by others in social interactions, irrespective of monetary payoffs or distributional aspects. Several aspects broadly related to intentions have been identified and experimentally tested in the economic literature, such as reciprocity (e.g., Falk, Fehr, and Fischbacher 2003; Falk and Fischbacher 2000; Rabin 1993), betrayal aversion (Bohnet and Zeckhauser 2004), process-dependent preferences (Sandbu 2004), and procedural fairness, as opposed to allocation fairness (Bolton, Brandts, and Ockenfels 2005). Despite similarities, there remain substantial differences from the concept of procedural utility. On the one hand, intentions are most closely related to the large literature on procedural fairness, but in terms of psychological content, research on the latter has developed a quite more detailed understanding of what intentions actually consist of in real-life relationships (see, e.g., Lind and Tyler 1988 for a survey). Economic experiments so far have employed a rather narrow view of intentions, typically showing that people judge a bad outcome distribution as more acceptable if it was produced by a random mechanism than if it was deliberately chosen by another person. On the other hand, the concept of procedural utility goes far beyond procedural fairness aspects alone. Importantly, it stresses that institutions at the societal level, like the market, democracy, or hierarchy, can have effects on human well-being beyond outcomes. Thus, the concept of procedural utility employs a comparative institutional approach, also encompassing the fundamental decision-making mechanisms that shape the organization of societies.

In sum, procedural utility is a concept that is distinct from outcome utility as traditionally studied in economics. It is based on well-researched foundations in the psychological literature; it emerges from sources of great relevance for economic analysis, like institutions at the level of society and, on a smaller scale, fair processes employed in social relationships; and it is distinct from related approaches that have received some attention in the economic literature, such as preferences for gambling, outcome fairness, and intentions.

8.3   The Relevance of Procedural Utility: Empirical Evidence

Whether or not procedural utility is a fruitful category ultimately rests on its empirical relevance. In this section, I discuss empirical evidence

from a broad range of areas where procedural utility has been shown
to matter. Eight areas seem particularly relevant for economics: consumption, work and employment, political participation, public good
provision, taxes, inequality and redistribution, organizations, and the
law.

8.3.1   Consumption

Consumption is probably an area where procedural utility would not
be expected: it generally takes place in well-functioning markets where
transactions are focused on material outcomes. Nevertheless, procedural utility has been found to play a role in consumer decisions. Frey
and Pommerehne (1993), in a study extending a famous investigation
by Kahneman, Knetsch, and Thaler (1986), analyze consumers' reactions to different allocation mechanisms in an excess demand situation.
In particular, they investigate how consumers rate different institutional mechanisms for allocating a limited number of water bottles to
hikers at a hilltop on a hot day. Seventy-three percent of the respondents surveyed consider a price increase for the water bottles to be an
unfair means of overcoming the shortage, and thus rate a normal functioning of the market mechanism as unacceptable. In contrast, other
decision-making mechanisms fare better. An allocation by "tradition"
(first come, first served) is considered by far fewer people to be unfair
(24 percent), and similarly an allocation by administrative procedures
(by the local authorities) is reckoned unfair by 57 percent. Only a random allocation fares worse than the price system; only to 14 percent of
the respondents does it appear to be acceptable. The study thus suggests that consumers' overall evaluations of allocations are not just dependent on outcomes. In particular, the market mechanism is opposed
as a rationing mechanism, despite the fundamental economic insight
that it leads to the most efficient results. Procedures seem to play an
independent role in consumers' utility, although it is not yet well
understood why alternative allocation mechanisms may serve innate
psychological needs of consumers better than the price system.

On a less institutional level, people have been found to care about
their perceived treatment as customers beyond outcome considerations. In an experimental study on consumer boycotts, for example,
Tyran and Engelmann (2005) show that boycotts in reaction to price
increases are often undertaken, although they fail to hold down prices
and are not profitable for consumers. They are also undertaken irrespective of whether collective action problems prevail (successful boy-

cotts are a public good). Rather, the experimental findings suggest that consumers undertake boycotts in order to punish sellers for apparently "unfair" price increases. People seem to be emotionally negatively affected when they perceive behavior towards them as exploitation, most likely because it undermines their status as consumers, who are presumed to be on an equal standing with producers. If consumers have such procedural concerns, this can impose a constraint on profit maximization by suppliers, affecting market equilibrium and even macroeconomic variables (see, e.g., Rotemberg 2005).

In addition, consumers may also care about more than just price and quality when buying a good. Kysar (2004) argues that consumers often have preferences about how a good is produced, in particular about whether the production process conforms to basic environmental standards or labor regulations. For example, people may prefer to buy an otherwise identical shoe when the production process respects certain worker rights. If by buying a good consumers satisfy not only material needs, but also the self-image of a conscious consumer, this makes a case for the mandatory provision of the relevant process information to consumers. Reliable knowledge about the characteristics of a good's production process helps consumers to purchase according to their procedural preferences; the resulting "political" consumption choice can even substitute for uniform regulations enacted in the political process.

Overall, probably the most interesting question related to consumption choices is whether the market mechanism, as the fundamental institution of capitalist economies, is a source of procedural utility. The evidence presented in Frey and Pommerehne (1993) suggests that in situations of excess demand, the use of market prices is often vigorously opposed by the individuals involved. But this does not mean that in more general situations, the market could not be valued by individuals as an attractive institution in procedural terms. Interestingly, related arguments have been made in the psychological literature, rather than by economists, who typically defend the market on efficiency grounds. A long tradition in social psychology has argued that freedom of choice, which is the defining characteristic of decision making on markets, satisfies an important basic psychological need of human beings (e.g., Brehm 1966; deCharms 1968; Heider 1958; White 1959). Empirical studies have repeatedly shown that individuals enjoy higher well-being if they can choose among alternatives, compared to a situation where an alternative is imposed from outside (irrespective of objective outcomes, see, e.g., Brehm 1966; Botti 2002; Cordova and Lepper 1996; Langer and Rodin 1976; Schulz and Hanusa 1978; Zuckerman et al. 1978). As a consequence, the psychological literature has largely reached a consensus that people value freedom of choice because it allows them to satisfy innate psychological needs of autonomy, control, and self-determination (but for contrasting views, see, e.g., Loewenstein 2000; Iyengar and Lepper 2000; Schwartz 2000). Thus the market mechanism cannot only be defended as an institution promoting outcome efficiency, as is typical in economics, but can also be seen as a source of procedural utility because it provides individuals with possibilities of self-determination.[3]

8.3.2   Work and Employment

When individuals act as income earners, they are often confronted with the institution of hierarchy. Hierarchy means that production and employment are integrated into an organization, and decisions are characterized by some degree of authority. Hierarchy can be considered the most fundamental institution by which decisions with respect to work organization and production are taken in society, and is thus an essential and widespread feature of the economy.

Does hierarchy involve procedural utility aspects? The theoretical arguments discussed in section 8.2 lead to a clear proposition: individuals prefer independence over being subject to hierarchical decision making. Hierarchy constitutes a procedural disutility because it interferes with innate needs of self-determination: autonomy and the experience of competence are generally restricted under hierarchy, and strongly related to independence.

Frey and Benz (2007) present an empirical test of whether individuals enjoy procedural utility from independence versus hierarchy. They exploit the idea that earnings can in principle be generated in two ways: in a hierarchy (as an employee) or independently (as a self-employed person). Using individual panel data from the United Kingdom, Germany, and Switzerland, they find that self-employed people indeed enjoy higher utility from their work (measured via job satisfaction) than employees, even if important outcomes like pay level, working hours, and many others are controlled for.[4] Benz and Frey (2003), moreover, show for a sample of twenty-three countries from different world regions that the higher job satisfaction of the self-employed can directly and fully be explained by their higher autonomy, and not by other, outcome-related factors. Self-employed people seem to enjoy their position as independent actors on the market and enjoy not being subject to a hierarchy for purely procedural reasons, because autonomy and independence are seen as characteristics of a good decision-making procedure.

There is also evidence for the related hypothesis that satisfaction is (ceteris paribus) lower the larger the hierarchy an employee is subject to. Frey and Benz (2003) show that in the United Kingdom, Germany, and Switzerland, people working in large firms are considerably less satisfied with their jobs than people working in small organizations. Idson (1990) finds a similar result for the United States and shows that the lower job satisfaction of workers in larger firms can mainly be explained by procedural factors: "workers in larger establishments have a significantly lower level of freedom on their jobs concerning what type of work they do and how they do it, and face significantly greater rigidity with regards to hours and days of work" (1013). Thus procedural utility seems to also be of great relevance for people working in dependent employment.

The notion that autonomy and job control are sources of procedural utility at work finds further support in the Whitehall studies undertaken by Michael Marmot and coauthors (e.g., Marmot et al. 1997; Marmot 2004). The Whitehall studies show that individuals working at lower levels of the British civil service have a considerably higher likelihood of developing coronary heart diseases than individuals working at the highest levels of the organizational hierarchy. Marmot et al. (1997) document that this "social gradient" in health can to a large extent be explained by procedural work aspects. While standard coronary risk factors, such as smoking, and factors acting early in life, as represented by physical height, account for a part of the social health gradient, the largest factor contributing to the higher frequency of coronary heart diseases among people in lower employment grades is their low job control. This finding suggests that a lack of autonomy at work does not only affect individuals' well-being in the form of low procedural utility, but that it also translates into substantially worse health.

Procedural aspects within hierarchies have also been studied in other contexts more related to the role of procedural fairness in work relationships. It is, for example, a well-known fact that workers often resist nominal pay cuts. The resulting downward wage rigidity has macroeconomic consequences because it can cause excess unemployment in recessions (e.g., Bewley 1999; Fehr and Götte 2005). For workers' resistance to pay cuts, not only do issues of outcome or distributional fairness seem to be crucial, but also process considerations. It has been shown, for example, that employees' reactions to pay cuts are less averse if this happens through fair processes; for example, when management thoroughly and sensitively explains the basis for the pay cuts (Greenberg 1990a). This finding has quite profound implications. It means that by applying fair procedures, firms could more easily implement necessary wage cuts in times of recession, which would reduce the rate of unemployment in the economy.

In sum, procedural utility seems to be an important factor in what individuals value in their work lives. On the one hand, procedural utility is the result of autonomy and control at work, or the absence of hierarchical decision making, which is valued by individuals beyond standard outcome considerations. On the other hand, procedural utility emerges if fair procedures are applied in work relationships (see also section 8.3.7). While labor economists and organizational economists usually do not deny that "bad working conditions" may cause disutility, the nonpecuniary aspects of autonomy, job control, and procedural fairness are typically not taken into account in formal models (see, e.g., Aghion and Tirole 1997; Baker, Gibbons, and Murphy 1999). Taking procedural utility seriously, however, may also enrich economic analyses of work and organizations.

8.3.3   Democratic Participation

In the realm of politics, the institution of democracy represents the fundamental mechanism by which decisions are made in society. Irrespective of the precise form of a democracy, citizens' rights to participate in political decisions are a crucial characteristic of any democratic constitution. Participation rights may be completely absent in an autocracy or dictatorship. In representative democracies, they typically comprise the right to vote in elections and to run for a seat in parliament, and in direct democracies, they additionally entail possibilities of launching and voting on referenda and initiatives. Citizens may gain procedural utility from such participation rights over and above the outcome generated in the political process because they provide a feeling of being involved and having political influence, as well as a notion of inclusion, identity, and self-determination. By being able to participate, citizens may feel that the political sphere takes their wishes into account in a fair political process; if participation is restricted, they may feel alienation and apathy toward the political institutions installed. Indeed, a large literature in the social sciences, especially in psychology, political science, and sociology, attributes a positive value to participation as it enhances individuals' perception of self-determination (for an extensive survey see Lane 2000, chapter 13).

Can it be empirically shown that citizens derive procedural utility from political participation rights? A study by Frey and Stutzer (2005) employs an empirical identification strategy based on the idea that the status of a national fundamentally differs from that of a foreigner. Nationals have the right to vote and to participate in political decision making, while foreigners do not. Nationals should thus derive more utility from political participation rights than foreigners, if they enjoy procedural utility. This hypothesis is tested econometrically using a survey based on more than six thousand interviews with residents of Switzerland, where there is a unique variation in the political participation rights among citizens. In addition to elections, citizens have access to direct democratic instruments (initiatives, referenda), which differ substantially from canton to canton. As a proxy measure for utility, an index of reported subjective well-being is used as the dependent variable. The estimated overall utility effect from more extended political participation rights, as reflected in reported life satisfaction, is in itself sizeable. Both citizens and foreigners living in jurisdictions with more developed political participation rights enjoy higher levels of subjective well-being. The positive effect on reported satisfaction with life, however, is smaller for foreigners, reflecting their exclusion from procedural utility. The positive effect of participation rights is about three times larger for the citizens than it is for the foreigners; in other words, a major part of the welfare gain from favorable political procedures seems to be due to procedural utility. The results hold, ceteris paribus, when a large number of determinants or correlates of subjective well-being (in particular sociodemographic characteristics, employment status, household income, and proxies for political outcomes) are controlled for.

The procedural utility of political participation rights may also be reflected in revealed behavior. In an experimental study before the elections to the German parliament in 1994, Güth and Weck-Hannemann (1997) investigated what amount of money would have to be paid to individuals in order to make them destroy their personal voting card, thereby giving up their right to vote in this particular election. Despite the fact that a single vote almost never changes the outcome of an election, most individuals are not willing to sell their

voting right even for high amounts of money: 63 percent of voters refuse to destroy their voting card even for the highest sum offered (200
deutsche mark (DM), approximately US$100 at the time), and only 5
percent agree to give up their voting right for less than DM 10 (approximately US$5). These findings show that individuals place a high value
on their voting right that goes beyond any outcome utility they may
get from altering the election result. Rather, political participation
rights seem to be a source of procedural utility because they enhance
individuals' possibilities of self- and codetermination.

8.3.4 Public Good Allocation

Governments often face resistance to public projects generally considered important and desirable, such as finding suitable locations for
psychiatric hospitals, for airports, or for nuclear waste facilities. Such
NIMBY projects are often supported by the general population, but nobody wants to see them in their neighborhood (hence "Not In My Back
Yard"). The economic approach suggests that the most straightforward
solution to this problem is to use a market mechanism: prospective
gainers must be taxed and the revenue must be redistributed to the
prospective losers hosting the public project (e.g., Kunreuther and
Kleindorfer 1986; O'Sullivan 1993). But in reality, procedures based on
the price system have been found to rarely, if ever, work (e.g., Frey and
Oberholzer 1997). Individuals seem to consider monetary compensation a bribe that disregards their sense of self as decent citizens and
seems to involve negative procedural utility. Other forms of compensation that do more justice to people's concerns have been found to work
better. For example, if compensation is offered along a predetermined
dimension (e.g., airport noise is compensated by helping people to
insulate their homes), the chances of project acceptance increase, although this form of transfer is inefficient, according to traditional welfare theory, because it's not fungible.

  More generally, different allocation procedures have been found to
greatly affect people's willingness to host a public project. A study by
Frey and Oberholzer (1996) investigates the acceptability of various
decision-making procedures for siting a noxious facility in Switzerland. The persons interviewed rank procedures in the following order:
negotiations (bargaining) are seen by 72 percent as an acceptable procedure for siting, 32 percent find referenda (democracy) to be acceptable, 26 percent a decision by lottery, and only a few see the price
system as an acceptable procedure (20 percent in the form of willing-

ness to accept, and 4 percent in the form of willingness to pay). Further analyses revealed that acceptability is seen by respondents as consisting of three components: security, local influence, and fairness. It transpired that the ranking in terms of fairness exactly mirrors the above given ranking in terms of acceptability. Thus, the results can clearly be interpreted in procedural terms. It is not only the implication for the outcomes (like the extent of local influence) that causes people to find a siting procedure more or less acceptable. Rather, individuals seem to attach an independent procedural value to the different allocation mechanisms. It is noteworthy that similar results have also been found for the allocation of publicly provided services to citizens and consumers, for example, in the area of health care (Wailoo and Anand 2005; Tsuchiya et al. 2005).

8.3.5 Taxes

The payment of taxes to finance the provision of public goods and redistributive measures is an important element in the relationship between citizens and the state. In principle, procedural utility can play a twofold role in this relationship. First, the political institutions used to determine tax rates and tax spending may influence citizens' satisfaction with the state's functioning beyond outcomes. Second, on a lower level, taxpayers may respond in a systematic way to how the tax authority treats them—for example, their willingness to pay taxes may be supported or even raised when the tax officials treat them in a procedurally fair way.

In recent years, empirical evidence for both channels of influence has been found, emphasizing the role of procedural aspects in taxation. With respect to institutional determinants, it has mainly been investigated how democratic participation rights affect people's willingness to pay taxes. Several experimental studies have shown that individuals evade fewer taxes if they have the opportunity to vote on tax measures (e.g., Alm, McClelland, and Schulze 1999; Feld and Tyran 2002; Torgler, Schaltegger, and Schaffner 2003). The impact of voting thereby holds over and above outcome aspects (factors like the probability of punishment for tax evasion, the size of the fine applied, the tax rate, individual incomes, and the "efficiency" of the state are carefully held constant in these experiments). Related results have been found in econometric field studies. For example, Pommerehne and Weck-Hannemann (1996) show that tax evasion is lower in those Swiss cantons where citizens have more extended direct democratic participation rights, and Torgler (2005) documents a similar finding using survey data on tax morale.

Procedural aspects also have been found to play a role in the direct relationship between citizens and tax authorities. Evidence reported in Feld and Frey (2002) and Frey and Feld (2002), using a sample of Swiss cantons in the years 1970–1995, suggests that individuals care about how they are treated by tax authorities. When tax collectors deal with citizens in a respectful way, people seem to avoid fewer taxes. Moreover, the tax authorities on average behave as if they were aware of the reaction of taxpayers to being treated with respect. For example, deterrence is only one of the motivational forces used by the authorities; often they rely on respectful tax collection procedures.

While procedural utility aspects in taxation certainly have to be investigated in more detail to corroborate their importance, the evidence discussed shows that new insights on tax compliance and tax evasion may be gained by taking procedural utility into account. Without a doubt, the procedural approach greatly extends the classical economic model of taxpayer behavior that is based on pure outcome considerations (Allingham and Sandmo 1972; Andreoni, Erard, and Feinstein 1998, 824–835; Slemrod and Yitzhaki 2002) and that has not been very successful in empirically explaining people's willingness to pay taxes (e.g., Alm, McClelland, and Schulze 1992, 22).

8.3.6   Redistribution and Inequality

Social inequality is a pervasive phenomenon in many societies. Most governments aim to reduce social inequality at least to some extent by applying redistributive measures that tax the rich and benefit the poor. What explains citizens' support of such redistributive measures, or rather, their opposition to them?

In economics, probably the most dominant view is that individuals' support of redistribution is dependent on their own position in the income distribution (i.e., being rich or poor) or, if they are forward-looking, on their prospects of upward income mobility (for an early account, see Hirschman 1973). Bénabou and Ok (2001) have proposed an influential model based on this outcome-oriented view, arguing that individuals oppose redistribution more if social income mobility is high. However, objective measures of upward income mobility have been found to explain individuals' demand for redistribution only to a limited extent (e.g., Alesina and La Ferrara 2005; Fong 2005). Rather, the empirical evidence suggests that individuals' support of redistributive measures depends on *how* the primary distribution was brought about. If people believe that success mainly depends on individual effort, they consider redistribution to be less necessary than when they believe that success mainly depends on luck; conversely, if people think that poverty is predominantly caused by factors beyond individual control, they will support redistribution (e.g., Fong 2001, 2005).

This evidence on individuals' demand for redistribution sheds a distinctly procedural light on the question of social inequality. People seem to judge a given income distribution not only in terms of individual outcomes or outcome fairness, but also to a considerable extent based on the social processes that brought it about. If social processes provide everyone with a fair chance to "make it," inequality is considered less of a problem than when social processes are biased and unfair. This suggests that "equality of opportunities" can be seen as a source of procedural utility. The theoretical arguments made in section 8.2 indeed support such an interpretation. On the one hand, people may value equality of opportunities in procedural terms because it gives everyone the chance to lead a self-determined life and to be the master of one's own fate. On the other hand, equality of opportunities signals that everyone in principle is considered a respected member of society. Individuals may care about both aspects beyond outcomes, because they address the innate needs of self-determination that form the basis of procedural utility. Recently, Bénabou and Tirole (2005) have included an aspect similar to this kind of procedural utility in a formal model of redistribution (which they call the "need to believe in a just world").

8.3.7 Organizations

Organizations are the field where aspects of procedural utility have been most intensely studied. As in hierarchies, many decisions are made in an authoritarian way; research has mainly focused on the effects of procedural fairness on well-being and behavior. The literature on procedural fairness or justice in organizations is so large that meta-analyses (e.g., Cohen-Charash and Spector 2001) already exist. The studies consistently find that concerns for procedural fairness are a highly relevant and widespread phenomenon in the employment relationship. It has been shown to matter for employees' behavior, satisfaction, and attitudes in areas like change (mergers and acquisitions, layoffs, restructuring, strategic planning) and human resources (personnel selection, performance evaluation, compensation; see Konovsky

2000 and Colquitt et al. 2001 for overviews, and Lind et al. 2000 for an exemplary empirical study). Procedural aspects that researchers have identified as important include organizational policies and rules, like providing advance notice for decisions and opportunities for voice (see, e.g., Greenberg 1990b; Lind and Tyler 1988), but they also encompass the interpersonal treatment of people (Bies and Moag 1986). Individuals generally have been found to value fair procedures over and above organizational outcomes. Procedural fairness effects prevail when individual outcomes, as well as aspects of distributional fairness, are controlled for in the analysis (e.g., Tyler and Blader 2000). Thus, procedural utility is without doubt a relevant part of what individuals value when working in organizations.

A study by Benz and Stutzer (2003) may serve as an empirical example for the relevance of fair procedures in work relationships. The authors study the satisfaction people derive from their pay, using a representative sample of over twenty-two thousand British workers. The results show that pay satisfaction is not only influenced by absolute outcomes (the compensation people get for a given input) or relative outcomes (people's pay in relation to comparable workers' pay), but most strongly by procedural factors. In particular, employees that are frequently consulted on pay issues by their superiors are, ceteris paribus, considerably more satisfied with their pay than workers who are never asked about matters of compensation. Thus, organizational procedures supporting a fair pay determination process are found to affect employees' well-being beyond material outcomes.

8.3.8   Law

Similar to organizations, procedural aspects are likely to be important in law because people are often subjected to decisions by authorities. Law is thus an area where procedural utility in the form of procedural fairness has been thoroughly studied. Many studies find that people react adversely to unfair legal procedures, irrespective of the objective judgment made by a court. Unfair procedures lead individuals to rate lower the legitimacy of authorities and their satisfaction with a trial, and it also affects subsequent compliance behavior (see, e.g., Tyler 1997, 2003 for overviews).

One study has already been summarized as an example in the introduction because it investigates real-life behavior and thus will be of most interest to economists. Lind et al. (1993) studied the acceptance of awards from court-ordered arbitration by real life litigants, which included corporate and individual litigants in federal courts. The authors find that litigants who judge the arbitration process as fair are much more likely to accept the court-ordered award (irrespective of the objective outcome). The decision to go on to have a formal trial was most strongly influenced by procedural fairness considerations. This is remarkable, as the disputes considered involved amounts of money of up to US$800,000. The objective size of the award and other outcome factors also predicted acceptance, although to a much lesser extent. Thus, the study shows that utility from procedures plays a role in lawsuits over and above outcome utility.

8.4   Concluding Remarks

People do not only care about outcomes, they also value the processes and conditions leading to outcomes. This "procedural utility" is a concept distinct from outcome utility as traditionally studied in economics. It is based on foundations that are well-researched in the psychological literature; it emerges from sources of great relevance for economic analysis, like institutions at the societal level and, on a smaller scale, fair processes employed in social relationships; and it is distinct from related approaches that have received some attention in the economic literature, like outcome fairness and intentions. Procedural utility has been found to play an important role for individuals' well-being in many areas of the economy, polity, and society. The empirical evidence discussed in this chapter suggests that people care about processes in their own right in their roles as consumers, employees, citizens, taxpayers, members of society, and individuals subject to various public and private authorities. As a consequence, economic science can gain from incorporating the concept of procedural utility more widely into economic theory and empirical research.

What could such an integration of procedural utility into the traditional economic approach look like? It has to be stressed that the concept of procedural utility in principle does not contradict the theoretical economic understanding of utility, which is based on the view that utility consists of everything that individuals value. However, procedural utility stands in contrast to how utility is usually defined in applications of economic theory to concrete problems and questions, and to how utility is used in many formal economic models. Therefore, an integration of procedural utility into the economic approach mainly requires an extended view of human well-being. In empirical research, a broader view seems relatively straightforward to implement. For example, the relative importance of "good procedures" and "good outcomes" can often be studied within the same empirical framework by using data on life or job satisfaction as measures for individual well-being, as illustrated in section 8.3. With respect to theoretical work, an integration of procedural utility into formal economic theory seems to be more of a challenge and remains to be addressed by future work. However, the development of formal models that take human concerns for processes and outcomes into account simultaneously may be guided by the theoretical considerations and psychological foundations outlined in section 8.2 (see also Frey, Benz, and Stutzer 2004 for a broader discussion).

While evidence discussed in this chapter inspires economic analysis and reasoning about economic policy in areas like consumption, work and employment, people's willingness to accept public undertakings or to pay taxes, and issues of social inequality, law, or organizational policies, there surely is room for promising further research in several so-far-unexplored directions. For example, the concept of procedural utility may be applied to other political institutions not considered in this paper, like fiscal federalism or majoritarian versus proportional electoral systems. Fiscal federalism may be a source of procedural utility because it allows for decentralized autonomous political decisions, and proportional electoral systems may be valued in procedural terms because they allow for a broader, more inclusive political representation. In the realm of economic organization, the notion that hierarchy involves procedural disutility might add to our understanding of the boundaries of the firm, and it might provide new insights into the organization of work. For example, not-for-profit firms tend to apply systematically different organizational procedures than for-profit firms, probably because procedural utility is a precondition for the particular pro-social motivation nonprofit workers have to possess (see, e.g., Benz 2005). For issues of redistribution, not only the social procedure of "equality of opportunities" might matter, but also whether transfers are in cash or in kind, or whether they are publicly or privately funded. Fair procedures are likely to shape conflict resolution, for instance, in bargaining between unions and firms. Finally, procedural aspects may be crucial for how people perceive discrimination in the workplace and in public life. An examination of these and related questions promises to add to a deeper understanding of human well-being and behavior beyond standard economic outcome considerations.

Notes

Much of the material contained in this chapter is based on ideas that were developed together with Bruno S. Frey and Alois Stutzer. I am grateful to them and to the participants of the CESifo Workshop on Economics and Psychology in Venice, July 18 and 19, 2005, for helpful remarks and discussions. I have also received valuable suggestions from two anonymous referees on how to improve the chapter.

1. Daniel Kahneman has coined the term "experienced utility" for this notion of utility, in contrast to traditional decision utility (Kahneman, Wakker, and Sarin 1997).

2. Self-determination theory by Deci and Ryan (2000) can be seen as a summary of manifold underlying theories that stress similar motives of the self. Related theories comprise, for instance, people's urge to master their environment for its own sake (White 1959) and their urge to be an original (DeCharms 1968), people's resistance to loss of control (Brehm 1966), and the reflection of perceived control in more effective behavior and higher positive affects (Bandura 1977; Peterson 1999; Seligman 1992). Based on similar reasoning on human functioning, several categorizations of the dimensions of well-being have been proposed; for instance, self-acceptance, positive relations with others, autonomy, environmental mastery, purpose in life, and personal growth (Ryff and Keyes 1995). In the literature on procedural justice, several psychological models have linked procedural justice to the human self, as in Tyler and Blader (2003).

3. In fact, this view is only defensively articulated in economics, if at all. A rare example for a procedural support of the market system by a liberal economist is by James Buchanan (1986, 22): "To the extent that voluntary exchange among persons is valued positively while coercion is valued negatively, there emerges the implication that substitution of the former for the latter is desired, on the presumption, of course, that such substitution is technologically feasible and is not prohibitively costly in resources."

4. Similar results on the job satisfaction of self-employed people have been found by Blanchflower and Oswald (1998); Blanchflower (2000); Blanchflower, Oswald, and Stutzer (2001); Hundley (2001); and Kawaguchi (2002). Moreover, Frey and Benz (2007), Kawaguchi (2002), and Hundley (2001) use an individual fixed-effects methodology in panel data to show that the higher job satisfaction of self-employed people is not due to different time-invariant personality characteristics. Nonmonetary benefits of self-employment and entrepreneurship are also documented in Hamilton (2000) and in Moskowitz and Vissing-Jorgensen (2002). For a general overview arguing that entrepreneurship should be seen as a non-profit-seeking activity, see Benz (2007).

References

Aghion, Philippe, and Jean Tirole. 1997. "Formal and Real Authority in Organizations." *Journal of Political Economy* 105, no. 1: 1–29.

Akerlof, George A., and Rachel E. Kranton. 2000. "Economics and Identity." *Quarterly Journal of Economics* 115, no. 3: 715–753.

Akerlof, George A., and Rachel E. Kranton. 2004. "Identity and the Economics of Organizations." *Journal of Economic Perspectives* 19, no. 1: 9–32.

Alesina, Alberto, and Eliana LaFerrara. 2005. "Preferences for Redistribution in the Land of Opportunities." *Journal of Public Economics* 89, nos. 5/6: 897–931.

Allingham, Michael G., and Agnar Sandmo. 1972. "Income Tax Evasion: A Theoretical Analysis." *Journal of Public Economics* 1, nos. 3–4: 323–338.

Alm, James, Gary H. McClelland, and William D. Schulze. 1992. "Why Do People Pay Taxes?" *Journal of Public Economics* 48, no. 1: 21–38.

Alm, James, Gary H. McClelland, and William D. Schulze. 1999. "Changing the Social Norm of Tax Compliance by Voting." *Kyklos* 52: 141–171.

Anand, Paul. 2001. "Procedural Fairness in Economic and Social Choice: Evidence from a Survey of Voters." *Journal of Economic Psychology* 22, no. 2: 247–270.

Andreoni, James, Brian Erard, and Jonathan Feinstein. 1998. "Tax Compliance." *Journal of Economic Literature* 36, no. 2: 818–860.

Baker, George, Robert Gibbons, and Kevin J. Murphy. 1999. "Informal Authority in Organizations." *Journal of Law, Economics and Organization* 15, no. 1: 56–73.

Bandura, Albert. 1977. "Self-Efficacy: Toward a Unifying Theory of Behavior Change." *Psychological Review* 84: 191–215.

Baumeister, Roy F. 1998. "The Self." In *The Handbook of Social Psychology*, vol. 1, ed. Daniel T. Gilbert, Susan T. Fiske, and Gardner Lindzey, 680–740. New York: Oxford University Press.

Bénabou, Roland, and Efe Ok. 2001. "Social Mobility and the Demand for Redistribution: The POUM Hypothesis." *Quarterly Journal of Economics* 116, no. 2: 447–487.

Bénabou, Roland, and Jean Tirole. 2005. "Belief in a Just World and Redistributive Politics." Working Paper No. 11208, National Bureau of Economic Research.

Benz, Matthias. 2005. "Not for the Profit, but for the Satisfaction?—Evidence on Worker Well-Being in Non-Profit Firms." *Kyklos* 58, no. 2: 155–176.

Benz, Matthias. 2007. "Entrepreneurship as a Non-Profit-Seeking Activity." Forthcoming in *International Entrepreneurship and Management Journal*.

Benz, Matthias, and Bruno S. Frey. 2003. "The Value of Autonomy: Evidence from the Self-Employed in 23 Countries." Institute for Empirical Research Working Paper No. 173, University of Zurich.

Benz, Matthias, and Alois Stutzer. 2003. "Do Workers Enjoy Procedural Utility?" *Applied Economics Quarterly* 49, no. 2: 149–172.

Bewley, Truman E. 1999. *Why Wages Don't Fall During a Recession*. Cambridge, MA: Harvard University Press.

Bies, R. J., and J. S. Moag. 1986. "Interactional Justice: Communication Criteria of Fairness." In *Research on Negotiation in Organizations*, vol. 1, ed. R. J. Lewicki, B. H. Sheppard, and B. H. Bazerman, 43–55. Greenwich, CT: JAI Press.

Blader, Steven L., and Tom R. Tyler. 2003. "A Four Component Model of Procedural Justice." *Personality and Social Psychology Bulletin* 29, no. 6: 747–758.

Blanchflower, David G. 2000. "Self-employment in OECD Coutries." *Labour Economics* 7, no. 5: 471–505.

Blanchflower, David G., and Andrew Oswald. 1998. "What Makes an Entrepreneur?" *Journal of Labor Economics* 16, no. 1: 26–60.

Blanchflower, David G., Andrew J. Oswald, and Alois Stutzer. 2001. "Latent Entrepreneurship Across Nations." *European Economic Review* 45, nos. 4–6: 680–691.

Bohnet, Iris, and Richard Zeckhauser. 2004. "Trust, Risk and Betrayal." *Journal of Economic Behavior & Organization* 55, no. 4: 467–484.

Bolton, Gary E., Jordi Brandts, and Axel Ockenfels. 2005. "Fair Procedures: Evidence from Games Involving Lotteries." *Economic Journal* 115, no. 506: 1054–1076.

Bolton, Gary E., and Axel Ockenfels. 2000. "ERC: A Theory of Equity, Reciprocity, and Competition." *American Economic Review* 90, no. 1: 166–193.

Botti, Simona. 2002. "Preference for Control and its Effect on Evaluation of Consumption Experience." Working Paper, Graduate School of Business, University of Chicago.

Brehm, Jack W. 1966. A *Theory of Psychological Reactance*. New York: Academic Press.

Buchanan, James M. 1986. *Liberty, Market and the State*. Brighton: Wheatsheaf.

Cohen-Charash, Yochi, and Paul E. Spector. 2001. "The Role of Justice in Organizations: A Meta-Analysis." *Organizational Behavior and Human Decision Processes* 86, no. 2: 278–321.

Colquitt, Jason A., Donald E. Conlon, Michael J. Wesson, Christopher Porter, and K. Yee Ng. 2001. "Justice at the Millenium: A Meta-Analytic Review of 25 Years of Organizational Justice Research." *Journal of Applied Psychology* 86, no. 3: 425–445.

Cooter, Robert, and Thomas Ulen. 2000. *Law and Economics*, 3rd edition. Reading, MA: Addison-Wesley.

Cordova, Diana I., and Mark R. Lepper. 1996. "Intrinsic Motivation and the Process of Learning: Beneficial Effects of Contextualization, Personalization, and Choice." *Journal of Educational Psychology* 88, no. 4: 715–730.

Dahl, Robert A., and Charles E. Lindblom. 1953. *Politics, Economics and Welfare: Planning and Politico-Economic Systems Resolved into Basic Social Processes*. New York: Harper.

DeCharms, Richard. 1968. *Personal Causation*. New York: Academic Press.

Deci, Edward L., and Richard M. Ryan. 2000. "The 'What' and 'Why' of Goal Pursuits: Human Needs and the Self-Determination of Behavior." *Psychological Inquiry* 11, no. 4: 227–268.

Diener, Ed, Eunkook M. Suh, Richard E. Lucas, and Heidi L. Smith. 1999. "Subjective Well-Being: Three Decades of Progress." *Psychological Bulletin* 125, no. 2: 276–303.

Falk, Armin, Ernst Fehr, and Urs Fischbacher. 2003. "On the Nature of Fair Behavior." *Economic Inquiry* 41, no. 1: 20–27.

Falk, Armin, and Urs Fischbacher. 2000. "A Theory of Reciprocity." Institute for Empirical Research in Economics Working Paper No. 6, University of Zurich.

Fehr, Ernst, and Lorenz Götte. 2005. "Robustness and Real Consequences of Nominal Wage Rigidity." *Journal of Monetary Economics* 52, no. 4: 779–804.

Fehr, Ernst, and Klaus M. Schmidt. 1999. "A Theory of Fairness, Competition, and Cooperation." *Quarterly Journal of Economics* 114, no. 3: 817–868.

Feld, Lars P., and Bruno S. Frey. 2002. "Trust Breeds Trust: How Taxpayers Are Treated." *Economics of Governance* 3: 87–99.

Feld, Lars P., and Jean-Robert Tyran. 2002. "Tax Evasion and Voting: An Experimental Analysis." *Kyklos* 55, no. 2: 197–222.

Fong, Christina. 2001. "Social Preferences, Self-Interest, and the Demand for Redistribution." *Journal of Public Economics* 82: 225–246.

Fong, Christina. 2005. "Prospective Mobility, Fairness, and the Demand for Redistribution." Working Paper, Carnegie Mellon University.

Frank, Robert H. 1985. *Choosing the Right Pond*. New York: Oxford University Press.

Frey, Bruno S., and Matthias Benz. 2007. "Being Independent is a Great Thing: Subjective Evaluations of Self-Employment and Hierarchy." Forthcoming in *Economica*.

Frey, Bruno S., Matthias Benz, and Alois Stutzer. 2004. "Introducing Procedural Utility: Not Only What, But Also How Matters." *Journal of Institutional and Theoretical Economics* 160, no. 3: 377–401.

Frey, Bruno S., and Lars P. Feld. 2002. "Deterrence and Morale in Taxation: An Empirical Analysis." Mimeo., Institute for Empirical Research in Economics, University of Zurich.

Frey, Bruno S., and Felix Oberholzer-Gee. 1996. "Fair Siting Procedures: An Empirical Analysis of Their Importance and Characteristics." *Journal of Policy Analysis and Management* 15, no. 3: 353–376.

Frey, Bruno S., and Felix Oberholzer-Gee. 1997. "The Cost of Price Incentives: An Empirical Analysis of Motivation Crowding-Out." *American Economic Review* 87, no. 4: 746–755.

Frey, Bruno S., and Werner W. Pommerehne. 1993. "On the Fairness of Pricing—An Empirical Survey among the General Population." *Journal of Economic Behavior and Organization* 20, no. 3: 295–307.

Frey, Bruno S., and Alois Stutzer. 2002a. *Happiness and Economics: How the Economy and Institutions Affect Human Well-Being*. Princeton, NJ: Princeton University Press.

Frey, Bruno S. and Alois Stutzer. 2002b. "What Can Economists Learn from Happiness Research?" *Journal of Economic Literature* 40, no. 2: 402–435.

Frey, Bruno S., and Alois Stutzer. 2005. "Beyond Outcomes: Measuring Procedural Utility." *Oxford Economic Papers* 57, no. 1: 90–111.

Greenberg, Jerald. 1990a. "Employee Theft as a Reaction to Underpayment Inequity: The Hidden Cost of Pay Cuts." *Journal of Applied Psychology* 75, no. 5: 561–570.

Greenberg, Jerald. 1990b. "Organizational Justice: Yesterday, Today, and Tomorrow." *Journal of Management* 16, no. 2: 399–432.

Güth, Werner, and Hannelore Weck-Hanneman. 1997. "Do People Care About Democracy? An Experiment Exploring the Value of Voting Rights." *Public Choice* 91, no. 1: 27–47.

Hamilton, Barton H. 2000. "Does Entrepreneurship Pay? An Empirical Analysis of Returns to Self-Employment." *Journal of Political Economy* 108, no. 3: 604–632.

Harsanyi, John C. 1993. "Normative Validity and Meaning of von Neumann-Morgenstern Utilities." In *Frontiers of Game Theory*, ed. Ken Binmore, Alan Kirman, and Piero Tani, 307–320. Cambridge, MA: MIT Press.

Heider, Fritz. 1958. *The Psychology of Interpersonal Relations*. New York: Wiley.

Hirschman, Albert O. 1973. "The Changing Tolerance for Income Inequality in the Course of Economic Development." *Quarterly Journal of Economics* 87, no. 4: 544–566.

Hundley, Greg. 2001. "Why and When Are the Self-Employed More Satisfied With Their Work?" *Industrial Relations* 40, no. 2: 293–317.

Idson, Todd L. 1990. "Establishment Size, Job Satisfaction and the Structure of Work." *Applied Economics* 22: 1007–1018.

Iyengar, Sheena S., and Mark R. Lepper. 2000. "When Choice is Demotivating: Can One Desire Too Much of a Good Thing?" *Journal of Personality and Social Psychology* 79, no. 6: 995–1006.

Kahneman, Daniel, Jack L. Knetsch, and Richard H. Thaler. 1986. "Fairness as a Constraint on Profit Seeking: Entitlements in the Market." *American Economic Review* 76, no. 4: 728–741.

Kahneman, Daniel, Peter P. Wakker, and Rakesh Sarin. 1997. "Back to Bentham? Explorations of Experienced Utility." *Quarterly Journal of Economics* 112, no. 2: 375–405.

Kawaguchi, Daiji. 2002. "Compensating Wage Differentials Among Self-Employed Workers: Evidence from Job Satisfaction Scores." Discussion Paper No. 568, Institute of Social and Economic Research, Osaka University.

Khalil, Elias L. 1996. "Respect, Admiration, Aggrandizement: Adam Smith as Economic Psychologist." *Journal of Economic Psychology* 17, no. 5: 555–577.

Konovsky, Mary A. 2000. "Understanding Procedural Justice and its Impact on Business Organizations." *Journal of Management* 26, no. 3: 489–511.

Konow, James. 2003. "Which Is the Fairest One of All? A Positive Analysis of Justice Theories." *Journal of Economic Literature* 41, no. 4: 1188–1239.

Köszegi, Botond. 2002a. "Ego Utility and Information Acquisition." Mimeo., University of California at Berkeley.

Köszegi, Botond. 2002b. "Ego Utility, Overconfidence, and Task Choice." Mimeo., University of California at Berkeley.

Kunreuther, Howard, and Paul R. Kleindorfer. 1986. "A Sealed-Bid Auction Mechanism for Siting Noxious Facilities." *American Economic Review* 76, no. 2: 295–299.

Kysar, Douglas A. 2004. "Preferences for Processes: The Process/Product Distinction and the Regulation of Consumer Choice." *Harvard Law Review* 118, no. 525: 526–624.

Lane, Robert E. 2000. *The Loss of Happiness in Market Economies*. New Haven, CT: Yale University Press.

Langer, Ellen, and Judith Rodin. 1976. "The Effects of Choice and Enhanced Personal Responsibility for the Aged: A Field Experiment in an Institutional Setting." *Journal of Personality and Social Psychology* 34, no. 2: 191–198.

Le Menestrel, Marc. 2001. "A Process Approach to the Utility for Gambling." *Theory and Decision* 50, no. 3: 249–262.

Lind, E. Allen, Jerald Greenberg, Kimberley S. Scott, and Thomas D. Welchans. 2000. "The Winding Road from Employee to Complainant." *Administrative Science Quarterly* 45, no. 3: 557–590.

Lind, E. Allen, Carol T. Kulik, Maureen Ambrose, and Maria V. de Vera Park. 1993. "Individual and Corporate Dispute Resolution: Using Procedural Fairness as a Decision Heuristic." *Administrative Science Quarterly* 38, no. 2: 224–251.

Lind, E. Allan, and Tom R. Tyler. 1988. *The Social Psychology of Procedural Justice.* New York: Plenum Press.

Loewenstein, George. 2000. "Is More Choice Always Better?" Working Paper, Carnegie Mellon University.

Marmot, Michael. 2004. *The Status Syndrome: How Social Standing Affects Our Health and Longevity.* New York: Times Books.

Marmot, Michael, Hans Bosma, Harry Hemingway, Eric Brunner, and Stephen Stansfeld. 1997. "Contribution of Job Control and Other Risk Factors to Social Variations in Coronary Heart Disease Incidence." *Lancet* 350, no. 9073: 235–239.

Marschak, Jacob. 1950. "Uncertain Prospects, and Measurable Utility." *Econometrica* 18: 111–141.

Moskovitz, Tobias J., and Annette Vissing-Jorgensen. 2002. "The Returns to Entrepreneurial Investment: A Private Equity Premium Puzzle?" *American Economic Review* 92, no. 4: 745–778.

Mueller, Dennis C. 2003. *Public Choice III.* Cambridge: Cambridge University Press.

O'Sullivan, Arthur. 1993. "Voluntary Auctions for Noxious Facilities: Incentives to Participate and the Efficiency of Siting Decisions." *Journal of Environmental Economics and Management* 25, no. 1: 12–26.

Oswald, Andrew J. 1997. "Happiness and Economic Performance." *Economic Journal* 107, no. 445: 1815–1831.

Pascal, Blaise. 1670. *Pensées.* Paris: Port-Royal.

Peterson, Christopher. 1999. "Personal Control and Well-Being." In *Well-Being: The Foundation of Hedonic Psychology,* ed. Daniel Kahneman, Ed Diener, and Norbert Schwarz, 288–301. New York: Russell Sage Foundation.

Pommerehne, Werner W., and Hannelore Weck-Hannemann. 1996. "Tax Rates, Tax Administration and Income Tax Evasion in Switzerland." *Public Choice* 88, nos. 1–2: 161–170.

Rabin, Matthew. 1993. "Incorporating Fairness into Game Theory and Economics." *American Economic Review* 83, no. 5: 1281–1302.

Rotemberg, Julio. 2005. "Customer Anger at Price Increases, Changes in the Frequency of Price Adjustment and Monetary Policy." *Journal of Monetary Economics* 52, no. 4: 829–852.

Ryff, Carol D., and Corey Lee M. Keyes. 1995. "The Structure of Psychological Well-Being Revisited." *Journal of Personality and Social Psychology* 69, no. 4: 719–727.

Sandbu, Martin. 2004. "Fairness and the Road Not Taken: An Experimental Test of Non-Reciprocal Set-Dependence in Distributive Preferences." Working Paper, Columbia University.

Schulz, Richard, and Barbara H. Hanusa. 1978. "Long-term Effects of Control and Predictability-Enhancing Interventions: Findings and Ethical Issues." *Journal of Personality and Social Psychology* 36, no. 11: 1194–1201.

Schwartz, Barry. 2000. "Self-Determination: The Tyranny of Freedom." *American Psychologist* 55, no. 1: 79–88.

Seligman, Martin E. P. 1992. *Helplessness: On Depression, Development, and Death.* New York: Freeman.

Sen, Amartya K. 1995. "Rationality and Social Choice." *American Economic Review* 85, no. 1: 1–24.

Sen, Amartya K. 1997. "Maximization and the Act of Choice." *Econometrica* 65, no. 4: 745–779.

Slemrod, Joel, and Shlomo Yitzhaki. 2002. "Tax Avoidance, Evasion, and Administration." In *Handbook of Public Economics*, vol. 3, ed. Alan J. Auerbach and Martin Feldstein, 1423–1470. New York: Elsevier.

Torgler, Benno. 2005. "Tax Morale and Direct Democracy." *European Journal of Political Economy* 21: 525–531.

Torgler, Benno, Christoph A. Schaltegger, and Markus Schaffner. 2003. "Is Forgiveness Divine? A Cross-Culture Analysis of Tax Amnesties." *Swiss Journal of Economics and Statistics* 139: 375–396.

Tsuchiya, Aki, Luis S. Miguel, Richard Edlin, Allan Wailoo, and Paul Dolan. 2005. "Procedural Justice in Public Healthcare Resource Allocation." *Applied Health Economics and Health Policy* 4, no. 2: 119–128.

Tyler, Tom R. 1997. "Procedural Fairness and Compliance with the Law." *Swiss Journal of Economics and Statistics* 133, no. 2: 219–240.

Tyler, Tom R. 2003. "Procedural Justice, Legitimacy, and the Effective Rule of Law." In *Crime and Justice—A Review of Research.* Vol. 30, ed. M. Tonry, 431–505. Chicago: University of Chicago Press.

Tyler, Tom R., and Steven L. Blader. 2000. *Cooperation in Groups: Procedural Justice, Social Identity, and Behavioral Engagement.* Philadelphia: Psychology Press.

Tyler, Tom R., and Steven L. Blader. 2003. "The Group Engagement Model: Procedural Justice, Social Identity, and Cooperative Behavior." *Personality and Social Psychology Review* 7, no. 4: 349–361.

Tyler, Tom R., Robert J. Boeckmann, Heather J. Smith, and Yuen J. Huo. 1997. *Social Justice in a Diverse Society.* Boulder, CO: Westview Press.

Tyran, Jean-Robert, and Dirk Engelmann. 2005. "To Buy or Not to Buy? An Experimental Study of Consumer Boycotts in Retail Markets." *Economica* 72, no. 285: 1–16.

von Neumann, John, and Oskar Morgenstern. 1944. *Theory of Games and Economic Behavior.* Princeton, NJ: Princeton University Press.

228   Matthias Benz

Wailoo, Allan, and Paul Anand. 2005. "The Nature of Procedural Preferences for Health-Care Rationing Decisions." *Social Science and Medicine* 60, no. 2: 223–236.

White, R. Winthrop. 1959. "Motivation Reconsidered: The Concept of Competence." *Psychological Review* 66, no. 5: 297–333.

Williamson, Oliver E. 1975. *Markets and Hierarchies: Analysis and Antitrust Implications.* New York: Free Press.

Zuckerman, Miron, Joseph Porac, Drew Latin, Raymond Smith, and Edward L. Deci. 1978. "On the Importance of Self-Determination for Intrinsically Motivated Behavior." *Personality and Social Psychology Bulletin* 4, no. 3: 443–446.

9   The Helping Hand—A Brief Anatomy

Felix Oberholzer-Gee

Imagine an organization whose employees are unwilling to help each other. No one stays late to finish a colleague's project, no one returns a misplaced document, warns the sales representative of a customer's peculiarities, or points out that another engineer is working on the same problem. Not a person in this organization holds doors open, moves a stack of papers a colleague might trip over, or points the pizza delivery person in the right direction. From the ordinary and mundane to critical business functions, the willingness of employees to support one another is critical for the performance of organizations.

Helping behavior, many social scientists argue, is best understood as motivated by reciprocity.[1] In economics, reciprocity is modeled as a willingness to help those who have helped us (Rabin 1993; Fehr and Gächter 2000; Charness and Rabin 2002). Sociologists, using a broader conception of reciprocity, distinguish restricted and generalized exchange (Blau 1964; Lévi-Strauss 1949; Malinowski 1922; Mauss 1925). Restricted exchange is reciprocity in the sense used in economics: *A* helps *B* because *A* expects *B* to support her. In generalized exchange, *A* gives to *B* because *A* expects help from *C*. Thus reciprocation is not mutual, but indirect. While direct reciprocity is of obvious importance in small groups and critical in companies, generalized exchange can enhance solidarity in more anonymous settings where individuals do not expect to interact in the future. For instance, most people are willing to help lost tourists (Rabinowitz 1997). Such helping behavior is hardly motivated by direct reciprocity since the local person is unlikely to ever see the tourist again. As groups and organizations get larger, supporting behavior is more likely due to generalized rather than direct exchange. For instance, in professional services firms, project teams frequently exchange information although no formal incentives support this type of exchange (Levine 2004). As there are many groups in these large companies, it is unlikely that a helpful team will require the assistance of those it has supported in the past. Rather, the provision of helpful information occurs in a system of generalized exchange.

The difference between direct and indirect reciprocity is also of interest because the two types can have very different consequences. Direct reciprocity is based on a quid pro quo mentality that holds actors accountable for the balance of transfers and often leads to conflict over the fairness of exchange (Ekeh 1974). In contrast, generalized reciprocity engenders trust and social solidarity (Uehara 1990).

While generalized reciprocity encourages helping behavior, there is no reason to believe that the resulting level of cooperation will be optimal. Thus, an important question concerns the types of incentives and interventions that can further encourage solidarity. Starting in the 1970s, social psychologists isolated numerous factors that encourage helping behavior. Unfortunately, many of these—gender and mood being notable examples—are difficult to manipulate. We know much about the forces affecting helping behavior, but little of what we know allows us to increase the likelihood that individuals will assist others (Latané and Nida 1981). To see if economic incentives can strengthen generalized exchange, I conducted an experiment that encouraged pro-social behavior with the help of monetary incentives. I test if subjects are more willing to let a hurried stranger cut in line if the stranger offers monetary compensation. I find that money does encourage helping behavior, but only because those waiting in line believe that a more hurried stranger offers more money. As I discuss in greater detail below, granting a favor in exchange for payment is no ordinary market transaction.

The first part of this chapter provides a brief survey of helping-hand research. I am particularly interested in factors that predict when generalized exchange is likely to arise. In section 9.2, I discuss the results of the waiting line experiment and section 9.3 offers concluding remarks.

9.1 Understanding the Helping Hand

The classic examples of generalized exchange are the Kula ring (Malinowski 1922) and matrilateral cross-cousin marriage (Lévi-Strauss 1949). Following these early studies, social scientists documented a number of instances in which generalized reciprocity appears to guide behavior. The examples include revolving credit associations, anonymous reviews, donations of blood, contributions to open-source software, and many instances of spontaneous help (Bearman 1997; von Hippel 2001; Osterloh and Rota 2005). In many of these examples, one can argue that individuals have private incentives to support the group. For instance, software developers who contribute open-source code might do so to signal their ability to future employers (Lerner and Tirole 2002). Private incentives, however, are not inconsistent with generalized exchange. Recall that A helps B because A expects help from someone else, a "selfish" motivation that distinguishes generalized reciprocity from altruism. Hence, to see if open-source software represents a system of generalized exchange, understanding employers' motivations in hiring open-source developers is critical. If this is simply a cost-effective way to identify talent, no reciprocity is in play. However, if the firm hires open-source programmers because it expects other members of the open-source community to be more helpful should it face technical challenges in the future, the hiring strategy is in fact consistent with a system of indirect reciprocity.

Research on helping behavior and generalized reciprocity has identified three factors influencing the likelihood of assistance: the cost and benefits of helping, information about the person who seeks help, and contextual variables. I discuss these factors in turn.

9.1.1 Cost and Benefits

Not surprisingly, individuals consider the cost and benefits of helping when they decide whether or not to offer assistance (Batson 1987; Dovidio 1984; Dovidio et al. 1991). For example, students are more likely to help classmates when their exams are not graded on a curve (Bell et al. 2001). Similarly, in companies with strong promotion incentives, employees are less likely to help one another (Drago and Garvey 1998). In both cases, competitive forces raise the price of supporting others and impede the helping hand. The benefits of helping also matter. For example, better-looking individuals are more likely to receive help, presumably because the benefits of helping are larger when assisting a good-looking person (West and Brown 1975; Benson, Karabenick, and Lerner 1976).

9.1.2 Information

What we know about the person seeking help is critical for two reasons. First, individuals are more willing to assist if the recipient bears no responsibility for his predicament (Weiner 1995; Fong 2004). For instance, a person who fell because he is sick is more likely to receive support than a person who fell because he is drunk (Piliavin, Rodin, and Piliavin 1969). Similarly, students are typically willing to help a classmate who was in an accident, but they often refuse to support a colleague who needs help because he was out partying (Betancourt 1990). Second, generalized exchange can persist as long as actors have reason to believe their own willingness to help is somehow linked to the help they will receive. For example, Takahashi (2000) studies a group whose members support a randomly chosen person, provided this person meets the giver's "sense of fairness." More generous members are more selective in their choice of recipient, reflecting an Aristotelian sense of fairness. With these simple rules, evolutionary simulation shows that robust generalized exchange will emerge among rational selfish actors. A critical ingredient in models of this type is information about the recipient. Unless the person who is asked for help knows something about the recipient, it is difficult to see how the helper would apply his sense of fairness. At this point, rational models of generalized exchange developed in sociology and neighboring disciplines can explain widespread cooperation in large businesses and stable communities where many members will have earned a reputation. Developing theoretical models of unilateral resource giving to a complete stranger, however, remains a task for the future (Takahashi 2000, 1129).

9.1.3   Contextual Factors

Many social psychologists see helping behavior as a function of the specific momentary situations in which bystanders find themselves when they are asked for help (Amato 1990). An important regularity is that individuals are less likely to help if there are many bystanders (Latané and Darley 1970), a rational response, because the bystanders feel less responsible (Harrington 2001). A second important contextual variable is the helper's mood (Batson 1998). Assistance is more likely when the sun shines (Schneider, Lesko, and Garrett 1980) and after individuals have watched a happy movie (Wilson 1981; Oswald 1996).

The cost of helping, information about the recipient, and contextual factors all influence the likelihood of assistance in predictable ways. However, there is no reason to believe that the resulting level of support for others will generally be optimal. Thus, it is interesting to study factors that might enhance general reciprocity. The simplest way to further generalized exchange is to reward those who are willing to assist others. The following section describes an experiment in which I use financial incentives to encourage helping behavior.

9.2 Monetary Incentives and the Helping Hand

Economists have studied the link between helping behavior and financial incentives in the context of multitasking models (Holmstrom and Milgrom 1991; Baker 1992). The basic idea is that linking an employee's financial compensation to imperfect measures of output will undercut his incentive to perform nonrewarded tasks such as helping. Similar effects ensue if compensation is based on relative performance. For instance, strong promotion incentives are likely to undermine cooperation (Lazear 1989; Drago and Garvey 1998).

These problems disappear if the financial incentives are linked to helping behavior itself. To see how individuals would react to monetary incentives for granting a favor, I conducted a simple field experiment in which I offered five hundred individuals who were waiting in line $0, $1, $3, $5, or $10 for letting me cut in (for a more detailed analysis of this experiment, see Oberholzer-Gee 2005). The experiment took place in a number of locations, including a university cafeteria, a train station, and a government office. In each instance, the experimenters approached a randomly chosen person who was waiting in line. In the treatments with positive offers, the opening statement was: "Can I go in front of you, I will pay you [$ amount]." All subjects who wanted the money were paid immediately.

Table 9.1 reports the results of this experiment. Sixty-two percent of all subjects waiting in line let the experimenter cut in. Stronger incentives clearly encourage helping behavior. Forty-five percent of subjects granted the request in the absence of monetary incentives, and 76 percent did so when offered $10. However, few people actually sell the right to jump the queue. In the $1 treatment, five out of the fifty individuals who granted the request took the money. No subject accepted an offer of $3, even though 65 individuals granted the request. Among those who let experimenters jump the queue, no clear trend in the probability of accepting the money across the four treatments is discernible. Twenty percent took the $5, 11 percent accepted $10.

Monetary incentives play an unusual role in this experiment. Prices normally fulfill two functions: they indicate scarcity and they compensate the owners of resources when they part with their assets. In the line experiment, prices play only the first role. For most subjects, no

Table 9.1
What fraction of requests are granted?

Offer ($)	# obs.	Requests granted	Positions sold (of # granted)
no money	100	0.45 (0.5)	
$1	100	0.5 (0.50)	0.1 (0.30)
$3	100	0.65 (0.48)	0
$5	100	0.75 (0.43)	0.2 (0.40)
$10	100	0.76 (0.43)	0.11 (0.31)

compensation takes place. The logic underlying this exchange is the logic of generalized reciprocity. Helping strangers requires no immediate payback; the reward for helpful assistance is the expectation to be helped when in need. Interestingly, the results of the line experiment indicate that individuals granting the request are not only willing to help without being compensated, but most of them feel that accepting money would actually make them worse off. Conditional on letting the experimenter jump the queue, a rational person only refuses payment if the value of money is negative. This behavior echoes findings in the literature on fair pricing. Many people feel that it is unfair to raise prices in situations of excess demand (Kahneman, Knetsch, and Thaler 1986; Frey and Pommerehne 1993).[2] As the queue experiment demonstrates, most individuals do indeed refrain from exploiting such a situation when given the opportunity to do so. Subjects pay up to $10 to live up to the rules of fairness.

The obligation to help increases when a person is in greater need. In a survey of empirical research studying fair exchanges, Konow (2003) argues that need, efficiency, and equity are the three principles guiding fairness judgments. Justice demands that the basic needs of all are met (Rawls 1971; Raphael 1980), but above this minimum, equity and efficiency guide fair allocations. There is much empirical evidence that individuals are more willing to help if the recipient is in greater need (Eckel and Grossman 1996; Gärtner, Jungeilges, and Neck 2001). In the line experiment, prices apparently "work" because they signal the need of those who are in a rush. The more pressing the demand, the greater is the willingness to pay to cut in. Since prices signal the degree of urgency, individuals are more willing to help when the experimenter is more hard pressed for time.

Theories of helping behavior predict that those waiting in line are more willing to grant a favor if the experimenter is not responsible for the emergency situation. To test this prediction, I approached fifteen individuals who had previously granted my request, asking them if I could cut in again. In all cases, I offered the same financial compensation. Everyone declined my request. Most subjects appeared upset, some were angry, and a few were outright hostile, suggesting it was probably not safe to continue the experiment.

By repeatedly requesting an identical favor, I undermined individuals' willingness to help. What had appeared to be an emergency the previous day was in fact planned and calculated, an act for which I was responsible. Note that this reaction is inconsistent with a simple model of altruism, a motivation often invoked to explain helping behavior. Altruists are better off when the welfare of others increases. Helping the same person repeatedly does not seem offensive to the altruist, but it is a violation of the rules of generalized exchange.

Preferences for outcomes that conform to some principle of distributive justice represent another possible explanation for the results of the line experiment. In this view, people let others cut in simply because it is the right thing to do. To distinguish such outcome-based preferences from generalized exchange, it is useful to consider a thought experiment. Suppose you lived in a country whose people are unwilling to let others cut in line. No matter how pressing your need, all requests to jump the queue are declined. How likely is it that you will let someone go in front? If a hostile environment of this sort diminishes one's willingness to extend favors, generalized reciprocity is a significant force in the explanation of helping behavior.

9.3   Conclusions

In recent research, economists have started to take seriously the idea that human interaction is often shaped by reciprocity. Direct reciprocity, which is based on a quid pro quo mentality, is the typical focus of this research.[3] Earlier contributions in sociology and anthropology, however, argued that direct *and* generalized exchange are important social forces. By studying situations in which strangers ask for favors, the literature on helping behavior has identified innumerable situations in which a large majority of persons will fulfill a stranger's request. The willingness to help varies in ways that are well understood.

Unfortunately, studies on helping behavior were less successful in identifying practical mechanisms that would increase solidarity. Financial incentives are a natural starting point to see how informal support systems can be strengthened. The news is mixed: more attractive offers elicit more help, but the exchange of favors is no ordinary market transaction. In the context of helping behavior, prices work because they signal urgency. Many people are more inclined to help if the recipient is in greater need. On the other hand, money does not reliably trigger greater assistance. Once helpers understand that the stranger willfully employs incentives to encourage assistance in a situation for which he bears responsibility, incentives prove ineffective. The rules of generalized exchange, it appears, include built-in safeguards that protect persons with good intentions from exploitation.

Notes

1. An alternative explanation is altruism. I discuss later why I believe altruistic motivations are inconsistent with the empirical results presented in this chapter.

2. These price increases are deemed unfair because the seller is not entitled to the extra profit. If the profit is given to a charity, most people no longer object to increases in price (Frey and Gygi 1998).

3. A few recent papers have begun to look at particular aspects of indirect reciprocity. For instance, Fehr and Fischbacher (2004) and Carpenter and Matthews (2004) study individuals' willingness to punish those who violate a social norm. Croson and Konow (2005) investigate if subjects are willing to reward another person who has been kind to someone else.

References

Amato, Paul R. 1990. "Personality and Social Network Involvement as Predictors of Helping Behavior in Everyday Life." *Social Psychology Quarterly* 53, no. 1: 31–43.

Baker, George P. 1992. "Incentive Contracts and Performance Measurement." *Journal of Political Economy* 100, no. 3: 598–614.

Batson, C. Daniel. 1987. "Prosocial Motivation: Is It Ever Truly Altruistic?" *Advances in Experimental Social Psychology* 20: 65–122.

Batson, C. Daniel. 1998. "Altruism and Prosocial Behavior." In *Handbook of Social Psychology*, vol. 2, ed. D. T. Gilbert, S. T. Fiske, and G. Lindzey, 282–316. New York: McGraw Hill.

Bearman, Peter. 1997. "Generalized Exchange." *American Journal of Sociology* 102: 1383–1415.

Bell, Jennifer, Jana Grekul, Navjot Lamba, Christine Minas, and W. Andrew Harrell. 2001. "The Impact of Cost on Student Helping Behavior." *Journal of Social Psychology* 135, no. 1: 49–56.

Benson, Peter L., Stuart A. Karabenick, and Richard M. Lerner. 1976. "Pretty Pleases: The Effects of Physical Attractiveness, Race, and Sex on Receiving Help." *Journal of Experimental Social Psychology* 12, no. 5: 409–415.

Betancourt, Hector. 1990. "An Attribution-Empathy Model of Helping Behavior." *Personality and Social Psychology Bulletin* 16: 573–591.

Blau, Peter M. 1964. *Exchange and Power in Social Life.* New York: Wiley.

Carpenter, Jeffrey Paul, and Peter Hans Matthews. 2004. "Social Reciprocity." Working Paper, Middlebury College.

Croson, Rachel, and James Konow. 2005. "Double Standards: Social Preferences and Their Self-Serving Biases." Working Paper, University of Pennsylvania.

Charness, Gary, and Matthew Rabin. 2002. "Understanding Social Preferences with Simple Tests." *Quarterly Journal of Economics* 117, no. 3: 817–869.

Dovidio, John F. 1984. "Helping Behavior and Altruism: An Empirical and Conceptual Overview." *Advances in Experimental Social Psychology* 17: 361–427.

Dovidio, John F., J. A. Piliavin, S. Gaertner, D. A. Schroeder, and R. D. Clark III. 1991. "The Arousal: Cost-Reward Model and the Process of Intervention: A Review of the Evidence." In *Prosocial Behavior: Review of Personality and Social Psychology*, ed. M. Clark, 86–118. Newbury Park, CA: Sage.

Drago, Robert, and Gerald T. Garvey. 1998. "Incentives for Helping on the Job: Theory and Evidence." *Journal of Labor Economics* 16, no. 1: 1–25.

Eckel, Catherine C., and Philip J. Grossman. 1996. "Altruism in Anonymous Dictator Games." *Games and Economic Behavior* 16, no. 2: 181–191.

Ekeh, Peter Palmer. 1974. *Social Exchange Theory: The Two Traditions.* London: Heinemann Educational.

Fehr, Ernst, and Urs Fischbacher. 2004. "Third-Party Punishment and Social Norms." *Evolution and Human Behavior* 25: 63–87.

Fehr, Ernst, and Simon Gächter. 2000. "Fairness and Retaliation: The Economics of Reciprocity." *Journal of Economic Perspectives* 14, no. 3: 159–181.

Frey, Bruno S., and Beat Gygi. 1998. "Die Fairness von Preisen." *Schweizerische Zeitschrift für Volkswirtschaft und Statistik* 124: 519–541.

Frey, Bruno S., and Werner W. Pommerehne. 1993. "On the Fairness of Pricing—an Empirical Survey Among the General Population." *Journal of Economic Behavior and Organization* 20: 295–307.

Fong, Christina. 2004. "Empathic Responsiveness: Evidence from a Randomized Experiment on Giving to Welfare Recipients." Working Paper, Carnegie Mellon University.

Gärtner, Wulf, Jochen Jungeilges, and Reinhard Neck. 2001. "Cross-Cultural Equity Evaluations: A Questionnaire-Experimental Approach." *European Economic Review* 45, nos. 4–6: 953–963.

Harrington, Joseph E. 2001. "A Simple Game-Theoretic Explanation for the Relationship between Group Size and Helping." *Journal of Mathematical Psychology* 45: 389–392.

Holmstrom, Bengt, and Paul Milgrom. 1991. "Multitask Principal-Agent Analyses: Incentive Contracts, Asset Ownership, and Job Design." *Journal of Law, Economics, & Organization* 7: 24–52.

Kahneman, Daniel, Jack L. Knetsch, and Richard Thaler. 1986. "Fairness as a Constraint on Profit Seeking: Entitlements in the Market." *American Economic Review* 76: 728–741.

Konow, James. 2003. "Which Is the Fairest One of All? A Positive Analysis of Justice Theories." *Journal of Economic Literature* 41, no. 4: 1188–1239.

Latané, Bibb, and John M. Darley. 1970. *The Unresponsive Bystander: Why Doesn't He Help?* New York: Appleton-Century Crofts.

Latané, Bibb, and S. Nida. 1981. "Ten Years of Research on Group Size and Helping." *Psychological Bulletin* 89: 308–324.

Lazear, Edward P. 1989. "Pay Equality and Industrial Politics." *Journal of Political Economy* 97, no. 3: 561–580.

Lerner, Josh, and Jean Tirole. 2002. "Some Simple Economics of Open Source." *Journal of Industrial Economics* 50: 197–234.

Lévi-Strauss, Claude. 1949. *Les structures élémentaires de la parenté.* Paris: Presses Universitaires de France.

Levine, Sheen S. 2004. "The Strength of Performative Ties: Network Exchange in a Knowledge Intensive Firm." Working Paper, Wharton School, University of Pennsylvania.

Malinowski, Bronislaw. 1922. *Argonauts of the Western Pacific.* London: Routledge.

Mauss, Marcel. 1925. *The Gift: Forms and Functions of Exchange in Archaic Societies.* London: Cohen & West.

Oberholzer-Gee, Felix. 2005. "A Market for Time: Fairness and Efficiency in Waiting Lines." Working Paper, Harvard Business School.

Osterloh, Margit, and Sandra Rota. 2005. "Open Source Software Development—Just Another Case of Collective Invention?" Working Paper no. 2005-8, Center for Research in Economics, Management, and the Arts.

Oswald, Patricia A. 1996. "The Effects of Cognitive and Affective Perspective Taking on Empathic Concern and Altruistic Helping." *Journal of Social Psychology* 136, no. 5: 613–624.

Piliavin, Irving M., Judith Rodin, and Jayne Allyn Piliavin. 1969. "Good Samaritanism: An Underground Phenomenon?" *Journal of Personality and Social Psychology* 13: 289–299.

Rabin, Matthew. 1993. "Incorporating Fairness into Game Theory and Economics." *American Economic Review* 83, no. 5: 1281–1302.

Rabinowitz, Frederic E. 1997. "Helpfulness to Lost Tourists." *Journal of Social Psychology* 137, no. 4: 502–509.

Raphael, David Daiches. 1980. *Justice and Liberty*. London: Athlone.

Rawls, John. 1971. *A Theory of Justice*. Cambridge, Mass.: Belknap Press.

Schneider, Frank W., Wayne A. Lesko, and William A. Garrett. 1980. "Helping Behavior in Hot, Comfortable, and Cold Temperatures: A Field Study." *Environment and Behavior* 12: 231–240.

Takahashi, Nobuyuki. 2000. "The Emergence of Generalized Exchange." *American Journal of Sociology* 105, no. 4: 1105–1134.

Uehara, Edwina. 1990. "Dual Exchange Theory, Social Networks, and Informal Social Support." *American Journal of Sociology* 96, no. 3: 521–557.

von Hippel, Eric. 2001. "Innovation by User Communities: Learning from Open-Source Software." *Sloan Management Review* 42, no. 4: 82–86.

Weiner, Bernard. 1995. *Judgments of Responsibility: A Foundation for a Theory of Social Conduct*. New York: Guilford Press.

West, Stephen G., and T. Jan Brown. 1975. "Physical Attractiveness, the Severity of the Emergency and Helping: A Field Experiment and Interpersonal Simulation." *Journal of Experimental Social Psychology* 11, no. 6: 531–538.

Wilson, D. W. 1981. "Is Helping a Laughing Matter?" *Psychology* 18: 6–9.

VI   Evaluation

10

Efficient Social Engineering and Realistic Cognitive Modeling: A Psychologist's Thoughts

Ralph Hertwig

Two decades ago, in 1985, an illustrious group of economists, psychologists, and other social scientists convened at the University of Chicago to discuss the implications of a growing body of experimental evidence documenting systematic departures from the dictates of rational economic behavior. The conference's proceedings, *Rational Choice: The Contrast Between Economics and Psychology*, included contributions from no fewer than two Nobel Prize laureates for economic sciences (Herbert A. Simon and Kenneth J. Arrow) and three future laureates (Daniel Kahneman, Robert E. Lucas, and Merton M. Miller). The book's two editors prefaced the contributions as follows:

The modern disciplines of economics and psychology are the direct descendants of a common body of philosophical ideas. As a result of their separate evolutions, however, the two disciplines interpret their ideas quite differently and generally pursue different research objectives using *disparate* methods of investigation and analysis. Nonetheless, since there are many areas of human activity where economists and psychologists study the same phenomena, it seems natural to ask whether the *present separation* is in the better interest of both disciplines.... *In other words, can the modern disciplines of psychology and economics learn from each other, and, if so, what?* (Hogarth and Reder 1987, 1; emphasis added)

This depiction of a somewhat estranged relationship between psychology and economics is a vivid reminder of a recent past in which, by conceptualizing rationality purely in terms of observable choices (substantive rationality), economics, according to Simon (1987, 26), took a path different from all other social sciences. In contrast, asserted Simon, psychology understands rationality in terms of the processes it employs, including "nonrational processes" (procedural rationality). These involve motivations, emotions, and simple approximate strategies used in reasoning to permit limited information-processing capabilities to cope with complex realities. Regardless of what different notions of rationality steered psychology and economics onto different paths, however, one need not be a naive idealist to believe that—merely twenty years after the Chicago conference—the question of whether psychology and economics can learn from each other is unambiguously answered: yes, they can.

Today, as Frey and Stutzer (chapter 1) point out, there are several vibrant research areas to which psychologists and economists jointly contribute. They include, for instance, behavioral economics, its applications to topics such as finance and game theory (see Camerer, Loewenstein, and Rabin 2004), motivational determinants of human behavior such as altruism and fairness (see Fehr and Schmidt 2003), the role of intrinsic motivation (Frey 1997), and the determinants of human happiness (e.g., Frey and Stutzer 2002; Kahneman, Diener, and Schwarz 1999; Layard 2005). Moreover, with the increasing acknowledgment of experimentation as a legitimate research tool in economics, even the previously disparate methods of investigation have become a bit less dissimilar.[1] Thus, the status quo renders the question of whether we can learn from each other superfluous. Today's challenge instead is not to be content with the interfaces that have evolved thus far but to search for others.

This is the goal of my chapter. Entrusted with the task of commenting on the contributions to this volume from a psychologist's vantage point, I focus on two themes, one in each discipline, that in my view deserve the attention of the other discipline. Both turn up in one form or another in several of this volume's chapters. The first theme relates to a great strength of economic analysis, namely, the efficient analysis and engineering of social institutions and the question of why psychology has so little to say about it. The second theme relates to a great strength of psychological analysis, namely, the analysis and modeling of observable behavior in terms of cognitive processes and the question of why economics has so little to say about it. Before I turn to these themes, allow me a brief digression into the twentieth-century history of both disciplines, simply because the roots of both themes lie there.

10.1 On Some Historical Roots of Two Sciences of Human Behavior

In the first half of the twentieth century, economics and psychology both underwent a conceptual revolution that redefined their respective foundations. Although both revolutions shared a kindred epistemological spirit (i.e., positivist philosophy of science), they appear to have unfolded side by side with little attention paid to events in the other field. To appreciate this behavioristic revolution, which started about 1913 in psychology, let us revisit the forces that helped to lead to it.[2] When scientific psychology was being founded in the nineteenth century, a key topic was consciousness. Indeed, such early luminaries as Wilhelm Wundt defined psychology as the quest for the understanding of conscious experience (Baars 1986), and for William James conscious experience, one of the most puzzling phenomena in psychology, was to be the foundation for a scientific psychology (Baars 1988). But building on a foundation that is itself puzzling and badly understood seems a recipe for futility. Matters were not helped when toward the end of the nineteenth century other scientific thinkers—notably Sigmund Freud—began to turn to even more elusive processes, and conjectured that unconscious processes can be inferred by analyzing psychological products such as slips of the tongue, motivated forgetting phenomena, dreams, and the like.

The behavioristic revolution of the early twentieth century was a revolution against a scientific psychology that espoused conscious experience as a legitimate scientific subject. Although not denying the existence of mental events, of course, behaviorists argued that mental events, whether conscious or unconscious, were not publicly observable. Therefore behaviorism—namely, a psychology understood as a science of behavior—limited itself to the study of observables. In B. F. Skinner's (1953) terms this meant the organism's present stimulation, its history of reinforcement, and its present response. Behaviorism thoroughly revolutionized psychology, and dominated American universities until the 1950s. George Miller (2003), whose *Plans and the Structure of Behavior* (jointly written with Galanter and Pribram in 1960) is considered to be one of the founding documents of modern cognitive psychology, described the behavioristic transformation of psychology as follows: "Perception became discrimination, memory became learning, language became verbal behavior, intelligence became what intelligence tests *test*" (141).

Unlike nineteenth and early twentieth century psychologists, economists were never interested in conscious mental events per se, whether they were feelings or thoughts. Instead, feelings and thoughts were meant to be instrumental in the prediction of behavior. However, because feelings and thoughts could not be independently and directly measured, but only assessed from behavior, they were eventually seen as useless intervening constructs. As Camerer, Loewenstein, and Prelec (2005) recounted:

In the 1940s, the concepts of ordinal utility and revealed preference eliminated the superfluous intermediate step of positing immeasurable feelings. Revealed preference theory simply equates unobserved preferences with observed choices. Circularity is avoided by assuming that people behave consistently, which makes the theory falsifiable; once they have revealed that they prefer A to B, people should not subsequently choose B over A. Later extensions...provided similar "as if" tools which sidestepped psychological detail. The "as if" approach made good sense as long as the brain remained substantially a black box. (10)

This condensed history of psychology and economics suggests there was a brief window in the middle of the last century during which, for different reasons, both disciplines espoused the study of observable behavior at the expense of unobservable, immeasurable mental events such as thoughts and feelings. In fact, the study of thoughts and feelings was at best perceived as unnecessary, at worst as unscientific. This epistemological parallelism, however, did not last long. It began to end when the young Noam Chomsky set out to strike what proved to be a severe blow to the supreme reign of behaviorism in American experimental psychology.

In 1957, Skinner, the most prominent behaviorist of his time, published a behavioristic account of language and communication, thus responding to Alfred North Whitehead's assertion that simple learning principles cannot account for verbal behavior. Chomsky, a young linguist at MIT, happened upon Skinner's *Verbal Behavior* and in a review of it (1959) challenged many of the assumptions therein. Generally speaking, he criticized Skinner's explanation of language acquisition as completely devoid of any reference to the built-in information-processing structures of the speaker. Skinner conjectured that external factors—in particular, the presence versus absence of reinforcing stimuli, their frequency, and their arrangement—suffice to explain how children master complex verbal behavior. In contrast, Chomsky concluded that "the fact that all normal children acquire essentially comparable grammars of great complexity with remarkable rapidity suggests that human beings are somehow specially designed to do this" (57).

Chomsky's critique of Skinner's attempt to generalize laws of operant behavior to linguistic behavior has often been viewed as the beginning of the end of behaviorism, a protracted process that was then advanced by events such as Garcia and Koelling's (1966) challenge to behaviorism's equipotentiality assumption, according to which any event could be associated equally well with any other event. As Miller (2003) recounted, in the wake of these criticisms it became apparent that behaviorism could not succeed: "If scientific psychology were to succeed, mentalistic concepts would have to integrate and explain the behavioral data" (142). And, indeed, that is what happened. Whereas in economics the notion of revealed preference, without reference to any mentalistic concept, was advanced and became triumphantly successful, psychology lived through the second conceptual shift of the twentieth century, the cognitive revolution. As a consequence, psychologists restored mental events as a legitimate object of study. The brain was no longer to be an impenetrable black box. But—and this is the thesis I would like to advance—in turning to the mental processes of the individual mind, psychology has also abandoned its behavioristic competence in engineering social institutions.

10.2   Social Engineering: A Forgotten Goal in Psychology

In reading this volume's chapters as a psychologist, I was struck by economists' potent analyses of issues regarding the efficient organization of social institutions. For instance, how can one increase people's willingness to contribute to a public good, a question that Stephan Meier (chapter 3) posed. Specifically, he studied whether an institutional arrangement, a matching mechanism, can foster people's willingness to donate money, certainly a key concern of many nongovernmental as well as governmental organizations (such as public universities). His study involved students at the University of Zurich who are asked at the beginning of each semester to donate money to two different causes, one supporting foreign students and one for students experiencing financial troubles. Anonymously, students can decide to donate nothing or to donate prefixed amounts of money to one or both funds. Can their willingness to donate at all, or to donate to two funds rather than just one, be boosted?

From the point of classic economic theory, the fact that people donate anything in a context in which their donation remains anonymous is difficult to explain. Yet, to the extent that people care for the well-being (utility) of others, reducing the costs of a donated monetary unit should stimulate donations, thus raising more money. The price of a donated unit is rendered cheaper either by a rebate (i.e., tax deductions for charitable contributions) or by a matching mechanism. Meier (chapter 3) focuses on the latter. You may be familiar with this mechanism if you listen to the United States' National Public Radio (NPR). A considerable part of NPR's operational expenses and infrastructure is financed by donations from its listeners. To encourage such donations, foundations or rich philanthropists offer to match listeners' contributions. In Meier's field experiment, students learned that an anonymous donor would match 50 percent (or 25 percent) of their contributions, but only if they decided to donate to both causes. Would this offer increase their willingness to donate to both causes? And, if so, would they continue to be generous even after the offer to match expired?

Meier (chapter 3) finds that although matching can hardly transform a previous nondonor into a donor, the 50 percent matching mechanism turns some of the *frugal* donors (giving money to only one cause) into *generous* donors (giving money to both causes). Interestingly, however, after the matching ends generous donors do not go back to being frugal donors, but stop donating altogether in the subsequent semester. Even people who were generous donors before the matching period stopped donating in the subsequent semester. Meier discusses different explanations of these results. The one most consistent with donors' behavior assumes that monetary incentives may crowd out pro-social behavior.

Regardless of any reservations one may have,[3] I was for several reasons excited to learn about this and related analyses of the impact of matching and other mechanisms on people's willingness to donate to a public good. One reason is that this research illustrates economists' readiness to tackle questions that are of immense importance for how a society organizes its institutions. Second, as well as studying institutions in the wild, economists have succeeded in finding ways to replicate these institutions in laboratory and field settings, thus enabling control of the myriad factors that are confounded with different real-world institutions (for instance, see Eckel and Grossman's 2003 laboratory experiment investigating the impact of a rebate and a matching mechanism on charitable giving). Third, economic theory provides a coherent framework and language, ranging from constructs such as price elasticity to the signal value of institutional arrangements, for analyzing and studying the behavioral impacts of a rebate and a matching mechanism. For illustration, take the notion that different institutions may signal different information. Monetary incentives to behave pro-socially can signal information about the nature of the task (see Bénabou and Tirole 2003). Matching, for instance, may signal that a charity has not been successful in raising money in the past, and now needs to resort to providing extra incentives. Alternatively, the fact that a donor matches people's contributions may be taken as a signal that the fund is trustworthy. Both interpretations imply that an institutional arrangement conveys information about the merits of the charity's cause, as well as about other people's willingness to donate money to this cause.

As has probably become obvious by now, psychologists are rarely, if ever, concerned with the analysis of institutions. Although we have a very rich theoretical framework to analyze and model the working of the mind, we have little to no language for describing institutions. Although we have gained a high level of experimental sophistication, we have rarely turned to the study of institutions in the laboratory. Although we are successful engineers of such diverse domains as people's workspace, their relationships, or their mental health, we appear to have no aspirations to efficiently engineer social institutions. This theoretical and experimental neglect of institutions, however, was not predestined. Possibly it was a little-noticed side effect of the cognitive revolution in psychology and the subsequent displacement of the behaviorist framework.

To appreciate this conjecture, let us again turn to history. From the outset, behaviorists defined their scientific objective not in terms of Dilthey's distinction of explanation and understanding (*Erklären und Verstehen*; von Wright 2004). Rather, they defined it in the terms used by Watson (1913): "Psychology as the behaviorist views it is a purely objective experimental branch of natural science. Its theoretical goal is the *prediction* and *control* of behavior" (158, emphasis added). True to this dictum, Skinner's (1957) analysis of "operant conditioning" focused on observable environmental events that predict and control behavior, in particular events preceding (e.g., discriminative stimulus) and succeeding (e.g., reinforcer) the target behavior.[4] In what behaviorists refer to as an experimental analysis of behavior, behavior is described in terms of a rich conceptual framework encompassing concepts such as punishment, avoidance, escape, discrimination, generalization, acquisition, and extinction—to name just a few. One of the key terms, "reinforcer," was defined by Skinner in *Beyond Freedom and Dignity* (1971) as follows: "When a bit of behavior is followed by a certain kind of consequence, it is more likely to occur again, and a consequence having this effect is called a reinforcer. Food, for example, is a reinforcer to a hungry organism; anything the organism does that is followed by the receipt of food is more likely to be done again whenever the organism is hungry" (27). In other words, whenever the consequence of behavior increases the frequency of behavior, the consequence is called a reinforcer. Analogously, when a consequence decreases the probability of behavior, the consequence is a negative reinforcer.

Based on his experimental analysis of behavior, Skinner (1971) was convinced that attributing human behavior to intentions, purposes, aims, and goals was futile. Instead, as he saw it in *Beyond Freedom and Dignity*: "We shall not solve the problems of alcoholism and juvenile delinquency by increasing a sense of responsibility. It is the environment which is 'responsible' for the objectionable behavior, and it is the environment, not some attribute of the individual, which must be changed" (122).

To the extent that environmental structures and, among these, institutional structures, underlie undesirable behavior, altering them is key in altering behavior. In other words, analysis and design of institutions is true to the behaviorist perspective. In fact, in his utopian novel *Walden Two*, Skinner (1948) went so far as to describe in detail the institutional structures of a small-scale community—its childcare facilities, its economic structures, and its political self-organization—that he thought to be conducive to the pursuit of happiness under conditions that, in today's jargon, are called sustainable. Indeed, his commentary to the second edition of *Walden Two* epitomized his unyielding aspiration to engineer efficient institutions. In words that sound eerily prescient of today's worries, Skinner (1976) wrote:

It is now widely recognized that great changes must be made in the American way of life. Not only can we not face the rest of the world while consuming and polluting as we do, we cannot for long face ourselves while acknowledging the violence and chaos in which we live. The choice is clear: either we do nothing and allow a miserable and probably catastrophic future to overtake us, or we use our knowledge about human behavior to create a social environment in which we shall live productive and creative lives and do so without jeopardizing the chances that those who follow us will be able to do the same. (xvi)

These quotes illustrate that in the heyday of behaviorism, scientists such as Skinner were committed to the engineering of environments and institutions. No doubt, by escaping into more applied fields such as clinical and educational psychology, some of this commitment has survived the demise of behaviorism. On a theoretical level, however, once it freed itself from behaviorism, mainstream experimental psychology resigned from the analysis and design of institutions. In other words, restoring cognition to scientific respectability exacted the price of losing sight of the world outside of the individual mind. The battle between behaviorism and cognitive psychology, however, has long been decided. Today psychology is a discipline that has greatly contributed to the understanding of the cognitive capacities and processes of the human mind. Bolstered by this achievement, it may now be more feasible than ever for psychologists to join economists in the analysis of behavior and cognition in institutional contexts, and to contribute constructs beyond the utility function.

10.3   Matching and Charitable Giving: A Look from a Behavioristic Framework

From psychology's point of view, one could begin such a return to institutional analysis by first investigating which of the behaviorist constructs could complement and enrich the economic analysis of institution. Take, for instance, the question of how a matching mechanism should be designed to bolster long-term charitable giving. In analyzing this question, it may be heuristically fruitful to treat the "offer to match" akin to a reinforcer.[5] To wit, matching is a reinforcer applied with the goal of increasing the frequency of pro-social behavior in terms of the likelihood of and the amount of donations. Matching is thus an instance of the most common type of instrumental conditioning, namely, positive reinforcement (as opposed to punishment and negative reinforcement), in which the display of the instrumental response yields a positive reinforcer (i.e., reward). Candy, money, praise, sensory stimulation, and social approval all may be strong rewards or reinforcers for some behaviors. One way to interpret the offer to match is in terms of a social reinforcer. This is a reinforcer that is socially mediated by others—for instance, teachers, parents, or peers—who express approval and praise for appropriate behavior.[6] In analogy, by offering to match a person's offer, an institution can express its appreciation of pro-social behavior. Metaphorically, it pats the donor on the back. At least during the period in which matching is offered, the pat seems to work: it fosters the desired instrumental behavior (Meier, chapter 3).

Having thus framed matching as a social reinforcer, one can now analyze the momentum of charitable giving using what behaviorists

know about the factors influencing positive reinforcements, such as reinforcement schedule, reinforcement delay, or contrast effects. Perhaps
the most important influence on instrumental conditioning is the reinforcement schedule, which determines how often a behavior results in
a reward. In natural settings, many rewards occur intermittently—
once a month, as with a paycheck, or after a variable number of days,
as with a return call from a friend, and so forth. Whether rewards
occur constantly or intermittently has a profound impact on the rate
and probability of the desired behavior. For instance, the response rate
in a "variable ratio schedule" (e.g., a variable ratio of 1:3 means that *on
average*, one out of every three behaviors will be rewarded) tends to be
higher than in other reinforcement schedules in which reinforcers are
presented after a fixed number of responses or within a fixed time interval (Tarpy and Mayer 1978).

The reinforcement schedule under which behavior is learned also
affects how robust it is. For instance, one of the most reliable phenomena in learning research is the partial reinforcement effect (Tarpy and
Mayer 1978). It describes the fact that resistance to extinction is stronger when behavior was originally acquired under intermittent rather
than continuous reinforcement. One possible reason is that under intermittent reward organisms have been conditioned to perform in the
presence of frustration. In contrast, the continuously reinforced organisms experience the full impact of aversive frustration for the first time
during extinction. Thus, according to one plausible speculation, they
cease to respond rather quickly.

If one accepts the analogy that matching donations acts like a reinforcer, then the partial reinforcement effect has immediate implications
for the matching regime. One prediction is that if the target behavior
—contributing to a public good—was learned under intermittent
reinforcement—here intermittent matching—then it will prove more
robust once all matching is removed. In other words, if making a charitable contribution is sometimes but not always reinforced by a matching offer, people will continue to contribute even if at some point
matching is no longer offered.

As the frequency of reward changes in real-world settings, the magnitude can fluctuate as well, thus creating a contrast effect. "Contrast"
is the term for what occurs when an organism learns a behavior under
one set of reward conditions and is then switched to a different set. In a
typical experiment, two groups of organisms are trained to make a response for a small reward, while two other groups receive a large

reward. Once the behavior is stabilized, one group in each reward regime receives the alternate reward magnitude, whereas the other group continues with the same reward. How does the learned behavior change as a consequence of the reward reversal? The typical result is that behavior in the alternate groups changes appropriately: the organisms who are shifted from low to high improve, while performance for those who are shifted from high to low deteriorates. More interesting, however, is the observation that the alternate organisms tend to overshoot and undershoot, respectively (compared to the high-high and low-low organisms). That is, after the shift, the low-high group performs even better than the high-high group. Similarly, the high-low group performs worse than the low-low one (Tarpy and Mayer 1978). This finding echoes Meier's (chapter 3) observation that when matching donations are stopped—thus switching from high reward to no reward—people appear to "overcompensate;" that is, they donate less than they did before.

Looking at the act of matching donations through the eyes of a behaviorist gives rise to still another interesting observation: the promise by the University of Zurich (in Meier's analysis, chapter 3) to match donations and the donors' responses may evolve into two mutually reinforcing behaviors. To appreciate this possibility, let us again assume that the offer to match fosters individuals' willingness to donate. At the same time, however, the behavior of the institution may also come to be controlled, at least partially, by donors' behavior. The increased likelihood of donations in response to the matching offer is likely to reinforce the behavior of the university, thus increasing the likelihood of matching donations in the future.

These few examples illustrate, I believe, that the rich behavioristic framework can be used as a heuristic tool when considering the efficient design and impact of social institutions such as matching mechanisms. To avoid misunderstandings, I am not pleading for a revival of behavioristic dogmatism in psychology, nor do I wish to imply that behavioristic constructs ought to supplant economic ones. Rather, I am convinced that by revisiting the behaviorist paradigm, cognitive psychologists will come across many theoretical constructs *and* empirical findings that promise to complement and enrich the economic analysis of institutions. Economists and behaviorists share the credo that behaviors are selected by their consequences. Perhaps this joint belief has given rise to theoretical frameworks offering commensurable sets of conceptual lenses. It is time to see whether they can be used in tandem.

In doing so, psychologists would also be offered an opportunity to make a larger contribution to the efficient engineering of the world.

10.4   Cognitive Modeling: A Neglected Goal in Economics

It is ironic that around the time economists turned away from psychological forces to focus on behavior, psychologists turned from overt behavior to psychological processes. Like behaviorists before them, economists became skeptical that psychological entities could be measured in any way other than inferring them through the observation of behavior. To escape from this tautology economists adopted another one that proved to be very productive, namely, that between unobserved utilities and observed (revealed) preferences. One price economists have paid for this premise is well known, at least in the eyes of many psychologists: a disregard for the psychological reality of people operating under constraints of time, information, and computational capacities. Simon (1987), perhaps the most outspoken critic of this neglect, wrote of neoclassical economics that, in its treatment of rationality, it differs from the other social sciences in its neglect of the "processes, individual and social, whereby selected aspects of reality are noticed and postulated as the 'givens'…for reasoning," and in its neglect the "computational strategies that are used in reasoning, so that very limited information-processing capabilities can cope with complex realities" (26).

One may fault the above depiction for outlining a view that was perhaps common early in the evolution of the field but is now long gone. Today many economists would agree that cognitive resources, time, and money are limited and would assert that economic models explicitly take such limits into account by, for instance, assuming a limited rather than unlimited search for information. Limited search requires a stopping rule, a way to decide when to stop looking for more information. Often put under the rubric of "optimization under constraints," one class of economic models assumes that the stopping rule *optimizes* search with respect to the constraints of time, computation, money, and other resources. According to this view, the mind should calculate the marginal benefits and the marginal costs of searching for further information and stop searching as soon as the costs outweigh the benefits (e.g., Sargent 1993; Stigler 1961). Although the rule "stop search when costs outweigh benefits" sounds plausible at first glance, optimization under constraints can demand even more knowledge and computation than classic models of unbounded rationality. This is because they assume that the decision maker takes into account not only cost-benefit calculations, but also opportunity costs and second-order costs for making those calculations (Conlisk 1996; see also Gigerenzer et al. 1989, 10–12).

It thus does not seem controversial to conclude that not only neo-classical economics but also many contemporary economic models pay little to no attention to the limited information-processing capabilities of the human actor. Psychologists, in contrast, often do. In fact, in doing so they have amassed a solid understanding of the cognitive constraints (e.g., in memory, processing capacity, and attention), as well as the cognitive processes that may have evolved in tandem with these constraints (see Hertwig and Todd 2003). In addition, psychologists have proposed models of cognitive processes underlying a wide range of behavior such as judgments, choice, inferences, and categorization. In what follows, I describe a very recent process model for risky choice, which, I believe, enriches our understanding of both the processes and the outcomes of judgments under risk and amplifies our predictive power. The same benefits, according to my thesis, could also be reaped in investigations that have enormous implications for economic theorizing, such as whether people mispredict future utilities.

10.5 The Priority Heuristic: Making Choices without Trade-Offs Heuristics in Risky Choice

One of the most consequential events in the history of decision theory occurred in the early eighteenth century and involved a perplexing gamble and two members of perhaps the most prominent family in the history of mathematics. In an epistolary exchange with Pierre Rémond de Montmort, Nicholas Bernoulli, a professor of law in Basel, Switzerland, posed the St. Petersburg gamble. In this gamble, a coin is tossed until heads occurs. If heads occurs on the first toss, the person will receive two coins; if it occurs on the second toss, the person will receive four coins. Thus the gamble's payoff is 2^k, where k is the number of tosses until heads comes up. Although this gamble has an infinite expected value (but see Jorland 1987), hardly anybody cared to pay more than small sums for the right to play the gamble.

To resolve the discrepancy between what was the then-dominant psychological theory of reasoning of the educated *homme éclairé* and people's good sense, Nicholas's cousin Daniel Bernoulli (1954) retained the core of the expected value theory—that is, the multiplication of monetary outcomes and their probabilities and maximization—but suggested replacing objective money amounts with subjective utilities. In his view, the pleasure or utility of money did not increase linearly with the monetary amount. Instead, the increases in utility declined (diminishing marginal utility), and he modeled this decline by assuming that the relation between objective and subjective values of money obeys a logarithmic function.

Daniel Bernoulli's resolution of the St. Petersburg paradox provided nothing less than the foundation of expected utility (EU) theory; however, it also introduced an influential precedent of how to solve discrepancies between theories of risky choice and behavior. As Bernoulli demonstrated so successfully, one can do this by adding one or more adjustable parameters to the original theory—in Bernoulli's case, the concept of utility—while retaining the original framework, that is, the notion that people behave as if they multiplied some function of probability and value, and then maximized.

To this day, myriad theories of risky behavior have been proposed that have wittingly or unwittingly adopted Bernoulli's strategy. Examples include disappointment theory (Bell 1985; Loomes and Sugden 1986), regret theory (Bell 1982; Loomes and Sugden 1982), the transfer of attention exchange model (Birnbaum and Chavez 1997), decision affect theory (Mellers 2000), prospect theory (Kahneman and Tversky 1979), and cumulative prospect theory (Tversky and Kahneman 1992). They represent a "repair" program that introduces psychological variables such as emotions and reference points in order to rescue the Bernoullian framework (Selten 2001). The originators of prospect theory, for instance, set themselves the goal "to assemble the minimal set of modifications of expected utility theory that would provide a descriptive account of ... choices between simple monetary gambles" (Kahneman 2000, x). Despite the additional dose of psychology, however, many of these modifications of EU theory have typically been interpreted to be as–if models because of the complex computations involved in them. That is, they describe and ideally predict choice outcomes, but do not explain the underlying process.

There is, however, a completely different way to react to empirical demonstrations that human behavior often contradicts EU theory. Rather than adding more psychology to the Bernoulli framework by way of more adjustable variables, one can step outside of the time-honored framework and explain people's choices as the immediate consequence of the use of a heuristic. That is the approach that Brand-stätter, Gigerenzer, and Hertwig (2006) have taken (for a related approach see Payne, Bettman, and Johnson 1993). Specifically, they investigated whether a sequential heuristic, the "priority heuristic," can predict both classic violations of EU theory and major bodies of choice data. Unlike outcome models, heuristics aim to model both the choice outcome and the process. To this end, they require a specification of (1) a process rule, (2) a stopping rule, and (3) a decision rule.[7]

To illustrate the priority heuristic, let us consider simple monetary gambles of the type "a probability p to win amount x; a probability $(1 - p)$ to win amount y" $(x, p; y)$. Here the decision maker is given four reasons: the maximum gain, the minimum gain, and their respective probabilities. All reasons are displayed simultaneously and they are available at no cost. The resulting choices are thus "decisions from description" and not "decisions from experience" (Hertwig et al. 2004). The "priority rule" refers to the order in which people go through these reasons, after screening all of them once, in order to make their decision. The heuristic describes the psychological process underlying a choice between two simple monetary gambles in terms of the following three steps:

1. *Priority rule*   Go through reasons in this order: minimum gain, probability of minimum gain, maximum gain.

2. *Stopping rule*   Stop examination if the minimum gains differ by 1/10 (or more) of the maximum gain; otherwise, stop examination if probabilities differ by 1/10 (or more) of the probability scale.

3. *Decision rule*   Choose the gamble with the more attractive gain (probability).

The term "attractive" refers to the gamble with the higher (minimum or maximum) gain and the lower probability of the minimum gain (see Brandstätter, Gigerenzer, and Hertwig 2006 for details on how the rules were derived from empirical evidence). The heuristic combines three different features. Its initial focus is on outcomes rather than on probabilities (Deane 1969; Loewenstein et al. 2001; Sunstein 2003). It is based on the sequential structure of the fast and frugal heuristic for inferences (see Gigerenzer 2004). Finally, the priority heuristic incorporates aspiration levels into its choice algorithm (Luce 1956; Simon 1983). The generalization of the priority heuristic to nonpositive and mixed prospects and to more than two outcomes is straightforward (see Brandstätter, Gigerenzer, and Hertwig 2006).

10.5.1   Certainty Effect

To illustrate how the priority heuristic works, let us turn to the certainty effect, a well-known violation of EU theory. According to Allais (1979, 441), the certainty effect captures people's "preference for security in the neighborhood of certainty." A simple demonstration is the following (Kahneman and Tversky 1979):

A:	4,000	with $p = 0.80$
	0	with $p = 0.20$
B:	3,000	with $p = 1.00$

A majority of people (80 percent) selected the certain alternative B.

C:	4,000	with $p = 0.20$
	0	with $p = 0.80$
D:	3,000	with $p = 0.25$
	0	with $p = 0.75$

Now the majority of people (65 percent) selected gamble C over D. Note that the choice of B implies that $u(3,000)/u(4,000) > 4/5$, whereas the choice of C implies the reverse inequality.

The priority heuristic starts by comparing the minimum gains of the alternatives A (0) and B (3,000). The difference exceeds the aspiration level of 1/10 of the maximum gain (4,000), thus examination is stopped, and the model predicts that people prefer option B, which is in fact the majority choice. Between C and D, the minimum gains (0 and 0) do not differ; in the next step, the heuristic compares the probabilities of the minimum gains (0.80 and 0.75). Because this difference does not reach ten percentage points (the threshold for the second reason), the last reason will be examined, and this reason—maximum gain—favors the choice of C over D.

The priority heuristic is simple in several respects. It typically consults only one or a few reasons; even if all are screened, it bases its choice on only one reason. Probabilities are treated as linear, and a 1/10 aspiration level is used for all reasons except the last, where the amount of difference is ignored. No parameters are built in for overweighting small probabilities and underweighting large probabilities, or for the value function.

10.5.2   Empirical Tests of the Priority Heuristic

Does this simple model account for people's choices as well as multi-parameter outcome models do? Brandstätter, Gigerenzer, and Hertwig (2006) found that the heuristic can account for a wide range of phenomena at variance with EU theory. Like the certainty effect, it can, for instance, predict the Allais paradox, the possibility effect, and intransitivities. To investigate the extent to which the heuristic can predict choices across a wide range of gambles, Brandstätter, Gigerenzer, and Hertwig tested the heuristic against four classes of gambles, namely, (1) simple choice problems (no more than two nonzero outcomes; Kahneman and Tversky 1979), (2) multiple-outcome gambles (Lopes and Oden 1999), (3) gambles inferred from certainty equivalents (Tversky and Kahneman 1992), and (4) randomly sampled gambles (Erev et al. 2002).

The four classes of gambles amounted to a total of 260 problems. The performance of the priority heuristic in predicting the modal choice in each of the 260 problems was compared to the performance of three modifications of expected utility theory: cumulative prospect theory (Tversky and Kahneman 1992), the security-potential/aspiration theory (Lopes 1987, 1995; for details, see Lopes and Oden 1999), and the transfer of attention exchange model (Birnbaum and Chavez 1997). Despite differences in their number and nature of parameters, all modifications retain the assumption that people behave as if they multiplied some function of probability and value, and then maximized. The priority heuristic was also compared to classic heuristics that have previously been proposed (see Thorngate 1980; Payne, Bettman, and Johnson 1993). For each strategy, its mean frugality (defined as the proportion of pieces of information that a model *ignores* when making a decision), and the proportion of correct predictions (i.e., prediction of the modal choice) were determined.

Figure 10.1 describes how well the different strategies can account for people's choices. Three clusters of strategies emerge: the modifications of expected utility and tallying, the classic choice heuristics, and the priority heuristic. The first cluster, involving the modifications of expected utility and tallying, could predict choice fairly accurately, but required the maximum amount of information. Specifically, security-potential/aspiration theory, cumulative prospect theory, and the transfer of attention exchange model correctly predicted 79 percent, 77 percent, and 69 percent of the majority choices, respectively. The second cluster, the classic heuristics, was fairly frugal but performed

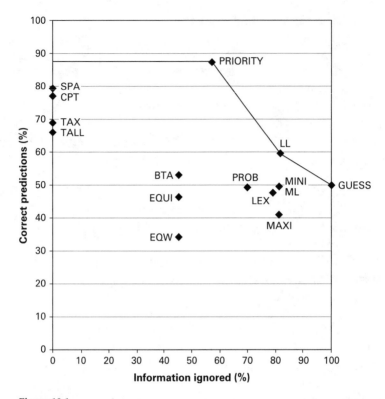

Figure 10.1
Predictability/frugality trade-off, averaged over 260 problems. The percentage of correct predictions refers to majority choices (including guessing).

PRIORITY: Priority heuristic	ML: Most likely heuristic
CPT: Cumulative prospect theory	BTA: Better than average heuristic
SPA: Security-potential/aspiration theory	EQUI: Equiprobable heuristic
TAX: Transfer of attention exchange model	PROB: Probable heuristic
TALL: Tallying	GUESS: Pure guessing
LEX: Lexicographic heuristic	MINI: Minimax heuristic
EQW: Equal-weight heuristic	MAXI: Maximax heuristic.
LL: Least likely heuristic	

For a description of the heuristics, see Brandstätter, Gigerenzer, and Hertwig (2006).
Source: Brandstätter, Gigerenzer, and Hertwig (2006). Reprinted with permission of the American Psychological Association.

dismally in predicting people's choices. Indeed, with the exception of the least likely heuristic (LL) and tallying (TALL), most classic heuristics' performance did not exceed chance level. For instance, the performances of the minimax and lexicographic rules were 49 percent and 48 percent, respectively. The priority heuristic represents the third and final cluster. This heuristic achieved the best predictive accuracy of all strategies (87 percent) while being relatively frugal.

To conclude, Brandstätter, Gigerenzer, and Hertwig's (2006) goal was to derive from empirical evidence a model that both predicts risky choice and spells out its underlying psychological processes. It does so by specifying (1) the order in which reasons—minimum outcomes, probability of minimum outcome, and maximum outcome—are examined, (2) the condition under which examination of reasons is stopped, and (3) a decision rule. Each of these process assumptions gives rise to empirical predictions over and above the predictions of outcomes. As a consequence, this model can be tested on two levels, on the level of choice and the level of processes (see Brandstätter, Gigerenzer, and Hertwig (2006) for a test of the latter). Notwithstanding its excellent performance in predicting people's choice in the examined set of gambles, the priority heuristic has, of course, limitations. For instance, additional results suggest that the priority heuristic does best when choices are difficult, due to similar expected values of the alternatives. In contrast, when choices become easy—due to widely discrepant expected values—expected value theory predicts choices as well as or better than the heuristic (see Brandstätter, Gigerenzer, and Hertwig 2006 for a discussion of this and other limitations).

10.6   Models of Heuristics for Predictions of Future Utilities

The priority heuristic is an instance of what Payne and Bettman (2004) describe as the "information processing approach to decision research." In contrast to the information-processing approach, the traditional focus in economic theorizing is on *what* decisions are made. This focus remains paramount even when economists challenge the standard economic model of rational choice, as Stutzer and Frey (chapter 7) do in their intriguing investigations of the economic consequences of misprediction utility. Standard economic theory assumes that individuals are able to accurately compare and predict the future utilities bestowed by consuming goods and activities, simply by determining the sum of the weighted values of the alternatives' characteristics, and then choosing the alternative promising the maximum predicted utility. In this view, ·people do not make systematic mistakes in their choice of goods and activities. People know what is good for them, now and in the future. In their incisive analysis, which is of utter relevance both for economists and psychologists, Stutzer and Frey challenge this dictum. Rather than consistently maximizing their utility, people, according to Stutzer and Frey, can and do make suboptimal consumptive decisions. The authors discuss such suboptimal consumer choice in the context of tobacco use, eating habits, TV watching, and commuting.

Why is that? According to Stutzer and Frey (chapter 7), people may do so because they struggle with self-control or lack thereof, or because they sometimes mispredict utilities in the future. Henceforth I will focus on the issue of misprediction. Drawing from research in psychology, Frey and Stutzer (2004) distinguish between intrinsic and extrinsic attributes of goods and activities. The former are associated with intrinsic needs such as relatedness and self-efficacy, whereas the latter are associated with extrinsic desires such as material possession and fame. In relation to extrinsic attributes, the intrinsic attributes are undervalued in the process of predicting future utility. Such undervaluation may arise because (1) adaptation (i.e., the fact that our affective responses to events wear off) may be more likely to be underestimated for extrinsic attributes than for intrinsic ones, (2) extrinsic attributes may yield briefer, yet more intense and thus more memorable, affective responses, (3) people may find it easier to justify extrinsic rather than intrinsic attributes toward themselves and others, and (4) people with predominantly extrinsic needs may be more likely to rely on false intuitive theories regarding the causes underlying their subjective well-being.

Among other contexts, Frey and Stutzer (2004) test their thesis of the relative neglect of intrinsic attributes in predicting future utilities in the context of an ubiquitous decision, namely, that of deciding between two jobs, one that offers more income but necessitates a longer commute, and the other that pays less but requires less time spent commuting. They hypothesize that commuting time and associated intrinsic attributes such as time spent with friends and family are underweighted, and extrinsic attributes such as more income and lower housing costs (thus enabling a higher level of consumption) are overweighted. Based on a maximization analysis (using commuters' reported life satisfaction as a proxy for individual utility), they then find that people who spend more time commuting are not fully compensated for their displeasure by higher income, lower rent, or nicer housing. Consistent with the notion that people overestimate the future utility from extrinsic attributes, when compared against their own preferences, people are not as content as they could be.

What would Frey and Stutzer's (2004) investigation have gained if they had aimed to model not only the outcome but also the process of choice? My conjecture is that a model of the process promises an even better understanding of *why* people systematically misjudge future utilities, and also of how and why people differ in this judgment. To illustrate this conjecture, let us do a thought experiment in which we look—in analogy to the choice between two gambles—at people's choice between two jobs. For the purpose of simplicity, let us assume that each job can be described with just three reasons: two tangible reasons, salary and commuting time (as a proxy for time lost on social activities), and a less tangible one, namely, anticipated social status. Job *a* pays more and promises more social status but requires a long commute. Job *b*, in contrast, pays less and promises less social status, but it offers a short commute. Which decision processes would lead people consistently to select job *a*, thus overweighting the satisfaction derived from the extrinsic attributes, income, and status?

The answer to this question depends on the class of heuristics used to examine the reasons. One class of heuristics examines reasons in order (a simple form of weighting)—the priority heuristic is an example—and then makes a decision on the basis of the first reason that discriminates. This is the class of "one-reason decision-making" heuristics (Gigerenzer 2004). Herein, extrinsic reasons would be privileged if they topped intrinsic reasons in the order of reasons. For instance, if salary is ranked higher than commuting time, and if the difference in salaries is good enough ("satisficing"), then examination of further reasons will be stopped. Consequently, other reasons such as commuting time will not enter the decision-making process. Within this class of heuristics, individual differences can enter through at least two sources. One source is the order of reasons. Some people—those who value intrinsic needs—may rank commuting time rather than salary as the most important reason. Another source is the aspiration level that stops examination. For instance, one may speculate that those who value extrinsic needs are satisfied with smaller salary differentials than those who value intrinsic needs.

A second class of heuristics dispenses with the simple ordering of reasons and simply adds up all reasons (until a threshold is met). This is the class of "tallying" heuristics (Gigerenzer 2004). In this class, extrinsic reasons would have an edge if more extrinsic than intrinsic reasons entered the decision-making process. Then, *ceteris paribus*, positive values on all intrinsic reasons for one job cannot make up for the other job's positive values on all extrinsic reasons. Alternatively, extrinsic reasons would also have an edge if they proved to be immediately available and quantifiable. Indeed, one typically knows the salaries of both jobs one is deciding between, but one may be less certain about each job's hours and how working overtime, for instance, would affect one's social life, and by extension, one's subjective well-being. If such an information asymmetry between intrinsic and extrinsic reasons exists, then extrinsic reasons, *ceteris paribus*, may have an edge simply because people are less likely to know the values for the intrinsic reasons.

These are just two classes of heuristics; others exist (see Payne, Bettman, and Johnson 1993). However, our thought experiment has already turned up some insights. For one thing, it shows that the reasons why people may misjudge future utilities can be manifold. Depending on the class of heuristics, the causes may lie, for instance, in the order of reasons, the ecological frequency of extrinsic and intrinsic reasons, or the lesser certainty and predictability of intrinsic reasons. Second, it is not so clear whether people's "misjudgment" is an instance of a cognitive bias: for instance, if people indeed possessed less reliable and certain knowledge of the intangible, intrinsic reasons than of the tangible, extrinsic reasons, then the relative edge of extrinsic over intrinsic reasons is due to this information asymmetry and not to erroneous processing of information. Third, by spelling out possible processes, various sources of interindividual differences become manifest: order of reasons, aspiration levels, relative number of intrinsic versus extrinsic reasons, and so on. Finally, the different heuristics give rise to different possible interventions: that is, if one aimed to enable people to make better choices—"better" measured in terms of their own preferences—then a person who systematically ordered extrinsic reasons over intrinsic would benefit from different feedback as compared to a person who examines reasons in no specific order but "suffers" from the uncertainty integral to intrinsic reasons.

10.7   Conclusion

For a very brief window of time during the twentieth century, psychology and economics shared, for related reasons, a focus on observable behavior. How would the two disciplines have cooperated had psychology not abandoned its behaviorist focus, or, alternatively, had economics not decided to sidestep psychological processes in favor of observed choices? We will never know. But perhaps there are ways of making up for some of the possibly missed interdisciplinary endeavors. In this chapter, I have described two, in my view particularly important and promising, future avenues. First, by reconciling with their behavioristic past, psychologists could access a rich theoretical repertoire of learning theories and empirical findings. By recruiting this framework and investigating how it maps onto, complements, and, perhaps, sometimes contradicts the constructs economists use to analyze and design institutions, they could join economists in a task as important as ever—social engineering.

Second, by recognizing constructs other than the utility function as worthy of consideration, economists could exploit psychology's existing and ever-evolving theories of cognitive processes—for instance, the science of heuristics. By opening up the black box of the human mind, economists and psychologists are likely to arrive at a more comprehensive understanding of, for example, whether, why, and when people mispredict future utilities. Augmenting our models by process assumptions renders it possible to test them both on the level of overt behavior as well as on the level of cognitive and affective processes. Last but not least, elucidating the processes driving suboptimal choice may also provide us with new tools to foster people's predictions of future utilities, thus fostering their well-being.

Notes

I would like to thank Alois Stutzer and two anonymous reviewers for constructive comments and Laura Wiles for valuable editorial input.

1. The practices of experimentation, however, are surprisingly different in economics and in areas of psychology relevant to both economists and psychologists, such as behavioral decision making (see Hertwig and Ortmann 2001; Ortmann and Hertwig 2002).

2. In 1913, J. B. Watson gave a lecture at John Hopkins University, Baltimore, that was to become one of the most famous lectures in the history of psychology. He called for a radical revision of the scope and method of psychological research.

3. All explanations discussed—intertemporal substitution, mental accounting, and crowding out—implicitly assume that six months later, people can still remember that in the previous period their donations were matched. But can they? Or does a person's behavior differ as a function of whether one is cognizant of this intervention?

4. Skinner's term "operant" reflects the idea that the organism actually operates, that it can have an effect on the environment.

5. Here I intentionally use the notion "heuristically fruitful" because there may be different ways of conceptualizing the offer to match from a behaviorist perspective. The institutional promise to match a person's offer can be seen as a contract between the donor and the benefactor in which the promise takes the form of a conditional reinforcer. I treat the offer to match as a positive reinforcer. But this mapping is not without problems, and conceivably there are other, better behavoristic models of the link between the matching offer and donors' behavior.

6. Verbal and written comments (e.g., "good job," "super") as well as nonverbal expressions of approval (e.g., smiling, a pat on the back) are all instances of social reinforcers.

7. The following paragraphs describing the priority heuristic are adapted from Brandstätter, Gigerenzer, and Hertwig (2006).

References

Allais, M. 1979. "Criticism of the Neo-Bernoullian Formulation as a Behavioural Rule for Rational Man." In *Expected Utility Hypotheses and the Allais Paradox*, ed. M. Allais and O. Hagen, 74–106. Dordrecht, Netherlands: Reidel.

Baars, B. J. 1986. *The Cognitive Revolution in Psychology*. New York: Guilford Press.

Baars, B. J. 1988. *A Cognitive Theory of Consciousness*. New York: Cambridge University Press.

Bell, D. E. 1982. "Regret in Decision Making under Uncertainty." *Operations Research* 30: 961–981.

Bell, D. E. 1985. "Disappointment in Decision Making under Uncertainty." *Operations Research* 33: 1–27.

Bénabou, R., and J. Tirole. 2003. "Intrinsic and Extrinsic Motivation." *Review of Economic Studies* 70: 489–520.

Bernoulli, D. 1954. "Exposition of a New Theory on the Measurement of Risk." *Econometrica* 22: 23–36. (Original work published in 1738.)

Birnbaum, M., and A. Chavez. 1997. "Tests of Theories of Decision Making: Violations of Branch Independence and Distribution Independence." *Organizational Behavior and Human Decision Processes* 71: 161–194.

Brandstätter, E., G. Gigerenzer, and R. Hertwig. 2006. "Priority Heuristic: Making Choices without Trade-Offs." *Psychological Review* 113, no. 2: 409–432.

Camerer, C., G. F. Loewenstein, and M. Rabin. 2004. *Advances in Behavioral Economics*. New York: Princeton University Press.

Camerer, C., G. F. Loewenstein, and D. Prelec. 2005. "Neuroeconomics: How Neuroscience Can Inform Economics." *Journal of Economic Literature* 43: 9–64.

Chomsky, N. 1959. "A Review of B. F. Skinner's Verbal Behavior." *Language* 35: 26–58.

Conlisk, J. 1996. "Why Bounded Rationality?" *Journal of Economic Literature* 34: 669–700.

Deane, G. E. 1969. "Cardiac Activity during Experimentally Induced Anxiety." *Psychophysiology* 6: 17–30.

Eckel, C. C., and P. J. Grossman. 2003. "Rebate versus Matching: Does How We Subsidize Charitable Giving Matter?" *Journal of Public Economics* 87: 681–701.

Erev, I., A. E. Roth, R. L. Slonim, and G. Barron. 2002. *Combining a Theoretical Prediction with Experimental Evidence to Yield a New Prediction: An Experimental Design with a Random Sample of Tasks*. Unpublished Manuscript, Columbia University and Faculty of Industrial Engineering and Management, Technion, Haifa, Israel.

Fehr, E., and K. Schmidt. 2003. "Theories of Fairness and Reciprocity: Evidence and Economic Applications." In *Advances in Economics and Econometrics: Vol. 1. Eighth World Congress of the Econometric Society*, ed. M. Dewatripont, L. P. Hansen, and S. J. Turnovsky, 208–257. Cambridge: Cambridge University Press.

Frey, B. S. 1997. *Not Just for the Money: An Economic Theory of Personal Motivation*. Cheltenham, UK: Edward Elgar.

Frey, B., and A. Stutzer. 2002. "What Can Economists Learn from Happiness Research?" *Journal of Economic Literature* 40: 402–435.

Frey, B. S., and A. Stutzer. 2004. "Economic Consequences of Mispredicting Utility." Working Paper no. 218, Institute for Empirical Research in Economics, University of Zürich.

Garcia, J., and R. A. Koelling. 1966. "Relation of Cue in Consequence to Learning." *Psychonomic Science* 4: 123–124.

Gigerenzer, G. 2004. "Fast and Frugal Heuristics: The Tools of Bounded Rationality." In *Handbook of Judgment and Decision Making*, ed. D. Koehler and N. Harvey, 62–88. Oxford: Blackwell.

Gigerenzer, G., Z. Swijtink, T. Porter, L. Daston, J. Beatty, and L. Krüger. 1989. *The Empire of Chance: How Probability Changed Science and Everyday Life*. Cambridge: Cambridge University Press.

Hertwig, R., G. Barron, E. U. Weber, and I. Erev. 2004. "Decision from Experience and the Effect of Rare Events." *Psychological Science* 15: 534–539.

Hertwig, R., and A. Ortmann. 2001. "Experimental Practices in Economics: A Challenge for Psychologists?" *Behavioral and Brain Sciences* 24: 383–451.

Hertwig, R., and P. M. Todd. 2003. "More Is Not Always Better: The Benefits of Cognitive Limits." In *Thinking: Psychological Perspectives on Reasoning, Judgment and Decision Making*, ed. D. Hardman and L. Macchi, 213–231. Chichester, England: Wiley.

Hogarth, R. M., and M. W. Reder, eds. 1987. *Rational Choice: The Contrast between Economics and Psychology*. Chicago: University of Chicago Press.

Jorland, G. 1987. "The Saint Petersburg Paradox 1713–1937." In *The Probabilistic Revolution: Vol. 1. Ideas in the Sciences*, ed. L. Krüger, G. Gigerenzer, and M. S. Morgan, 157–190. Cambridge, MA: MIT Press.

Kahneman, D. 2000. "Preface." In *Choices, Values, and Frames*, ed. D. Kahneman and A. Tversky, ix–xvii. Cambridge: Cambridge University Press.

Kahneman, D., E. Diener, and N. Schwarz, eds. 1999. *Well-Being: Foundations of Hedonic Psychology*. New York: Russell Sage Foundation Press.

Kahneman, D., and A. Tversky. 1979. "Prospect Theory: An Analysis of Decision under Risk." *Econometrica* 47: 263–291.

Layard, R. 2005. *Happiness: Lessons from a New Science.* London: Allen Lane.

Loewenstein, G. F., E. U. Weber, C. K. Hsee, and N. Welch. 2001. "Risk as Feeling." *Psychological Bulletin* 127: 267–286.

Loomes, G., and R. Sugden. 1982. "Regret Theory: An Alternative Theory of Rational Choice under Uncertainty." *Economic Journal* 92: 805–824.

Loomes, G., and R. Sugden. 1986. "Disappointment and Dynamic Consistency in Choice under Uncertainty." *Review of Economic Studies* 53: 271–282.

Lopes, L. L. 1987. "Between Hope and Fear: The Psychology of Risk." *Advances in Experimental Social Psychology* 20: 255–295.

Lopes, L. L. 1995. "Algebra and the Process in the Modeling of Risky Choice." *The Psychology of Learning and Motivation* 32: 177–220.

Lopes, L. L., and G. C. Oden. 1999. "The Role of Aspiration Level in Risky Choice: A Comparison of Cumulative Prospect Theory and SP/A Theory." *Journal of Mathematical Psychology* 43: 286–313.

Luce, R. D. 1956. "Semiorders and a Theory of Utility Discrimination." *Econometrica* 24: 178–191.

Mellers, B. A. 2000. "Choice and the Relative Pleasure of Consequences." *Psychological Bulletin* 126: 910–924.

Miller, G. A. 2003. "The Cognitive Revolution: A Historical Perspective." *Trends in Cognitive Science* 7: 141–144.

Miller, G. A., E. Galanter, and K. H. Pribram. 1960. *Plans and the Structure of Behavior.* New York: Holt, Rhinehart and Winston.

Ortmann, A., and R. Hertwig. 2002. "The Costs of Deception: Evidence from Psychology." *Experimental Economics* 5: 111–131.

Payne, J. W., and J. R. Bettman. 2004. "Walking with the Scarecrow: The Information-Processing Approach to Decision Research." In *Handbook of Judgment and Decision Making,* ed. D. Koehler and N. Harvey, 110–132. Oxford: Blackwell.

Payne, J. W., J. R. Bettman, and E. J. Johnson. 1993. *The Adaptive Decision Maker.* New York: Cambridge University Press.

Sargent, T. J. 1993. *Bounded Rationality in Macroeconomics.* Oxford: Oxford University Press.

Selten, R. 2001. "What Is Bounded Rationality?" In *Bounded Rationality: The Adaptive Toolbox,* ed. G. Gigerenzer and R. Selten, 13–36. Cambridge, MA: MIT Press.

Simon, H. A. 1983. *Reason in Human Affairs.* Stanford, CA: Stanford University Press.

Simon, H. A. 1987. "Rational Decision Making in Business Organizations." In *Advances in Behavioral Economics: Vol. 1,* ed. L. Green and J. H. Kagel, 18–47. Norwood, NJ: Ablex.

Skinner, B. F. 1948. *Walden Two.* New York: Macmillan.

Skinner, B. F. 1953. *Science and Human Behavior.* New York: The Free Press.

Skinner, B. F. 1957. *Verbal Behavior.* Acton, MA: Copley Publishing Group.

Skinner, B. F. 1971. *Beyond Freedom and Dignity*. New York: Alfred A. Knopf.

Stigler, G. J. 1961. "The Economics of Information." *Journal of Political Economy* 69: 213–225.

Sunstein, C. R. 2003. "Terrorism and Probability Neglect." *Journal of Risk and Uncertainty* 26: 121–136.

Tarpy, R. M. and R. E. Mayer. 1978. *Foundations of Learning and Memory*. Glenview, IL: Scott, Foresman and Company.

Thorngate, W. 1980. "Efficient Decision Heuristics." *Behavioral Science* 25: 219–225.

Tversky, A., and D. Kahneman. 1992. "Advances in Prospect Theory: Cumulative Representation of Uncertainty." *Journal of Risk and Uncertainty* 5: 297–323.

von Wright, G. 2004. *Explanation and Understanding*, rev. ed. Ithaca, NY: Cornell University Press.

Watson, J. B. 1913. "Psychology As the Behaviorist Views It." *Psychological Review* 20: 158–177.

Index